90 0575825 6

International Financial Market Regulation

International Financial Market Regulation

Edited by Benn Steil
The Royal Institute of International Affairs, London

John Wiley and Sons
Chichester • New York • Brisbane • Toronto • Singapore

Chapters 1, 3, 4, 6, 7 and 8 were originally published in the *Financial Review* (June 1994), Institute of Fiscal and Monetary Policy, Ministry of Finance, Japan.

Other Wiley Editorial Offices

John Wiley & Sons, Inc., 605 Third Avenue,
New York, NY 10158-0012, USA

Jacaranda Wiley Ltd, 33 Park Road, Milton,
Queensland 4064, Australia

John Wiley & Sons (Canada) Ltd, 22 Worcester Road,
Rexdale, Ontario M9W 1L1, Canada

John Wiley & Sons (SEA) Pte Ltd, 37 Jalan Pemimpin #05-04,
Block B, Union Industrial Building, Singapore 2057

Library of Congress Cataloging-in-Publication Data

International financial market regulation / edited by Benn Steil.
p. cm.
Includes bibliographical references and index.
ISBN 0-471-94401-7
1. Capital market. 2. International finance. 3. International finance—Law and legislation. 4. Banks and banking, International—Law and legislation. I. Steil, Benn.
HG4523.1594 1994
332'.042—dc20 94–31600
CIP

British Library Cataloguing in Publication Data

A catalogue record for this book is available from the British Library

ISBN 0-471-94401-7

Typeset in 10/12 pt Times in Great Britain by Mackreth Media Services, Hemel Hempstead
Printed and bound in Great Britain by Biddles Ltd, Guildford, Surrey

Contents

List of Contributors

CORINNE BRONFMAN
Assistant Professor of Finance, Department of Finance and Real Estate, College of Business and Public Administration, University of Arizona, USA.

RICHARD DALE
Professor of International Banking and Financial Institutions, Department of Accounting and Management Science, University of Southampton, UK.

JEAN DERMINE
Professor of Banking and Finance, INSEAD, Fontainebleau, France.

KENNETH LEHN
Professor of Business Administration, Joseph M. Katz Graduate School of Business, University of Pittsburgh, USA

ROBERT A. SCHWARTZ
Professor and Yamaichi Faculty Fellow, Department of Finance, Leonard N. Stern School of Business, New York University, USA.

BRIAN SCOTT-QUINN
Professor and Director of the ISMA Centre for Education and Research in Securities Markets, University of Reading, UK.

BENN STEIL
Senior Research Fellow, International Economics Programme, The Royal Institute of International Affairs, London, UK.

LAWRENCE J. WHITE
Arthur E. Imperatore Professor of Economics and Department Chairman, Leonard N. Stern School of Business, New York University, USA.

Preface

This book represents the first effort to draw together original and independent economic analysis of regulatory developments in the United States, in the European Community (EC), and at the wider international level. This is an extremely valuable and timely endeavor, given the prominence which regulatory issues have recently assumed in public debate over the evolution of the financial markets, and the necessarily fragmented perspectives which have heretofore emerged from diverse interests reacting to narrow issues or local developments.

Previous books in this area have either focused on a single national market, or have compiled short conference papers, many by authors representing specific institutional interests, in order to cast the net over a wider geographic area. In creating this book, the editor has specially commissioned all of the contributions from noted American and European academic economists with expert knowledge in US, EC, and international banking and securities regulation. The resulting volume should be of great interest to market practitioners and regulators alike, as well as students and researchers studying regulation in particular, and financial markets and institutions more generally.

This volume has its genesis in a project which the editor undertook for the Institute of Fiscal and Monetary Policy (IFMP) of the Japanese Ministry of Finance, to devote an entire issue of their quarterly journal, the *Financial Review*, to the subject of financial market regulation. The six papers commissioned for the June 1994 issue (No. 32) comprise, with minor changes, Chapters 1, 3, 4, 6, 7, and 8 of this book. The editor and the contributors are very grateful to the IFMP for supporting the research.

The editor would also like to acknowledge the support of The Leverhulme Trust, which has funded much of his research on securities regulation over the past year and a half. Finally, this project would not have been possible without the backing of The Royal Institute of International Affairs. A research center of considerable international standing, the Institute has long been at the forefront of scholarly debate on major issues of international political economy.

Benn Steil
September 1994
London

1

Introduction: Effective Public Policy in a World of Footloose Finance

BENN STEIL

When the subject is financial markets, the terms "regulate" and "regulation" are beginning to sound anachronistic.

To "regulate," according to Webster's Universal Dictionary, is "to control or direct by a rule, principle, method, etc." Few major market participants, or indeed regulators, would accept that the markets can be "controlled" or "directed" in the same sense that they were two decades ago. Indeed, events such as the 1987 stock market crash, the 1991 BCCI scandal, and the 1993 collapse of the European Exchange Rate Mechanism (ERM) worry policymakers, practitioners, and investors largely because no one appears to be "in control."

It is therefore not surprising that policymakers in the US, the EC, and internationally are now beginning to rethink not just "regulations," but the fundamental parameters of effective *public policy* toward the markets. "Public policy," which Webster's defines as "the fundamental policy on which laws rest," does not simply deal with questions such as whether banks should be allowed to trade equity derivatives, but addresses far more fundamental questions, such as whether a regulatory distinction between banks and nonbanks is actually meaningful. The growing debate about "level playing fields" for financial services firms is essentially a public policy debate, and the way it is resolved may have considerable implications for the efficiency and

International Financial Market Regulation. Edited by B. Steil

stability of the markets. This is not to say that the implications will be what the regulators *intend*: market participants do not passively conform to regulatory edicts. Regulatory arbitrage works in strange and mysterious ways.

The purpose of this brief introduction is not to introduce new semantic distinctions into the regulatory debate, but to highlight the fact that the enormous developments in the markets over the past fifteen years or so have forced us to reevaluate fundamentally why it is we regulate and how we can do it effectively in a drastically altered environment. Most significantly, it is no longer clear what the contours of "the market" actually are — in terms of geography, providers, or products. Is the trading of Japanese equity derivatives simply a question for Japanese securities regulators? What about when they are traded in Singapore or Chicago? What about when they are traded by German banks? Cash and derivative products are traded in different marketplaces by different traders according to different trading mechanisms, but should they be "different markets" from a regulatory perspective? When Chicago futures prices lead NYSE cash prices, which product is, economically speaking, a "derivative" of which? And who should care? The SEC? The CFTC? The Federal Reserve? These are the types of questions with which policymakers are now grappling.

THE NEW MARKET ENVIRONMENT

The contributions to this volume examine the major regulatory debates and developments taking place in the US, the European Community (EC), and internationally, in light of the new market environment. This environment is marked by a proliferation of products and providers, and a rapidly increasing integration of national and product markets. It is worthwhile first to consider the factors which have served to create this environment; factors which may be clearly distinguished, but which operate in a dialectical fashion with one another.

Competition. The economic, political, technological, and regulatory context in which the markets operate can change dramatically over time, but the relentless operation of competitive forces is a constant. All of the factors listed below can be extremely influential in shaping the outcomes of market competition, but competition cannot be "scripted" in the way in which legislators and regulators too often believe it can. The birth of the Eurobond market in the mid-1960s was certainly not anticipated by the US authorities when capital controls and new tax laws were imposed, yet it has developed into a huge international market without any formal direct regulatory oversight or guidance. Likewise, the collapse of the Bretton Woods system in

1973 provided a major impetus for the development of the foreign exchange markets, but they have since grown into the world's largest — with daily turnover of around $1 trillion — without any of the standard trappings of exchanges or self-regulatory umbrellas.

Deregulation. Deregulation is both a liberator of market forces and a product of them. National authorities relinquish formal controls and prohibitions when they perceive economic benefits from freer competition, but authorities likewise find themselves forced to dismantle such measures when regulatory arbitrage produces unintended consequences. The US and, since the mid-1980s, the UK, have generally been the leaders in deregulating their national markets, but the trend has spread widely in recent years. The removal of the last remaining barriers to capital flows among the developed economies has, in particular, played an enormous role in integrating markets cross-border. Passive capital and unexploited investment opportunities can no longer be kept apart for a significant space of time.

Technology. Advances in computer and telecommunications technology have been a major driving force behind market integration, both cross-border and cross-product. Arbitrage opportunities can now often be spotted and exploited in a matter of seconds. The huge daily volume of trades in the major markets is wholly dependent upon the proper functioning of hardware systems of enormous capacity and software configurations of rapidly growing complexity. In the bull markets of the mid-1980s, systems analysts began to achieve star status in major securities houses, as overcoming technology constraints on trading volume became one of the major factors in determining profitability.

Securitization and disintermediation. Institutions are ever in search of cheaper ways to finance their operations and better ways to mitigate their financial exposure risks. The past decade has witnessed a major shift away from intermediated financing through bank lending toward securitized financing through the capital markets. Large corporate borrowers have turned to commercial paper and repurchase agreements for short-term borrowing. Banks are customizing interest rate and currency risk profiles with swaps, and securitizing and selling off their mortgages and personal loans. Finally, investors are shifting savings out of bank deposits into liquid money market and mutual funds. US mutual fund assets now represent about 85 percent of the value of bank deposits, up from about 10 percent in the early 1980s.

Finance theory. The Black–Scholes option pricing formula, published in 1973, is arguably the most significant contribution to finance theory in the past quarter century. The formula, together with its subsequent refinements and adaptations, has spawned major new derivatives markets around the globe and a revolution in thinking about the risks which market participants bear in everyday transactions. The quantitative techniques of finance theory are essential for the pricing of complex new instruments, the effective management of financial risk, and the identification of speculative and arbitrage opportunities. Modern portfolio theory, which is largely based on the work of Harry Markowitz in the 1950s, has had an enormous impact on the way mutual and pension funds manage their assets through diversification.

Macroeconomics. With minimal regulatory and technological barriers to shifting capital, the markets have become extremely sensitive to changes in macroeconomic conditions. Savers are now highly yield-sensitive, and growing increasingly sophisticated with regard to investment vehicles. The easing of US monetary policy which began in late 1990 motivated a huge shift in American private savings toward domestic and foreign equity markets and long-term bonds. In 1993, Americans poured about $1 billion a day into mutual funds. Changes in national fiscal and monetary conditions also provoke large and rapid shifts in the pattern of net flows of international savings and investment. The marked rise in cross-border activity has in turn increased sensitivity to currency risks, and fuelled demand for derivative instruments to control them.

Politics. With the end of the Cold War, the poorer countries of Eastern Europe, Asia, and Latin America are making huge strides toward the establishment of market-based economies. International institutional investment in emerging markets has rocketed as a consequence, rising from just 2 percent of international funds in 1989 to 13 percent in 1993. International investors have been extremely sensitive to political conditions in these countries. In Latin America, in consequence, Mexico, Chile, and Argentina have attracted very substantial investment, while Nicaragua, where property rights are still tenuous, has attracted almost nothing.

Institutions. The "institutionalization" of the markets is perhaps the defining trend of recent years. The US mutual fund industry in 1993 had over $2 trillion in assets; nearly double the level in 1990, and 15 times the level in 1980. There has been tremendous debate raging over the effects of this shift. Concerns have been expressed particularly over whether the huge pool of new fund investors will keep its nerve in the midst of a "market correction," or whether they will cut and run, sending the funds scrambling for liquidity. At the very least, market institutionalization must force regulators to reevaluate the distinction between "retail" investors and institutions. Retail investors have long been assumed to require far more regulatory protection because of their lack of sophistication, but when their main investment vehicle becomes a multibillion dollar mutual fund, the distinction becomes extremely blurred. There is also a slowly advancing institutionalization of international financial market regulation, under the auspices of the Basle Committee of the Bank for International Settlements (BIS) and the International Organization of Securities Commissions (IOSCO).

THE NEW REGULATORY ENVIRONMENT

Regulators in all major markets are struggling to adapt to these significant market developments. What follows is a brief look at the critical regulatory issues facing the US, the EC, and markets across the world.

The United States

Banking

The very business of banking is undergoing a sea change in the US. Fierce competition from the capital markets has cut margins on corporate lending to razor-thin levels. At Bank of America, for example, lending and cash management services account, respectively, for 43 percent and 33 percent of revenues, yet only 30 percent and 15 percent of net income. Corporate finance and capital market activities, in contrast, account for only 24 percent of revenues, but 55 percent of net income.[1] Major banks are, not surprisingly, moving rapidly into the trading and securities business. Chemical Bank achieved trading revenues of over $1 billion in 1993, up from $47 million in 1980. Bankers Trust has chosen to abandon corporate lending altogether. The shift away from traditional lending activities did not come quickly or painlessly: the major banks lost prodigious sums on high-risk loan defaults in the late 1980s — loans that had been made at the beginning of the decade when margins had begun to fall. Even those banks which continue to do major lending business now do so with the expectation that borrowers will be led into more profitable lines of bank services.

Banks have also been forced to react to the severe erosion of their deposit bases, as individual investors continue to shift savings into mutual funds. The US household sector's holdings of bank deposits and money market funds has fallen from 50 percent of total discretionary spending in 1975 to about 30 percent in 1993. One response has been for the banks to move into the mutual fund business, in effect to move laterally with their customers in the hope of keeping their business. Mellon Bank, for example, acquired the

Boston Company private banking and mutual fund group in 1992 and then moved to acquire the Dreyfus mutual fund group in 1993. Thus, while continental European countries featuring universal banking systems are moving more toward the bank-disintermediated Anglo-American style of financing, the US is, in a sense, simultaneously developing a universal banking model of its own based on mutual funds.[2]

This change would appear to have regulatory implications, but it is not clear whether, on balance, they are negative or positive. On the one hand, banking regulators are concerned that investors may be generally unaware that their mutual funds are not risk-free government-backed investments. On the other, higher-yielding assets offered through banks are weaning customers off the segment of the banking system supported by the Federal Reserve's safety net, leaving only those customers who are unwilling or unable to manage their own financial asset risks remaining with low-yield government-backed deposits.

As the transmutation of the banking system continues, the government is trying simultaneously to simplify the regulatory structure with a primary aim of increasing its effectiveness. The Treasury would like to see the four federal regulatory agencies consolidated into an umbrella Federal Banking Commission. The chairman of the US Federal Reserve, however, continues to press his case that the central bank must maintain its responsibilities as an independent regulator. This, he claims, is essential to ensure that the Fed has detailed knowledge of market conditions that could impact on the entire financial system. While this view has been widely echoed by commentators, critics point out that the German Bundesbank functions with no such regulatory powers. The Treasury's proposal would, in any case, leave intact America's curious "dual banking system," which accommodates separate regulatory structures for state-chartered and nationally chartered banks.

In Chapter 2, Lawrence White documents the complicated, multilayered and multipurpose American regulatory structure, and analyzes its operation according to three broad regulatory functions:

- *Economic regulation* generally involves price, entry, and so-called "must serve" requirements.
- *Health–safety–environment (H–S–E) regulation* covers product characteristics and production processes; *safety-and-soundness (or prudential) regulation* is the variant that applies specifically to banks.
- *Information regulation* focuses on information disclosure in the provision of services.

Discussing regulatory developments since the 1970s, he notes that while economic regulation has been relaxed in certain areas, the scope of information regulation has increased and, in the early 1990s, the grip of safety-and-soundness regulation was considerably tightened. Looking ahead,

White strongly advocates further relaxation of economic regulation, particularly with regard to branching restrictions. He recommends specific reforms of safety-and-soundness regulation to increase its effectiveness while removing barriers to banks' pursuit of legitimate competitive opportunities. Changes are particularly needed in the way bank capital is calculated and capital requirements formulated. He notes that the renewed prosperity in the industry is likely to dull incentives for regulatory changes, but urges the US authorities to lay the groundwork for reforms now.

Securities Markets

Competition for trading volume in the US equity markets has stiffened dramatically in recent years, and it is therefore no surprise that market structure issues have been thrust to the top of the regulatory agenda. The New York Stock Exchange (NYSE), once considered the unshakeable monolith of US equity trading, now faces increasingly fierce competition from a growing array of effective marketplaces, such as the regional exchanges and the American Stock Exchange (AMEX), the over-the-counter (OTC) market, proprietary trading systems (PTSs), nonintermediated markets, and overseas markets. The US regulatory structure is geared to a bygone era of overwhelming NYSE dominance. Dramatic changes in trading technology, trading strategies, and the role of institutional investors are reshaping the structure of the US equity markets, and therefore necessitate a thorough rethinking of why and how trading should be regulated.

In Chapter 3, Bronfman, Lehn, and Schwartz provide a timely and incisive economic analysis of the role of the Securities and Exchange Commission (SEC) in the regulation of the US equity markets, focusing particularly on present SEC thinking as reflected in the Division of Market Regulation's Market 2000 Report. The Report addresses some critical market structure issues, a number of which are also beginning to feature in EC debates related to the establishment of a "single European market" in financial services. Among the questions which motivated the Market 2000 study were the following:

- Does intermarketplace competition act as a welcome catalyst to greater innovation and efficiency in securities trading, or by "fragmenting" order flow does it reduce liquidity and impair price discovery?
- What is the proper role of a statutory regulator with regards to promoting market "transparency"?
- Are practices such as "payment for order flow" and "soft dollars" legitimate competitive tools, or abusive practices interfering with a broker's obligation to secure "best execution"?
- From the perspective of statutory regulation, what is "an exchange"?[13]

Bronfman, Lehn and Schwartz provide a clear and concise critique of the Report's major recommendations, and address the larger question of the SEC's proper role in regulating market structure. They conclude that technological change and competitive forces are significantly increasing the contestability of the US "market for equity markets," and that Congress should therefore consider downgrading the SEC's role in regulating market structure in favor of a greater reliance on intermarketplace competition.

We recognize that market structure issues are becoming increasingly complex in the present trading environment, and so we have covered them separately in Chapter 4. Robert Schwartz analyzes the eight central regulatory issues in market design: transaction costs, price discovery, transparency, consolidation of order flow, liquidity, price volatility, immediacy, and regulatory simplicity. He then provides an evaluation of the structural changes which the securities industry is undergoing, focusing particularly on the advent of electronic call market trading. He concludes that the US must avoid allowing market structure to be designed by the regulatory process, as this is apt to impair the efficiency of competition, to the detriment of the market's buy-side participants. His analysis should serve as a warning to the EC against top-down control of Europe's own developing market structure.

The European Community

The EC legislative framework for financial markets is grounded in a concept known as "competition among rules," which takes the continuing reality of separate and distinct national legal and regulatory systems as given. The principle outlined in the European Commission's 1985 White Paper supporting competition among rules is that of *mutual recognition*, according to which all member states agree to recognize the validity of each other's laws, regulations, and standards, and thereby facilitate free trade in goods and services without the need for prior harmonization. Directly derived from this principle is the Second Banking Coordination Directive provision for a *single passport*, under which credit institutions incorporated in any EC member state are permitted to carry out a full range of "passported services," detailed in the Directive's annex, throughout the Community.[4] Similar guidelines are laid down for the provision of investment services cross-border in the Investment Services Directive. Reinforcing the market-opening effect of mutual recognition is the assignment of *home-country control*, which attributes the primary task of supervising a given financial institution to its home-country authorities. Home-country control provides further assurance that foreign EC firms will not be put at a competitive disadvantage by host-country authorities seeking to protect domestic firms.

A second major principle enshrined in the White Paper is *harmonization of minimum standards*, which acts to limit the scope for competition among rules by mandating member state conformity with some base-level Community-wide requirements. The principle is intended to ensure that "basic public interests" are safeguarded in a single market with different national rules and standards. Whether this principle facilitates or inhibits the free movement of goods, capital, and labor depends wholly upon the manner in which it is applied. It can, on the one hand, facilitate free competition by stopping member states from erecting "standards barriers" against one another's products and services, while on the other it can inhibit free competition by barring certain products or practices from the market altogether.

The minimum harmonization principle represents a major question mark in the drafting of EC legislation, since the Commission has never been explicit either about what sorts of rules do and do not require harmonization, or about how the "minimum" is to be determined. Reading the Commission's version of history in the White Paper, it is clear that the minimum harmonization principle is not seen simply as a necessary response to negative externalities deriving from free competition among rules. Rather, competition among rules is itself seen as a necessary but regrettable consequence of the Commission's inability to legislate full harmonization.

Banking

In Chapter 5, Jean Dermine provides an economic analysis of the EC regulatory framework for banking services, focusing particularly on the two major areas of debate: the allocation of regulatory responsibility between home and host country authorities, and the determination between regulatory harmonization and regulatory competition.

In dealing with the problem of *imperfect information and consumer protection*, Dermine concludes that competition among national regulators is desirable where market participants are capable of evaluating the quality of regulatory systems. To the extent that there exists a significant class of "uninformed" investors, he concludes that harmonization of essential standards is an appropriate solution. The degree of harmonization could, in principle, vary across different activities and classes of investors. An alternative to harmonization is to allow some measure of host-country regulatory control where host authorities believe that certain investors are not adequately protected by foreign regulation or supervision. This approach has been taken by the European Commission, which allows for host-authority intervention for reasons of "public interest."

With regard to *bank runs and systemic risk*, Dermine also calls for a measure of host-country control. Domestic central banks must necessarily concern themselves with the stability of their financial markets, and therefore require some measure of supervisory authority over the solvency of banks operating in their jurisdiction. Since solvency of a foreign branch or even subsidiary would depend on the solvency of the entire group, Dermine recommends a system of joint supervision by home and host authorities. He further recommends modification of the deposit insurance scheme agreed by the Council of Ministers in 1993: insured deposits should be made a "first order" claim so as to increase monitoring incentives for uninsured deposits.

Finally, Dermine addresses the thorny area of *"fair trade"* in international banking. Harmonization of regulations, he concludes, should only be pursued in order to limit implicit public subsidies which confer competitive advantages on national institutions.

Securities Markets

"To harmonize, or not to harmonize," is also the critical question with regard to Community-level securities markets regulation. While the Investment Services Directive (ISD) is popularly seen as being synonymous with the pro-competitive "single passport" principle, there are in fact several major (and controversial) provisions in the Directive which act explicitly to constrain competition through the imposition of "minimum standards." These relate explicitly to market structure issues, which, as we pointed out earlier, were also the central focus of the SEC's Market 2000 study. One such provision concerns minimum trade reporting and publication requirements intended to ensure that all regulated markets are sufficiently "transparent." The battle between Paris and London over the transparency requirements brings to the fore very different conceptions of "fair" and "efficient" markets. In Chapter 6, Brian Scott-Quinn teases out the many strands of the debate, such as the liquidity–transparency trade-off, differences in the operation of continuous auction and competing dealer markets, and the "public goods" versus "property rights" view of a securities exchange. A second contentious provision which Scott-Quinn addresses is the *concentration principle*, which reflects the view of a number of member states that trading in a given security should be "concentrated" on a "regulated market." This is defended both as a means of ensuring efficient price discovery and protecting investors, although opponents attack it as a protectionist barrier to legitimate intermarketplace competition. Since the ISD will not come fully into force until 1996, it remains to be seen precisely how member states supporting the concentration principle intend to apply its specific provisions.

International Regulation

Banking

The international nature of the disturbances surrounding the collapse of the German Bankhaus Herstatt in 1974 provided a major impetus to the institutionalization of cross-border regulatory coordination and cooperation. The Committee on Banking Regulation and Supervisory Practices (now known as the "Basle Committee") was created the following year under the auspices of the Bank for International Settlements (BIS), and has since then established itself as the locus of debate and standards-setting in international banking regulation. The organization's concerns and approaches have evolved considerably since its founding, and Richard Dale's analysis of its role and performance is very timely given the importance of the issues now on the agenda.

As Dale documents in Chapter 7, the focus of the Basle Committee has shifted over time from the development of guidelines for the division of regulatory responsibility among national authorities to the establishment of minimum regulatory and supervisory standards, with more recent concerns being directed specifically at questions of competitive equality across financial institutions. He provides a penetrating critique of specific Basle agreements, particularly the famous Capital Adequacy Accord of 1988, as well as the organization's evolving approach to international harmonization. He draws an important distinction between *regulatory* harmonization and *supervisory* harmonization. The 1991 collapse of BCCI was specifically a supervisory failure, and further regulatory harmonization (along the lines of the capital accord) will do little to prevent further episodes of this type in the absence of coordinated moves to buttress supervisory standards across jurisdictions.

Concerning competitive equality, Dale focuses on the Committee's attempts to remove competitive distortions across national banking industries. Differential capital requirements across national jurisdictions have been a central concern of the committee, but harmonization of such requirements does nothing to address the critical distortion arising from differences in national financial "safety nets;" that is, the deposit insurance and lender of last resort support provided by national authorities. Such support severely complicates the "level playing field" agenda, particularly when that agenda is extended to the area of securities operations. Dale concludes that the Basle Committee's policy of partial harmonization — in dealing with the determination of capital standards, regulatory and supervisory standards, and the establishment of competitive equality — has left significant gaps in the regulatory agenda which need to be addressed.

Securities Markets

Formal international coordination in securities regulation is considerably less advanced than in banking. The International Organization of Securities Commissions (IOSCO) is more of a giant "tent" for international discussion and debate than an effective multinational standards-setting regime, like the

Basle Committee. It is certainly true that IOSCO's structure and operating procedures make it harder to achieve formal harmonization of specific rules and standards, but observers should avoid the temptation to equate harmonization with greater regulatory effectiveness. As we stress in Chapter 8, harmonization does not necessarily enshrine the "best" standards. Harmonized rules which are poorly structured or badly implemented can actually serve to *undermine* market efficiency and stability. Regulatory diversity is not in and of itself a bad thing, given that we cannot always know *ex ante* what is "best practice." To the extent that IOSCO contributes to ensuring that regulators are making informed decisions in an increasingly complex regulatory environment, it is hardly clear that it has been less "effective" than the Basle Committee.

Despite IOSCO's formal status as a world body of securities regulators, it would be a great error to focus the lion's share of attention on IOSCO affairs. There have been a large number of organizations which have been instrumental in concentrating regulatory attention on critical areas of market operation. The private sector has been at the forefront, with the Group of Thirty (G-30) providing valuable analysis of clearance and settlement issues and derivatives markets, and the International Accounting Standards Committee (IASC) working to facilitate cross-border equity issues.

In Chapter 8, we look at four issues in particular which have been under the regulatory spotlight. *Capital adequacy standards* for securities firms have been the subject of fierce debate, particularly within IOSCO. It is not clear, however, that this debate is being driven by economic imperatives, since the case for international capital standards is much weaker for securities firms than for banks. Since the Basle Committee showed that capital agreements were both politically feasible and media-worthy, it is not surprising that the issue rose rapidly up the IOSCO agenda. The explosion in *derivatives trading* has also prompted enormous international attention, amid fears that such instruments may destabilize the markets and pose new risks on the operation of the financial system. We examine the different types of risk implicit in derivatives trading — market risk, liquidity risk, credit risk, and legal risk — and then analyze the systemic risk concerns of regulatory authorities. While the trading practices of institutions such as hedge funds have been the subject of some excessive suspicion, concern will not be alleviated until regulators are able to achieve more transparency for off-balance-sheet activities. Stock index trading is also worthy of regulatory attention, but any actions taken should always be geared to ensuring that cash and derivatives markets remain integrated in turbulent markets. *Clearance and settlement* is not as sexy a subject as derivatives, but would appear to represent a far more significant source of systemic risk in cross-border operations. We suggest a number of mechanisms for mitigating the many sources of risk in clearance and settlement. Finally we focus on *multinational disclosure and accounting.*

This issue featured prominently at the 1993 IOSCO Conference, and will become increasingly important with further growth in international equity issues. We analyze three developments which are accompanying the growth in cross-border activity: acceptance of International Accounting Standards, mutual recognition agreements, and increasing use of US accounting standards.

THE FUTURE

Trying to divine the future shape of the financial markets is a fairly hopeless venture. Nonetheless, there would seem to be some general trends to which market participants and regulators will have to adapt.

First of all, the distinction between different types of financial institution will become increasingly blurred as the process of securitization and disintermediation continues to develop. Indeed, the distinction between "financial" and "nonfinancial" institutions will itself become less and less meaningful as companies like General Electric and General Motors take on more and more characteristics of major credit institutions. Regulation will in consequence become an even more complicated task, particularly with regard to controlling the size and scope of the financial safety net.

Secondly, "convergence theories" of market structure will be rudely challenged by events. Different classes of investors tend naturally to gravitate toward different types of trading systems. There will be more diversity and more competition in market structures, and this will force regulators to address some very difficult questions. In particular, will greater intermarketplace competition lower the cost of capital by driving down transaction costs, or will it simply "fragment" the market, undermining liquidity and damaging the price discovery process? The US and the EC would appear to be moving in opposite directions on this question. The Market 2000 Report has, on balance, given the Division of Market Regulation's blessing to the new competition posed by proprietary trading systems, while the market "concentration" provisions in the EC's Investment Services Directive reflect a deep skepticism toward (or a protectionist avoidance of) competition to the primary national exchanges.

Thirdly, institutional participants will increase their dominance in the markets. Small investors will buy and sell mutual funds as they now buy and sell shares. Fund portfolios are managed by experienced traders who are becoming highly trading-cost conscious in a fiercely competitive environment. Regulators will therefore have to reevaluate the distinction between "retail" and "wholesale" market participants, and the implications for how they balance the need for transactional efficiency with appropriate investor protection. Despite reassuring signs during the March/April 1994 stock market declines, we have yet to see firm evidence of how the rapidly growing body of unsophisticated fund holders behaves in a highly turbulent market. It is not clear whether liquidity problems are more or less likely in this considerably changed investment environment. Regulators, including central banks, will at the very least need to do some quiet but thorough scenario planning.

Finally, markets will continue to integrate cross-product and cross-border. This should be a very welcome development from the perspective of effective portfolio management, but it must also raise legitimate concerns among regulators. They must look first and foremost to ensure that neither statutory regulation nor self-regulation acts in any way to disconnect cash and related derivatives markets in periods of turbulence. This not only requires effective coordination between different regulatory bodies within countries, but across them as well, since "domestic" derivative products are being traded in an increasing number of foreign jurisdictions. Financial shocks which might have remained localized in a much simpler trading environment will become considerably more difficult to contain.

We live in interesting times. This is the Chinese curse under which market regulation must operate.

ENDNOTES

1. Figures are from Goldman Sachs, as reported in 'When to Throw 'em Back,' *The Economist*, March 12, 1994, p. 105.
2. Remarked upon by David Hale of Kemper Financial Services in 'Re-Inventing US Banking,' *Financial Times*, December 9, 1993.
3. See Ruben Lee, 'What is an Exchange?' Capital Markets Forum Discussion Paper No. 1, 1992.
4. The institution must be authorized to carry out an activity in its home state before it can invoke its passport rights to carry out the activity in other Member States.

2
US Banking Regulation

LAWRENCE J. WHITE*

INTRODUCTION

The regulatory structure for banks in the US defies easy description. Banks are subject to multiple layers of regulation from multiple regulatory authorities, with multiple goals. Further, there are a number of types of depository institutions, each subject to a different set of regulatory rules and authority. Diagrammatic efforts to explain the forms and functions of US bank regulation usually resemble a modern abstract painting or, alternatively, a radio wiring diagram.[1] Despite some deregulatory actions in the 1970s and 1980s, banks remain among the most heavily regulated entities in the US economy of the 1990s.[2]

This chapter will provide an overview of the US bank regulatory system. Our goals will be first to clarify its structure and describe its instruments, then to discuss its recent history and important developments, and finally to highlight the important challenges that lie ahead for banks and bank regulation. Unless otherwise indicated, our discussion will focus on the regulation of *commercial banks*;[3] a complete and comparable treatment of other depositories will be left for another day.[4]

We will proceed as follows. In the next section we provide a few summary statistics to indicate the relative size and importance of the banking sector in the US economy. Then we establish a taxonomy for types of regulation and

*I would like to thank Dana Jaffe, Michael Klausner, and Benn Steil for valuable comments on an earlier draft.

International Financial Market Regulation. Edited by B. Steil

identify the major regulatory agencies. We describe the recent history and important developments of the regulatory system. And prior to drawing a brief conclusion, we discuss the major issues and challenges ahead.

SOME RECENT DATA ON BANKING

At year-end 1992 there were 11,461 commercial banks[5] in operation in the US, with $3,506 billion in assets. Table 2.1 shows that the numbers of banks have diminished since 1980, while their aggregate assets have grown, though not as rapidly as US GDP.

Table 2.1 Numbers and Assets of US Commercial Banks, 1980–1992

		1980	1985	1990	1992
Banks	Number	14,435	14,417	12,345	11,461
	Assets ($ billions)	1,856	2,731	3,389	3,506
US GDP ($ billions)		2,708	4,039	5,546	6,038
Bank assets/GDP		0.69	0.68	0.61	0.58

Sources: FDIC, Council of Economic Advisers (CEA).

Among the other types of depository that operate in the US are savings and loan (S&L) associations, savings banks, and credit unions. As is shown in Table 2.2, the assets of commercial banks constitute over 70 percent of the assets of all depositories. Thus, commercial banks are clearly the dominant form of depository in the US.

Table 2.3 provides data on the numbers and assets of US banks classified by the asset sizes of banks. In 1992 over one-fifth of US banks had less than $25 million in assets, and almost half had less than $50 million. Although

Table 2.2 Numbers and Assets of All US Depository Institutions, 1992

	Number	Assets (Billions of Dollars)
Commercial banks	11,461	3,506
Savings and loan associations and savings banks*	2,367	1,065
Credit unions	12,688	299
Total	26,516	4,870

*Includes institutions operated by the Resolution Trust Corporation.
Sources: FDIC, Office of Thrift Supervision (OTS), National Credit Union Administration (NCUA).

Table 2.3 Size Distribution of Commercial Banks, 1992

	Number	Percent	Assets (Billions of Dollars)	Percent
Less than $25 million	2,556	22	41	1
$25–50 million	2,949	26	107	3
$50–100 million	2,785	24	197	6
$100–500 million	2,539	22	503	14
$500 million to $1 billion	252	2	177	5
$1–3 billion	202	2	350	10
$3–10 billion	127	1	684	20
$10 billion or more	51	1	1,446	41
Total	11,461	100%	$3,505	100%

Source: FDIC.

these small banks account for only a tiny fraction (less than 5 percent) of all US bank assets, their large numbers make them a prominent part of the banking landscape, both as an important consequence of one type of bank regulation and as a continuing significant influence on that regulation.

THE STRUCTURE OF REGULATION

Regulation, at first glance, may appear to be an undifferentiated mass of governmental interventions in private decision-making and marketplace outcomes. There are, however, broad regulatory categories that can be used to classify types of intervention and that will prove useful in understanding bank regulation.

Before providing this classification and its application to banking, we will first describe the governmental structure in the US that applies to bank regulation. We can then develop the regulatory classification scheme and describe "who does what" in the American regulatory system.

The Regulators

American regulatory authority with respect to banks is split between the federal government and the governments of the individual states. The tradition of state regulation began over two hundred years ago, at the founding of the Republic. Indeed, until the 1860s the individual states were the sole regulators of banks and banking.

In 1863 the first permanent[6] federal regulatory presence in banking began with the establishment of the Office of the Comptroller of the Currency

(OCC). The succeeding 130 years have seen a substantial expansion of federal regulatory powers, frequently at the expense of (i.e., superseding) state regulatory powers. Two additional federal regulatory agencies, the Federal Reserve System (established in 1913) and the Federal Deposit Insurance Corporation (FDIC) (established in 1933), together with the OCC currently share the federal regulatory authority over banking.[7]

Regulatory Form and Function

It is useful to classify regulation into three broad categories: economic regulation, health–safety–environment regulation, and information regulation.

Economic Regulation

This form of regulation usually involves controls over prices, profits, and/or entry, as well as "must-serve" requirements. It is often justified as a governmental response or counterbalance to a perceived market imperfection—market (monopoly) power. But the American experience with economic regulation generally has shown that it is often a means by which specific interest groups can use government to create or buttress market imperfections to benefit that group.[8]

Economic regulation is pervasive in US banking:

Prices. From the mid-1930s until the mid-1980s the Federal Reserve maintained a system (in a set of regulations known as "Regulation Q") of *maximum* interest rates on bank deposits. A current remnant of those regulatory restraints continues to prevent banks from paying interest on commercial checking deposits.

A number of state governments, at various times, have placed usury ceilings on the interest rates that can be charged on some types of loans, and some states continue to do so today. Also, many states place limits on the fees surrounding loan transactions, such as late fees on credit card payments.

Entry. Entry into banking is restricted both by the federal government and by the states. The establishment of a new bank requires a charter, which can be granted either by the OCC (in which case the bank is a *national bank*) or by a state regulatory agency (in which case the bank is a *state bank*). In either case, the bank must also obtain deposit insurance from the FDIC. Any of the relevant agencies can withhold its permission on the basis of its doubts about the prospective safety and soundness of the bank's operations (see below) or its belief that the "convenience and needs of the community" are already being adequately served; the latter grounds have an obvious protectionist potential.

Further, federal legislation prevents banks from owning or being owned by securities firms, insurance firms, or firms in general manufacturing or commerce.[9] But exceptions have been carved out for some lines of insurance and some securities services. In essence, banks (or their holding companies) can only be owned by individuals and can only engage in financial activities and services that are closely related to traditional commercial banking.

Once a bank has been established, the geographical location of its headquarters determines its jurisdiction with respect to state regulation of deposit-taking branch locations. This state regulation applies to national banks as well as state banks. Some states allow an unlimited number of branch locations within their borders; others place greater or lesser restrictions on branching, although the trend is toward fewer restrictions. Interstate banking is increasingly tolerated; e.g., an out-of-state bank is increasingly able to buy an in-state bank and operate it as a subsidiary.[10] But yet to arrive is true interstate *branching*, in which a bank headquartered in one state could easily operate *branches* (rather than separate subsidiaries) in other states. In essence, though banks headquartered in one state can transact with loan and deposit customers who are located in other states and can even establish *loan production* offices in other states, the banks cannot yet establish deposit-taking branches in other states. The restrictions on deposit-taking branches hinder banks in offering depository services over wider geographic areas. They also hinder loans, since deposits and loans are often complementary services from the perspective of the customer, who can enjoy the advantages of "one-location" service, and the bank, which may be able to take advantage of production synergies, including the use of deposit activity information to help it monitor its risks with respect to a borrower.[11]

"Must-serve" Requirements. Since 1977 federal legislation has required banks to "serve the needs" of their local communities. Banks are also forbidden (as are all other lenders), under 1975 legislation, from discriminating against customers on the basis of race, color, religion, national origin, sex, marital status, or age.

Health–Safety–Environment (H–S–E) Regulation

This form of regulation involves changes in product characteristics or production processes. It is frequently justified as a governmental response to the market imperfections arising from externality (spillover) effects or from the existence of asymmetric or inadequate information among the parties involved in transactions. But, similar to economic regulation, H–S–E regulation can be a means for specific interest groups to use government to distort market outcomes in ways that benefit themselves at the expense of others.[12]

"Safety-and-soundness" regulation[13] is the predominant form of this regulation for banks. It is enforced by both federal and (for state banks) state regulatory agencies.[14] Banks are restricted as to the types of assets they can hold, the types of liabilities they can offer, and the types of activities in which they (or their holding companies) can engage. They are required to maintain minimum levels of capital, as a buffer against unexpected cost shocks, and they are required to have competent management, who are of good character (felons cannot own or manage a bank) and who have sound operating systems. The primary goal of safety-and-soundness regulation is to maintain the solvency of banks and thereby to protect depositors. The latter are also protected by a system of deposit insurance provided by the FDIC; the current maximum insured amount is $100,000.

The day-to-day enforcement of this regulation is performed by field forces of *examiners*, who perform on-site audits, and *supervisors*, who assess the information yielded by the on-site audits and by the quarterly balance sheet and income data filed by the banks. The agencies' assessments are frequently characterized in terms of *c*apital adequacy, *a*sset quality, *m*anagement, *e*arnings, and *l*iquidity (CAMEL).

Information Regulation

This form of regulation requires that specific types of information must accompany the provision of goods and services. It is frequently justified as a governmental response to problems of asymmetric information or of customers' transactions costs when the relevant information is not presented in a consistent, standardized form by all sellers.[15]

Federal legislation, beginning in 1968, has required banks to provide borrowers with standardized information with respect to interest rates and other fees charged in connection with loans (especially consumer, credit card, and mortgage loans) and to provide depositors with standardized information with respect to interest paid (and any fees or relevant conditions) on deposits. The information requirements also extend to advertisements and other solicitations with respect to loans or deposits.

These three categories of regulation are not airtight or mutually exclusive. Some of the asset or activities restrictions on banks could be interpreted as either economic regulation or safety-and-soundness regulation. The restrictions may even have multiple motivations. Capital requirements, and other safety measures, surely have consequences for the pricing of bank services and thereby have indirect effects that are similar to the direct effects of economic regulation. Nevertheless, these categories are useful as broad organizing devices for discussing and evaluating the course and consequences of bank regulation.

RECENT REGULATORY DEVELOPMENTS

The late 1970s and the 1980s were a period of deregulation — of rolling back *economic* regulation — in the US economy generally.[16] In banking, the legislative elimination of most of the Regulation Q deposit interest rate ceilings in the early 1980s constituted a major rollback of economic regulation. Also, bank regulators were more inclined to grant new charters to entrants; and other depositories, especially S&Ls, were increasingly permitted to offer financial services that were similar or identical to many of the services offered by commercial banks. Further, many states that had previously restricted intrastate branching began easing those restrictions, and virtually all states began to open their borders to bank acquisitions by out-of-state banks.[17]

With respect to securities activities, sharp-eyed bank lawyers (and sympathetic federal regulators) were able to find loopholes in the 1933 legislation (the Glass–Steagall Act) that had separated commercial and investment banking. As a consequence, during the late 1970s and the 1980s banks were able to enter some securities activities, such as discount (no frills) securities brokerage, mutual fund management and distribution, and even (in a limited way) corporate securities underwriting.

Finally, other sharp-eyed lawyers in the late 1970s noticed that most of the legislative definitions of banks described them as institutions that accepted deposits *and* made *commercial* loans. Armed with this knowledge, over one hundred firms that would otherwise have been ineligible (e.g., securities firms, insurance firms, firms in general commerce, and even out-of-state banks) bought small commercial banks, sold off their commercial loan portfolios, and operated them as "non-bank banks" that accepted deposits (FDIC insured) and made only consumer loans. This loophole was closed in 1987, and no new "non-bank banks" have been established since then.

These deregulation actions came on the heels of major *extensions* of economic regulation earlier in the 1970s — notably a significant tightening of bank holding company restrictions in 1970, and the creation of "must-serve" obligations to banks' local communities in 1977. The vigor of this latter regulation, the Community Reinvestment Act (CRA), was noticeably increased in the early 1990s.[18] Also, information dissemination requirements became more extensive throughout the 1970s and 1980s.

In the early 1990s the grip of safety-and-soundness regulation of banks tightened considerably. This tightening was the product of a number of influences. First, in the late 1980s the federal regulators agreed that the Basle (Bank for International Settlements) capital standards — requiring banks to maintain a minimum capital-to-assets ratio of 8 percent, with assets weighted according to their default risk — should become applicable to US banks in the early 1990s. Second, well over a thousand S&Ls became insolvent during the 1980s and early 1990s, bankrupting their deposit insurance fund[19] and requiring a massive ($150–200 billion, on a present discounted value basis) taxpayer contribution to honor the federal government's insurance guarantees to S&L depositors. Excessively lax safety-and-soundness regulation of S&Ls was clearly responsible for much of this debacle.[20] Legislators and regulators wanted the lessons of this experience applied to banks.

Third, commercial banks also suffered well over a thousand insolvencies during this same period. Though the aggregate costs to the FDIC of bank insolvencies were substantially less than those of S&L insolvencies, the specter of taxpayer contributions to support the bank insurance fund appeared substantial in 1991, and legislation enacted at the end of that year was intended to toughen the perceived laxness in safety-and-soundness regulation that was responsible for these bank insolvencies.

As a consequence, the examination and supervision staffs of the regulatory agencies were expanded, and the frequency of bank examinations (audits) was increased. Criteria for "classifying" loans that had or would likely generate losses were tightened, which meant that increased reserves (which reduced a bank's capital) were required. Banks' asset choices were narrowed slightly. The Basle capital requirements came into effect, and the federal regulatory agencies formally adopted a tiered approach to capital adequacy, whereby well-capitalized banks were allowed greater flexibility in their operations and successively thinner levels of capitalization would cause increasingly tighter regulatory scrutiny and restrictions and eventual closure.[21]

In sum, the two decades since the mid-1970s have been a period of conflicting regulatory trends. There has been some relaxation of economic regulation; elimination of most of Regulation Q's restrictions counts as a significant achievement. But the stepped-up attention to CRA regulation in the early 1990s clearly offsets this trend to deregulation. The reach of information regulation has grown steadily broader during this period, and the grip of safety-and-soundness regulation became noticeably tighter in the early 1990s.

THE ISSUES AND CHALLENGES

The major issues and challenges for bank regulation in the 1990s primarily concern economic regulation and safety-and-soundness regulation. To put this discussion in context, we first address the competitive environment in which banks are embedded.

The Growing Competition in Financial Services

As late as the 1960s most banks in the US, and especially those located outside metropolitan areas, operated in relatively sheltered and legally protected local market environments. The regulatory structure severely discouraged competition among banks: Regulation Q limited the price competition among banks for deposits. The state branching restrictions of many states prevented banks headquartered in one part of the state from establishing branches elsewhere in that state, thereby limiting the competition that otherwise might have occurred.[22] Branching across state boundaries, or even establishing deposit-taking subsidiaries across those boundaries, was impossible. In addition, regulation generally discouraged new entry and prevented other depositories from offering services that competed with those of banks.[23]

Erosion of this protected position began in the 1970s and accelerated in the 1980s. The changes came from three sources. First, the basic technologies underlying financial services — data processing and telecommunications — were changing rapidly. The improved technologies meant that banks, and other financial services firms, could more easily offer a wider variety of services to larger numbers of customers over greater geographic distances. These changes alone would have meant that banks would be increasingly in competition with each other and with nonbanks.[24]

Second, the US economy's growing involvement in and exposure to international trade and finance attracted increasing numbers of foreign banks to American shores. They came to provide financial services for the US trade and production activities of their home-country customers and to participate in US financial services markets generally. The rapidly improving technologies made it easier for foreign banks to operate US branches, and their rising share is shown in Table 2.4.

The third source of change, which strongly reinforced the first two, was the group of deregulation measures described in the previous section. These actions meant that banks could compete more directly for deposits because

Table 2.4 Assets of Foreign Banking Offices in the US as a Share of All Bank Assets in the US, 1978–1992

	Percent
1978	5.0
1980	6.6
1985	6.0
1990	10.9
1992	13.5

Source: Federal Reserve.

they could compete on price (i.e., deposit interest rates) and because they could establish more deposit-taking branch locations. More branch locations allowed banks to compete more effectively for loans as well. And the deregulation measures meant that other depositories (and the nonbank banks) could compete more effectively with banks.

Accordingly, the 1990s represent a far more competitive environment for banks than was generally true in the 1960s. In addition to the heightened competition among themselves, banks are now just one group of financial intermediaries among many groups, including S&Ls, savings banks, insurance companies, pension funds, mutual funds, industrial finance companies, and consumer finance companies. And the process of *securitization*, another result of the improved technologies, has meant that loans that were previously the preserve of banks and other depositories[25] can now be originated and bundled in standardized packages whose claims can be sold to other intermediaries or to individual investors. Banks' special roles as originators and portfolio holders of these loans have been diminished.[26]

Table 2.5 The Sources of Credit Market and Trade Credit Debt Outstanding to the Domestic Nonfinancial Sectors of the US Economy, Percentage Shares, 1980–1992

	1980	1985	1990	1992
Commercial banks	29	26	24	23
S&Ls and savings banks	16	14	10	7
Credit unions	1	1	1	2
Total depositories	46	41	35	32
Insurance companies	11	11	13	13
Pension funds	7	8	9	9
Other financial sector lenders	8	12	17	19
Nonfinancial sector lenders	16	19	19	18
Trade credit	11	9	8	8
Total	100%	100%	100%	100%
Total assets (billions)	$4,416	$7,632	$11,628	$12,732

Source: Federal Reserve.

Table 2.5 shows the relative position of banks as lenders to the rest of the economy. Since 1980 banks' share of lending has declined steadily. Banks now provide less than a quarter of the credit extended to the rest of the economy (and all depositories now account for less than a third of all lending). This is consistent with Table 2.1. Though the banking sector is growing, its growth has been relatively slow.

We now turn to the regulatory issues.

Economic Regulation

A possible motive for economic regulation is the need to offset market (monopoly) power. Indeed, the fears of market power are routinely cited by defenders of branching limitations and of other restrictions on bank activities.[27] But, ironically, branching restrictions have been a major *source* of protective market power for individual incumbent banks, especially in smaller towns and rural areas.[28]

Branching restrictions have been a continuing expression of the nineteenth century American populist sentiment toward banks: They are powerful providers of (vital) credit, and they therefore should be kept small and locally oriented. This sentiment meshed conveniently with the interests of the incumbent bankers, who were thereby protected from branch entry by neighboring banks. The legacy of this approach has been the preservation of the thousands of small banks shown in Table 2.3 (whose owners and managers continue to fan the political flames of localism and restricted branching), an inefficient banking structure, and pockets of market power.

One of the latest manifestations of these localism sentiments has been a renewed emphasis on the local "must-serve" obligations embodied in the CRA.[29] However, if serving the local community is profitable for a bank, the CRA obligations are redundant. And if the local service is unprofitable, then the CRA obligations require cross-subsidy from above-normal profits of the bank's other activities.[30] But in the increasingly competitive banking environment of the 1990s, there are unlikely to be above-normal profits earned in "other" activities. Consequently, enforcement of the CRA (where it is binding) is likely to lead to a combination of shirking, frustration, and/or bank losses. The CRA is a localistic anachronism in a world of widening and increasingly competitive financial services markets.

Though banking in the US may not fit the textbook model of perfect competition, it is also far from the textbook model of monopoly that might justify corrective economic regulation. The actual economic regulation that has permeated banking has generally prevented, rather than encouraged, the development of efficient and competitive banking markets. The best hope for an efficient banking sector that can adapt to the competitive 1990s would be the rapid removal of most, if not all, of the specific economic regulatory provisions that bind the industry. Though the current trend with respect to branching restrictions is in the right direction, progress is nevertheless slow; and the renewed emphasis on the CRA is clearly a major step in the wrong direction.[31] The day when banking might be treated economically and politically like most other industries — subject to the antitrust, antidiscrimination, and other broad-sweep laws of the US but not singled out for special economic regulation — still seems to be a long time away.

Safety-and-Soundness Regulation

In the late 1980s and early 1990s, as the banking industry experienced hundreds of insolvency failures and as the FDIC bank insurance fund itself teetered on the edge of failure, the discussion concerning the proper structure of banks, of deposit insurance, and of safety-and-soundness regulation reached a fever pitch.[32] A dramatic improvement in the economic climate for banks in late 1991 and continuing through 1993 — notably, as is shown in Table 2.6, a substantial drop in the level of short-term interest rates and a steepening of the yield curve — caused bank profits to increase strongly,[33] bank failures to decline sharply, and the FDIC insurance fund to grow rapidly (Table 2.7). There has been a commensurate decrease in the volume of discussion of these structural issues. But this favorable economic climate is unlikely to be permanent, and rocky times could well return. These structural questions are therefore worth addressing.

Table 2.6 Interest Rates (Percent) on US Treasury Obligations, 1989–1993

	Three-month Bills (1)	Three-year Notes (2)	Ten-year Bonds (3)	Thirty-year Bonds (4)	Difference (2) − (1)	Difference (3) − (1)	Difference (4) − (1)
1989	8.12	8.55	8.49	8.45	0.43	0.37	0.33
1990	7.51	8.26	8.55	8.61	0.75	1.04	1.10
1991	5.42	6.82	7.86	8.14	1.40	2.44	2.72
1992	3.45	5.30	7.01	7.67	1.85	3.56	4.22
1993	3.02	4.44	5.87	6.59	1.42	2.85	3.57

Source: CEA.

Table 2.7 The Financial Experience of US Banks and the FDIC, 1989–1993

	Bank Profits (Billions of Dollars)	Bank Profits ÷ Bank Assets	Number of Bank Failures	Assets of Failed Banks (Billions of Dollars)	Net Income of FDIC (Billions of Dollars)	Net Assets of FDIC (Billions of Dollars)
1989	15.6	0.49	207	29.2	−0.9	13.2
1990	16.0	0.48	169	15.7	−9.2	4.0
1991	17.9	0.53	127	63.0	−11.1	−7.0
1992	32.0	0.93	122	46.2	6.9	−0.1
1993	43.4	1.21	42	3.8	13.1	13.2

Sources: FDIC, Rehm (1994).

Why regulate?

A justification for safety regulation could be a finding of significant externality or asymmetric information problems affecting the relevant market. These kinds of arguments can indeed be made for banking.

Banks are special not because of their loan assets but because of the characteristics of their deposit liabilities.[34] As Table 2.8 indicates, banks (and other depositories) are still important providers of deposits to the rest of the US economy. Deposits are treated as money or near-money and are expected by households and businesses to be liquid and to hold their value. Most depositors, however, are not capable of monitoring the performance of their banks so as to assure themselves of the safety of their deposits. This inadequate (asymmetric) information problem could provide one justification for governmental intervention.[35]

Table 2.8 Deposits and Money Market Mutual Fund Accounts, 1980–1992

	1980	1985	1990	1992
Commercial banks ($ billion)	1,088	1,697	2,301	2,435
S&L and savings banks ($ billion)	665	1,034	1,050	853
Credit unions ($ billion)	62	126	201	243
Total, all depositories ($ billion)	1,815	2,857	3,552	3,531
Money market mutual funds	76	244	498	544
Grand total ($ billion)	1,891	3,101	4,050	4,075
Banks as a fraction of total depositories (%)	60	59	65	69
Banks as a fraction of grand total (%)	58	55	57	60
All depositories as a fraction of grand total (%)	96	92	88	87

Source: Federal Reserve.

A second justification based on externalities follows from the first.[36] With inadequate information, depositors may be nervous about the solvency (safety) of their bank and may be excessively prone to withdrawing their funds. Since banks' loan assets are generally less liquid than their deposit liabilities, other depositors may fear that the first group's withdrawals would deprive them (the second group) of the liquidity of their deposits, and they rush to the bank to try to withdraw their funds. Depositor runs can thus make individual banks, even healthy banks, unstable; and, in a world of poorly informed depositors, runs might spread from bank to bank, in a contagion effect.

Effective safety-and-soundness regulation, by forestalling bank insolvencies, would protect depositors and thereby prevent losses and avoid runs.[37] Deposit insurance could provide an extra layer of assurance for depositors, in the event that safety-and-soundness regulation failed to prevent insolvencies, and thereby further dampen the tendency toward runs and contagion. With deposit insurance present, the safety-and-soundness regulatory framework has an alternative interpretation — the set of rules that protects the deposit insurance fund. It is worth noting, however, that the practice of safety-and-soundness regulation in the US long preceded the establishment of deposit insurance; and even where governments elsewhere do not have deposit insurance schemes, they nevertheless have systems of safety-and-soundness regulation. It is also worth noting that it was the inability of state and federal safety-and-soundness regulation in the US to prevent the failures of thousands of banks and S&Ls in the late 1920s and early 1930s that led to the creation of the federal deposit insurance schemes in the 1930s. Also, even in instances where countries do not have formal deposit insurance schemes, their governments are usually unwilling to let depositors bear the losses from bank failures and thus are operating implicit deposit insurance systems.[38]

The preceding discussion can now be used to illuminate the links between the major positions advocated in the "structural" (banks, regulation, and deposit insurance) debates and the underlying beliefs of the advocates.[39]

Those who advocate a system of unregulated banks for the US (and an absence of government deposit insurance) tend to believe that depositors are capable of monitoring banks effectively (and that government agencies are not) and that depositor runs and bank instability are not major problems (or that private deposit insurance or other market mechanisms would be adequate to handle them).

Those who advocate a strong safety-and-soundness regulatory system and a continuation (or even an expansion) of government deposit insurance tend to believe that depositors cannot effectively monitor banks (and that governments, though not perfect, can monitor more effectively than can depositors) and that runs and bank instability are serious potential problems.

The advocates of "narrow banks" try to stake out a middle ground: "Narrow banks" could accept deposits that would be government-insured, but these funds could be invested only in high-quality, short-term, low-risk assets (e.g., Treasury bills and high-quality commercial paper);[40] in essence, a "narrow bank" would have the characteristics of a money market mutual fund. All other "deposits" would be explicitly uninsured and could fund any type of assets. The advocates believe that government cannot monitor banks effectively, but neither can many depositors; the latter can still have a safe (but low-yielding instrument), while those who choose uninsured deposits will be those who are better at monitoring; bank instability and runs among these uninsured depositors are not seen as major problems.

As noted above, the improved health of the banking system (as of early 1994) has quieted the discussions of structural reform. The current system of extensive safety-and-soundness regulation and deposit insurance is likely to persist, at least until the next crisis in banking.[41]

Improving the Effectiveness of Regulation

Until the late 1980s the safety-and-soundness regulatory system was entirely in the form of "command and control:" Specific targets (e.g., minimum capital levels) or prohibitions (e.g., a ban on the holding of below-investment-grade "junk" bonds) were mandated on a uniform basis for all banks, and banks were expected to stay within the limits or be subject to substantial penalties. Even the rate structure of premiums that banks paid in return for deposit insurance was flat rate (i.e., all banks paid the same amount per hundred dollars of domestic deposits) and did not vary according to the risks of loss that they posed to the FDIC. Though this "command and control" approach has been typical across the entire American regulatory landscape,[42] it is not the only way that regulation could be implemented. An alternative approach would be one that relied more on the use of economic incentives and mechanisms to promote efficiency. Examples from the environmental (externality) regulation area would be the use of effluent fees and tradable effluent permits.

In the late 1980s and early 1990s bank regulation took modest steps in this second direction. The federal regulatory agencies adopted the Basle (BIS) risk-based capital standards. Banks are now required to maintain capital-to-asset ratios of at least 8 percent, where a bank's assets are weighted according to their default risks, with the weights ranging from 0 percent for government securities to 100 percent for commercial loans. Thus, in principle, the unweighted minimum capital-to-assets ratios for banks now vary according to the riskiness of their portfolios.[43] And in 1992 the federal regulators adopted a tiered approach to capital adequacy, with well-capitalized banks having greater operating flexibility.

Also in 1992, the FDIC adopted its first set of variable, risk-related deposit insurance premiums. A bank's premium can vary between $0.23 per $100 of domestic deposits and $0.31 per $100, depending on its capital level and the evaluations (based on the CAMEL criteria) of its regulatory supervisors.

These initiatives are a welcome start, but much more needs to be done. First, and most important, the accounting framework that serves as the basic information system for bank regulation and that determines how a bank's capital is calculated must be changed. That framework, generally accepted accounting principles (GAAP), relies far too heavily on backward-looking, historical cost-based valuations. It provides far too much leeway for banks to overstate the value of their assets and thus overstate their capital. It needs to be replaced by an accounting framework that focuses on current (market) values.[44] Also, the capital requirements themselves should be imposed on a continuous (real-time) basis, rather than just at the end of each quarter; this is necessary because banks can get into financial difficulties at any time, not just at the end of each quarter.

Second, regulators' choices in setting standards should rely as heavily as possible on empirical evidence with respect to bank behavior and riskiness, rather than relying on intuitive "judgement" that may have little or no empirical basis. For example, the risk weights for assets in determining capital standards and the structure of risk-related deposit insurance premiums should each reflect the available empirical evidence.

Third, more encouragement of the use of subordinated debt as a component of bank capital would bring into banks' governance structure a set of stakeholders whose interests, like those of the regulators, are in avoiding risky operating strategies that could lead to insolvency. In important respects, the use of subordinated debt has many of the same favorable properties as having a private insurer cover a fraction of the liabilities; but the subordinated debt plan has the advantage of obtaining the guarantee funds initially, whereas a private insurance scheme leaves unaddressed the question of the ultimate soundness of the private insurer.

Fourth, consistent with the spirit of economic deregulation advocated above, a bank holding company should be unrestricted in its choices of assets or activities, with only one crucial caveat: Because the transfer of assets from the bank to its holding company is so easy and because such transfers can endanger the solvency of the bank, all transactions between the bank and its holding company must be monitored closely. With respect to the suitability of an asset or activity for the bank itself, the main criterion should be whether bank regulators believe that they can determine its risk characteristics (and can thereby assign appropriate capital levels and insurance premiums). But even if an asset or activity were deemed unsuitable for the bank, the holding company should always be a suitable place for it.

These changes would allow safety-and-soundness regulation to become more effective while simultaneously allowing efficient, well-capitalized firms to take advantage of cost-reducing and profit-enhancing opportunities.

CONCLUSION

Bank regulation in the US is a multifaceted phenomenon that has a long history and quite likely has a long future. There are important distinctions among the types of regulation, and substantially different policies are appropriate for these different categories.

The US banking industry will be facing an environment that can only become more competitive in the remainder of the 1990s and in the twenty-first century. Inappropriate regulation could easily impede the industry's adaptation to this environment.

This chapter has suggested some major reforms of economic regulation and of safety-and-soundness regulation that would allow the industry to adapt and perform effectively. These changes will not be easy. Many entrenched interest groups would be challenged, and the Washington cliché, "If it ain't broke, don't fix it," is likely to be voiced about an industry that has achieved a renewed prosperity in the mid-1990s. But to delay reform until the next crisis is to encourage hasty actions and poor timing. This is one of the lessons of the S&L debacle. Banking, and the US economy, deserve better.

ENDNOTES

1. See, for example, Bloch (1985) or White (1991a).
2. Only electric utilities would seem to be close in terms of the extent and pervasiveness of regulation.
3. Other treatments of commercial banks can be found, for example, in Kane (1985), White (1986), Benston et al. (1986), Litan (1987), and Macey and Miller (1992).
4. A discussion of savings and loan associations, for example, can be found in Brumbaugh (1988), Kane (1989), White (1991a), and Barth (1991).
5. This count is of separate bank charters. Since many (nominally) separate banks are subsidiaries of multiple-bank holding companies, the number of separate banking *organizations* is somewhat smaller, around 8,500.
6. Earlier efforts to establish a federal central bank did not succeed permanently.
7. The federal regulator of savings and loan associations is the Office of Thrift Supervision, which in 1989 became the successor organization to the Federal Home Loan Bank Board (which was established in 1932). The National Credit Union Administration is the regulator of credit unions; it was established in 1970, though federal regulation of credit unions first began in 1934.
8. This is frequently described as rent-seeking or rent-creating behavior. See Stigler (1971), Posner (1971, 1974), Krueger (1974), and, for a survey, Noll (1989).
9. Sharp-eyed lawyers have been able to carve out a few modest exceptions, but the basic principle still holds.
10. Some states, though, have placed maximum market share limits (usually measured in terms of deposits) on the in-state size that out-of-state banks can reach.
11. See Nakamura (1993).
12. For a discussion and references, see White (1993c).
13. Outside the US this is frequently described as *prudential* regulation.
14. The OCC has sole responsibility for national banks. The states and the Federal Reserve share responsibility for state banks that are members of the Federal Reserve. The states and the FDIC share responsibility for state banks that are nonmembers. Also, the Federal Reserve has responsibility for all bank holding companies. As this chapter is being written in early 1994, the Clinton administration has proposed a major consolidation of federal bank and S&L regulation; the proposal's political prospects are uncertain.

15. This latter concern focuses on issues of standardization. See, for example, Braunstein and White (1985) and Economides and White (1994) and the references in the latter article.
16. For surveys, see Joskow and Noll (1994) and White (1993c, 1994).
17. Initially, however, only banks from neighboring or regional states were permitted to enter; most states were fearful of entry by the large New York banks.
18. See White (1993b).
19. This was the Federal Savings and Loan Insurance Corporation (FSLIC). S&Ls are currently insured by the FDIC.
20. See White (1991a, 1993a).
21. This approach had been followed informally and somewhat erratically by regulators prior to the 1990s; it was formally codified in the early 1990s. This approach had been strongly advocated by Benston and Kaufman (1988a, 1988b).
22. In some *unit bank* states such as Illinois and Texas, banks were limited to a single headquarters location. In other *limited branching* states, such as New York and New Jersey, banks could establish branches only within specified areas.
23. S&Ls, for example, could only offer passbook savings accounts and make home mortgage loans.
24. For example, credit cards are typically offered to customers nationwide from a single issuing location.
25. This process has proceeded farthest with home mortgage loans, but it is used extensively for credit card and other consumer loans and is spreading to commercial real estate and other commercial loans.
26. Banks may still be relatively important originators and portfolio holders of loans to small and medium-size businesses; see Hannan (1991). Over time, however, securitization or other creative forms of finance may erode even this stronghold for banks; see Smith (1993).
27. The initial advocates of the Regulation Q restrictions defended them on safety-and-soundness grounds. It was claimed that banks would compete excessively for deposits, raising their interest costs and forcing them to earn the necessary revenue by making excessively risky loans.
28. Repeated studies have shown that interest rates on loans are higher and interest rates are lower in local markets where entry is difficult and seller concentration is high. See Gilbert (1984), Berger and Hannan (1989, 1992), and Hannan (1991).
29. CRA applies also to S&Ls and savings banks.
30. See White (1993b).
31. In the absence of the elimination of the CRA, an ameliorating step would be to transform its vague obligations to "serve the needs of the community" into *specific* target obligations, which could then be traded among banks or with other financial services providers (similar to the system of tradable emissions rights that is developing among the major emitters of some air pollutants). The banks that were less efficient at meeting these obligations could pay other (more efficient) banks or other parties to fulfill them, with the result that any aggregate set of specific obligations placed on the banking system could be fulfilled at a lower aggregate cost. See Klausner (1994).
32. A flavor of that discussion can be found in Litan (1987), Haraf and Kushmeider (1988), Benston et al. (1989), Kane (1989), Barth (1991), England (1991), Pierce (1991), White (1991a), Barth, Brumbaugh, and Litan (1990), Barth and Brumbaugh (1992), Kaufman and Litan (1993), and Klausner and White (1993).
33. Bank profits increased both because the steeper yield curve permitted wider spreads (between loan yields and deposit costs) and because the lower interest

rates on long-term securities allowed banks to reap capital gains on the sale of older (higher interest rate) securities in their portfolios.

34. This discussion applies also to the deposits of S&Ls, savings banks, and credit unions.
35. It is noteworthy that the US Securities and Exchange Commission requires that money market mutual funds maintain portfolios of high-quality, low-default-risk securities.
36. See Diamond and Dybvig (1983) and Postlewaite and Vives (1987).
37. Though a lender of last resort alone is capable of forestalling runs, it would quickly want to install a system of safety-and-soundness regulation, so as to protect itself from the losses of lending to banks that may become insolvent.
38. In late 1993 and early 1994, for example, the governments of Spain, Venezuela, France, and Japan all took steps (with financial costs for each government) with respect to specific insolvent banks in each country that resulted in depositors' not bearing the losses of these banks.
39. See White (1992).
40. There have been two versions of a "narrow bank" advocated. One would require a separate, free-standing entity that would be identified as a narrow bank; the other would simply require that banks collateralize these insured deposits with high-quality short-term assets. See Litan (1987), Benston et al. (1989), and Pierce (1991); see also White (1988).
41. The Washington cliché, "If it ain't broke, don't fix it," will surely discourage any efforts at reform prior to the next crisis.
42. See White (1981).
43. The Basle standards, though, are far from perfect: (a) the risk weights have no empirical basis; (b) the risk weights ignore covariance and portfolio considerations; (c) the risk weights ignore interest rate risk; and (d) the entire calculation of capital is based on the traditional cost-based accounting framework rather than on a market value accounting framework.
44. See White (1991a, 1991b).

REFERENCES

Barth, J.R. (1991) *The Great Savings and Loan Debacle*. Washington, D.C., American Enterprise Institute.

Barth, J.R. and Brumbaugh, R.D., Jr., eds. (1992) *The Reform of Federal Deposit Insurance*. New York, Harper Collins.

Barth, J.R., Brumbaugh, R.D., Jr. and Litan, R.E. (1990) *The Banking Industry in Turmoil: A Report on the Condition of the US Banking Industry and the Bank Insurance Fund*, presented to the Financial Institutions Subcommittee of the Committee on Banking, Housing and Urban Affairs, US House of Representatives, December 17, 1990.

Benston, G.J., Brumbaugh, R.D., Jr., Guttentag, J.M., Herring, R.J., Kaufman, G.G., Litan, R.E. and Scott, K.E. (1989) *Blueprint for Restructuring America's Financial Institutions: Report of a Task Force*. Washington, D.C., Brookings Institution.

Benston, G.J., Eisenbeis, R.A., Horvitz, P.M., Kane, E.J., Kaufman, G.G. (1986) *Perspectives on Safe and Sound Banking: Past, Present and Future*. Cambridge, Mass., MIT Press.

Benston, G.J. and Kaufman, G.G. (1988a) *Risk and Solvency Regulation of*

Depository Institutions: Past Policies and Current Options. Monograph Series in Finance and Economics no. 1988-1, Salomon Brothers Center for the Study of Financial Institutions, New York University.

———. (1988b) 'Regulating bank safety and performance', in W.S. Haraf and R.M. Kushmeider, (eds.) *Restructuring Banking and Financial Services in America*. Washington, D.C., American Enterprise Institute.

Berger, A.N. and Hannan, T.H. (1989) 'The price-concentration relationship in banking.' *Review of Economics and Statistics*, **71**, May, 291–299.

———. (1992) 'The price-concentration relationship in banking: a reply.' *Review of Economics and Statistics*, **74**, May, 376–379.

Bloch, E. (1985) 'Multiple regulators: their constituencies and policies,' in Y. Amihud, T.S.Y. Ho and R.A. Schwartz, (eds.) *Market Making and the Changing Structure of the Securities Industry*. Lexington, Mass., Heath.

Braunstein, Y. and White, L. (1985) 'Setting technical compatibility standards: an economic analysis. *The Antitrust Bulletin*, **30**, Summer, 337–355.

Brumbaugh, R.D., Jr. (1988) *Thrifts under Siege: Restoring Order to American Banking*. Cambridge, Mass., Ballinger.

Diamond, D.W. and Dybvig, P.H. (1983) 'Bank runs, deposit insurance, and liquidity.' *Journal of Political Economy*, **91**, June, 401–419.

Economides, N. and White, L.J. (1994) 'Networks and compatability: implications for antitrust.' *European Economic Review*, **38**, March, 651–662.

England, C., ed. (1991) *Governing Banking's Future: Markets vs. Regulation*. Boston, Kluwer.

Gilbert, A. (1984) 'Studies of bank market structure and competition: a review and evaluation.' *Journal of Money, Credit and Banking*, **16**, 617–644.

Hannan, T.H. (1991) 'Bank commercial loan markets and the role of market structure: evidence from surveys of commercial lending.' *Journal of Banking and Finance*, **15**, February, 133–149.

Haraf, W.S. and Kushmeider, R.M. eds. (1988) *Restructuring Banking and Financial Services in America*. Washington, D.C., American Enterprise Institute.

Joskow, P.L. and Noll, R.G. (1994) 'Economic regulation: deregulation and regulatory reform during the 1980s,' in M. Feldstein, (ed.) *American Economic Policy in the 1980s*. Chicago, University of Chicago Press.

Kane, E.J. (1985) *The Gathering Crisis in Federal Deposit Insurance*. Cambridge, Mass., MIT Press.

———. (1989) *The S&L Insurance Mess: How Did it Happen?* Washington, D.C., Urban Institute Press.

Kaufman, G.G. and Litan, R.E., eds. (1993) *Assessing Bank Reform: FDICIA One Year Later*. Washington, D.C., Brookings.

Klausner, M. (1994) 'Letting banks trade CRA obligations would offer market-based efficiencies. *American Banker*, January 21, 26.

Klausner, M. and White, L.J., eds. (1993) *Structural Change in Banking*. Homewood, Ill., Business One Irwin.

Krueger, A.O. (1974) 'The political economy of the rent-seeking society.' *American Economic Review*, **66**, June, 291–303.

Litan, R.E. (1987) *What Should Banks Do?* Washington, D.C., Brookings Institution.

Macey, J.R. and Miller, G.P. (1992) *Banking Law and Regulation*. Boston, Little Brown.

Nakamura, L.I. (1993) 'Commercial bank information: implications for the structure of banking' in M. Klausner and L.J. White, (eds.) *Structural Change in Banking*. Homewood, Ill., Business One Irwin.

Noll, R.G. (1989) 'Economic perspectives on the politics of regulation' in R. Schmalensee and R.D. Willig, (eds.) *Handbook of Industrial Organization*, vol. 2. Amsterdam, North Holland.

Pierce, J.L. (1991) *The Future of Banking*. New Haven, Conn., Yale University Press.

Posner, R.A. (1971) 'Taxation by regulation.' *Bell Journal of Economics and Management Science*, **2**, Spring, 22–50.

———. (1974) 'Theories of economic regulation.' *Bell Journal of Economics and Management Science*, **5**, Autumn, 335–358.

Postlewaite, A. and Vives, X. (1987) 'Bank runs as an equilibrium phenomenon.' *Journal of Political Economy*, **95**, June, 485–491.

Rehm, B. (1994) '42 banks failed last year, smallest number since 1982.' *American Banker*, January 5, 3.

Smith, S.D. (1993) 'Comment' in M. Klausner and L.J. White (eds.) *Structural Change in Banking*. Homewood, Ill, Business One Irwin.

Stigler, G.J. (1971) 'The theory of regulation.' *Bell Journal of Economics and Management Science*, **2**, Spring, 3–21.

White, L.J. (1981) *Reforming Regulation: Processes and Problems*. Englewood Cliffs, N.J., Prentice Hall.

———. (1986) 'The partial deregulation of banks and other depository institutions' in L.W. Weiss and M.W. Klass, (eds.) *Regulatory Reform: What Actually Happened*. Boston, Little, Brown.

———. (1988) 'Litan's *What Should Banks Do*? a review essay.' *Rand Journal of Economics*, **19**, Summer, 305–315.

———. (1991a) *The S&L Debacle: Public Policy Lessons for Bank and Thrift Regulation*. New York, Oxford.

———. (1991b) 'The value of market value accounting for the deposit insurance system.' *Journal of Accounting, Auditing, and Finance*, **6**, April, 284–301.

———. (1992) 'What should banks *really* do?' *Contemporary Policy Issues*, **10**, July, 104–112.

———. (1993a) 'A cautionary tale of deregulation gone awry: the S&L debacle,' *Southern Economic Journal*, **59**, January, 496–514.

———. (1993b) 'The Community Reinvestment Act: good intentions headed in the wrong direction.' *Fordham Urban Law Journal*, **20**, Winter, 281–292.

———. (1993c) 'Competition policy in the United States: an overview,' *Oxford Review of Economic Policy*, **9**, Summer, 133–153.

———. (1994) 'Government-business relationships in the US in the 1980s,' in M. Feldstein and Y. Kosai, (eds.) *US–Japan Economic Forum*, vol. 2. Chicago, University of Chicago Press.

3

US Securities Markets Regulation: Regulatory Structure

CORINNE BRONFMAN, KENNETH LEHN, and ROBERT A. SCHWARTZ

INTRODUCTION

The industrial organization of US equity markets has changed remarkably in recent years. The New York Stock Exchange (NYSE) remains the dominant marketplace for trading US equity securities,[1] but it faces stiff competition from a variety of other market centers, including regional exchanges,[2] the American Stock Exchange,[3] the over-the-counter market,[4] proprietary trading systems,[5] nonintermediated markets,[6] and overseas markets.[7] The proportion of total trading volume in US equities accounted for by the NYSE has declined substantially during the past decade.[8] As Blume, Siegel, and Rottenberg (1993) point out, the erosion of the NYSE's dominant market position in recent years parallels that of other large US business enterprises, such as General Motors and IBM.[9]

It is generally agreed that several factors account for the change in market structure, including the increased importance of institutional investors, the development of new trading strategies, and technological innovations in the trading of financial assets. These factors have affected both the demand and supply sides of the market for trading services in ways that have encouraged the entry and growth of enterprises which compete with the NYSE.

International Financial Market Regulation. Edited by B. Steil

For example, it is likely that the growth of institutional investors has altered the demand for trading services. If some large institutional investors (e.g., index or pension funds) use portfolio strategies that require less immediacy than that demanded by other investors, they will be reluctant to pay for the high degree of immediacy provided in continuous markets such as that provided by the NYSE. Instead, they may find it more appealing to trade in electronic call markets (e.g., the Arizona Stock Exchange) which provide less immediacy but have lower trading costs. Some of the increase in the trading of NYSE-listed stocks off the NYSE undoubtedly reflects product differentiation that meets the changing demands of investors.

Concurrent with demand changes, advances in communications technology have substantially reduced the cost of producing trading services and facilitated the entry of new enterprises into the market. Many of the new entrants employ electronic-based trading systems that have become possible in recent years because of advances in interactive communications technology. For example, the proprietary trading systems allow subscribers to anonymously submit bids and offers for individual stocks electronically, and they provide trade execution services as well. As former SEC Chairman Breeden wrote in a letter to Congressman Markey in 1991, "markets no longer are, or need be, only physical places."[10]

The change in market structure and the factors behind this change have rekindled some old debates, and triggered some new ones, about the regulatory environment in which US equity markets operate. In July 1992, the US Securities and Exchange Commission's Division of Market Regulation, which oversees the trading environment for securities in the US, issued a "concept release"[11] that surveys the major regulatory issues relating to the industrial structure of US equities markets. Most prominently, the Securities and Exchange Commission (SEC) release stimulates the following questions:

1. Does the growth in trading on markets other than primary markets represent healthy competition? Or is it fragmenting order flow and impairing liquidity and price discovery?

2. Is it in the "public interest" for regulators to promote greater dissemination of real time trade and quote information (i.e., greater "transparency") in equity markets? Or, should market centers have private property rights to this information and be allowed to contract freely with those who want to buy it?

3. Does the payment for order flow (by dealers or specialists to brokers) enhance competition and serve the interests of investors? Or does the practice represent free-riding (by dealers or specialists off the NYSE's price quotations) which diminishes liquidity and price discovery, while

providing customers with poor trade execution?

4. Does the present regulatory structure put exchanges at a competitive disadvantage in relation to new marketplaces that are regulated as broker-dealers? If so, should regulation of exchanges be reduced? Or should regulation of the new marketplaces be increased? Should neither be done? Or both?

In short, when should the decisions of regulators replace the decisions of firms in the industry? How is the public interest best served? Simply stated, should the SEC play a larger or a smaller role in shaping market structure?

In January 1994, the SEC issued the Market 2000 Report which contains the Division of Market Regulation's policy responses to these and other questions. In a letter transmitting the report to the commission, Division Director Brandon Becker, claims that although "radical reform of how equity trading is conducted or regulated is not necessary . . . regulation has not kept pace with changes in the existing market structure". (SEC Release 34-30920, letter from Brandon Becker to the SEC commissioners.) The report makes several recommendations for SEC action in order to "ensure fair treatment of investors, increase market transparency, foster competition, and expand market access". (SEC Release 34-30920, letter from Brandon Becker). The recommendations include a mix of increased disclosure and reporting requirements; suggested changes in rules and procedures of self-regulatory organizations; and enhanced intermarket linkages.

Although the immediate proposals in the Market 2000 Report do not appear to be dramatic, the report envisions that the Commission will continue to play a prominent role in regulating both the rules and procedures of market centers as well as competition between market centers. This regulatory response is not surprising, given the statutory constraints imposed on the SEC by the 1934 Act and the 1975 National Market System Amendments, as well as an institutional bias of regulators to regulate. However, it is hard to justify a large role for the SEC in regulating market structure at a time when technological change and competitive forces are increasing the contestability of the "market for equity markets."

We view market centers such as the NYSE as business enterprises which supply securities trading services, and argue that the regulation of this industry should be guided by two principles: the elimination of anticompetitive price-fixing (i.e., collusion between market centers in the pricing of their transaction services); and mitigation of externality problems. Note that, unlike the Division's report, our definition of anticompetitive practices does not include *intrafirm* restrictions, such as the NYSE's off-board trading or delisting restrictions. It also does not justify subsidizing rivalry between market centers through mandated intermarket linkages or other methods of enhanced disclosure, although it should allow voluntary linkages, subject to normal antitrust constraints (similar to airline reservation systems, for example, which are not mandated by the Department of Transportation, but are the outcome of voluntary agreements between airlines and travel agents).

Without revisiting the debate over whether or not the NYSE's previous dominant market position once resulted in anticompetitive pricing, one point is clear — as in other industries highly reliant on telecommunications technology, this industry has become quite contestable in recent years.[12] The increase in contestability should suggest a greater reliance on competition between market centers, and a lesser role for regulation, in the securities industry. Just as the increasing contestability of the local telephone market has prompted a policy debate about reducing regulation of the Baby Bells, one can argue that competitive developments in the securities markets should lead the SEC and Congress to rethink the basic premises of securities market regulation.[13]

Despite the special "quasi-governmental" status that Congress has bestowed on self-regulatory organizations, these institutions are, in essence, business enterprises which are now competing with less regulated entities in a market characterized by rapid technological change. We argue that these conditions suggest a smaller, not larger, role for SEC regulation of market mechanisms and market structure, in order to facilitate desirable innovation, experimentation, and adaptation to the new technology. The Commission's regulation of self-regulatory organizations (SROs) and proprietary trading systems (PTSs) should be modelled after its regulation of registered corporations. The SEC does not regulate the governance structure and business decisions of registered companies; instead, its regulation of these companies is confined largely to the disclosure of information. The SEC should regulate enterprises which "produce" market centers in a similar manner.

However, focusing disproportionately on the SEC's behavior ignores the incentives created for the Commission by the 1934 Act and the 1975 Amendments. We further argue that it is timely for Congress to reconsider the rationale for regulating the rules, procedures, and governance structure of SROs and other "producers" of trading services. In a period of rapid technological change, Congressional and SEC control over the organizational structure and business decisions of these enterprises is likely to impede the development of lower-cost ways of trading securities.

After describing the structure of securities market regulation, we describe and critique the SEC's Market 2000 Report. We then provide some concluding comments.

REGULATORY STRUCTURE

Regulation by the SEC

Following the stock market crash of 1929, Congress passed two pieces of legislation that continue to serve as the cornerstone of US securities laws. The Securities Act of 1933 is largely a disclosure law, requiring issuers of securities to disclose information that purportedly allows investors to make informed investment decisions. In addition to its disclosure provisions, the 1933 Act also prohibits the fraudulent sale of registered securities.

The Securities Exchange Act of 1934 (SEA) extends the reach of federal securities laws beyond the disclosure and antifraud provisions of the 1933 Act. Whereas the 1933 Act regulates the primary issuance of securities, the 1934 Act regulates the secondary markets in which securities trade. The SEA also authorizes the SEC, as an independent regulatory agency; prior to this, the 1933 Act was administered by the Federal Trade Commission. Under the 1934 Act, the SEC has legislative authority to regulate exchanges, broker-dealers, and disclosures in secondary markets through its rule-making and enforcement powers. In 1938, Congress passed the Maloney Act, which extended the SEC's regulatory jurisdiction to the over-the-counter (OTC) market.

Independent regulatory agencies in the US are designed to be autonomous from both the executive and legislative branches of the federal government. Like other independent regulatory agencies, the SEC is governed by five commissioners who are nominated by the President and confirmed by the Senate. The President selects a chairman, presently Arthur Levitt, from among the five commissioners. The selection of a chairman does not require Senate confirmation. The purported independence of the SEC from the executive branch derives largely from two institutional features: no more than three commissioners may come from the same political party; and the commissioners' terms are not coterminous with the President. A majority vote of the commissioners is required for rule changes, enforcement actions, legislative proposals, and administrative proceedings.

The SEC has several operating divisions which specialize in different areas of securities regulation.[14] The Division of Market Regulation is largely responsible for regulatory issues pertaining to the microstructure of securities markets, including the regulation of exchanges and broker-dealers. As the SEC's 1990 annual report describes, the Commission's "Division of Market Regulation, together with [its] regional office examination staff, oversees the operations of the nation's securities markets and market professionals."[15] The SEC's Market 2000 Report was produced by the Division of Market Regulation.

Congress retains oversight over the operations of the SEC both through the budget appropriations process and through public hearings, which it holds periodically on issues that appear to have public interest considerations. A large body of scholarly literature argues that independent regulatory agencies can be viewed as agents of Congress, even though ostensibly they are "independent."[16] According to this view, if regulatory agencies prefer larger to smaller budgets, then Congress can affect the behavior of regulatory agencies through the budget appropriations process.

The principal Congressional committees with oversight jurisdiction over the SEC are the Committee on Energy and Commerce in the US House of Representatives, chaired by John Dingell (Democrat from Michigan), and the Committee on Banking and Finance in the US Senate, chaired by Donald S. Riegle (Democrat from Michigan). The respective subcommittees with SEC oversight jurisdiction are the Subcommittee on Telecommunications and Finance, chaired by Edward Markey (Democrat from Massachusetts), and the Subcommittee on Securities, chaired by Christopher Dodd (Democrat from Connecticut). These committees and subcommittees have held several hearings on the structure of securities markets in recent years. Most recently, Chairman Markey's Subcommittee on Telecommunications and Finance held hearings during the spring of 1993 on the national market system (April 14, 1993), inducements for order flow (May 13, 1993), and proprietary trading systems (May 26, 1993), three topics addressed in the SEC's Market 2000 release.

After the passage of the Maloney Act in 1938, the next major legislative event affecting the SEC's authority to regulate market structure occurred in 1975, with the passage of amendments to the 1934 Act. The Amendments, often referred to as the National Market System Amendments, require the SEC to facilitate the development of a national market system for trading securities. In addition, the Amendments bring clearinghouses and suppliers of financial information under SEC jurisdiction, and they strengthen the SEC's authority over rule-making by self-regulatory organizations. For example, the Amendments state that

> Self-regulatory organizations must display a greater responsiveness to their statutory obligations and to the need to coordinate their functions and activities. In the new regulatory environment created by this bill, self-regulation would be continued, but the SEC would be expected to play a much larger role than it has in the past to ensure that there is no gap between self-regulatory performance and regulatory need and, when appropriate, to provide leadership for the development of a more coherent and rational regulatory structure to correspond to and to police effectively the new national market system.

Congress and the SEC initially disagreed over how much authority the Commission should have to regulate market structure in the securities industry. Congressional oversight committees preferred to grant the SEC more authority to promote "competition" among marketplaces through the development of a national market system for trading securities. Khademian (1992, p. 74) describes the Congressional desire by quoting a former staff member of the SEC who participated in the drafting of the 1975 Amendments.

> For [Representative] Moss [chairman of the House Subcommittee] and particularly [Senator] Williams [chairman of the Senate Subcommittee], they wanted to abolish the floor of the New York Stock Exchange, and create this kind of... black box trading system, set up to [receive orders to trade stock and] disseminate information at the speed of light. There would be no coming together of people on the New York Stock Exchange.

In contrast, the Commission resisted the Congressional demands for it to micromanage the design of a national market system, preferring instead to rely on a combination of disclosure and incremental rule-making to promote "competition." For example, Khademian (1992, p. 73), cites the following passage from an SEC letter transmitting the Institutional Investor Study (Securities and Exchange Commission 1971):

> We do not believe ... that it is either feasible or desirable for the Commission or any other agency of the government to predetermine and require a particular structure, and still less to specify now particular procedures for the markets of the future. It is better to observe and, if necessary, to modify the structure which evolves through the ingenuity and response of the marketplace.

The SEC largely prevailed, as the 1975 Amendments establish goals for a national market system, but refrain from directing the SEC to micromanage the structure of equity markets. Becker and Angstadt (1994) describe the mandate given to the SEC by the 1975 Amendments.

> Congress did not define what the NMS [national market system] was or what it should be. Instead, Congress believed that it was best to provide the Commission maximum flexibility and discretion in working out specific details, and that the NMS should evolve through the interplay of competitive forces as unnecessary restrictions were removed. The Commission was expected, in those situations where competition was not sufficient, to use the powers granted to it to act promptly and effectively to ensure the NMS was put in place.

The Amendments establish five goals of a national market system, including (1) fair competition among brokers and dealers, among exchange markets, and between exchanges and other marketplaces; (2) economically efficient executions of securities transactions; (3) availability to brokers, dealers, and investors of information with respect to quotations for and transactions in securities; (4) opportunities for best trade execution; and (5) the opportunity for the execution of customer orders without dealer intervention. Congress also called for the linking of markets for qualified securities through communication and data processing facilities.

The 1975 Amendments potentially expand the SEC's role in affecting the industrial organization of US equity markets. In 1975, the year the Amendments were passed, the commission adopted a rule phasing out fixed brokerage commission rates on grounds that agreements among exchange members to fix commission rates are anticompetitive. Since the 1975 Amendments, the major SEC actions affecting market structure include an attempt to foster intermarket competition through the adoption of Rule 19c-3, which allows exchange members to act as dealers in stocks that were newly listed on an exchange after April 26, 1979; and attempts to make markets more transparent through the development and refinement of intermarket linkages, such as the Intermarket Trading System (which displays quotation information at participating markets and provides order routing facilities), the Consolidated Transactions Tape (which disseminates last sale price and volume information for exchange listed stocks), and the Consolidated Quotations System (which disseminates best bids and offers in exchange-listed stocks to vendors).

Regulation by SROs

As noted above, US securities regulation is a mixture of federal oversight and reliance on the self-regulatory organizations. US exchanges are SROs with rules designed to "prevent fraudulent acts and practices, to promote just and equitable principles of trade, to foster cooperation and coordination with persons engaged in regulating, clearing, settling, processing information with respect to, and facilitating transactions in securities."[17] Section 6(b)(1) of the 1934 Act provides that the criteria for registration as a national securities exchange include a determination by the SEC that, among other things, an exchange has the organization and capacity to comply, and to enforce compliance by its members and persons associated therewith, with the provisions of the 1934 Act, the rules promulgated by the SEC under the 1934 Act, and the rules of the exchange.

In addition, Section 19(g)(1) of the Act requires that an exchange enforce compliance by its members and associated persons with such provisions. Market professionals (brokers, dealers, investment managers) are required to register with the SEC. Brokers and dealers are also required to be members of a self-regulatory organization which is responsible for supervising their trading activity and assuring that it conforms with federal securities laws.

Congress views securities exchanges as quasi-governmental institutions. This role was stated explicitly in a report by the Committee on Banking, Housing, and Urban Affairs associated with the 1975 Amendments.

> The Committee has found a common and serious misunderstanding of the nature and limits of the concept of self-regulation . . . self-regulation is thought to mean that the securities industry regulated itself and therefore is not

> regulated by the government . . . this fails to recognize the essential and continuing role of the federal government. Industry regulation and governmental regulation are not alternatives, but complementary components of the self-regulatory process . . . The SEC is charged with supervising the exercise of this self-regulatory power.

The interface between self-regulation and SEC oversight underlines much of the rule-making discussed in the Market 2000 Report and this paper.

The self-regulatory role is well illustrated by the specialist's job description contained in the NYSE's Floor Official Manual,[18]

> An exchange member registered as a specialist is accountable to the Exchange for the quality of the Exchange markets in the securities in which the specialist is registered . . . The specialist helps ensure that such markets are fair, orderly, operationally efficient and competitive with other markets in those securities. A "fair" market is free from manipulative and deceptive practices and affords no undue advantage to any participant. An "orderly" market is characterized by regular, reliable operation, with price continuity and depth, in which price movements are accompanied by appropriate volume, and unreasonable price variations between sales are avoided . . . As is true of all exchange members, the specialist is expected to adhere to all applicable Federal laws and regulations, and Exchange rules and policies, including the provisions that apply to specialists in Section 11(b) of the Securities Exchange Act of 1934.

The NYSE's Division of Enforcement is part of its regulatory group that also includes the Division of Member Firm Regulation, responsible for conducting periodic examinations of member firms and monitoring their financial condition, operations, and sales practices; and the Division of Market Surveillance, responsible for monitoring the trading activities of members, member firms, and their customers.[19] In 1991, there were 476 people with regulatory responsibilities at the NYSE, 95 in surveillance alone. The primary role of the surveillance group is the monitoring of trade data and the investigation of abuses relating to insider trading, market manipulation, front-running, specialists' obligations (both affirmative and negative as discussed below), member firms' proprietary trading, and rules governing the NYSE's trading floor.

The Intermarket Surveillance Information System (ISIS) is an extensive data base containing more than twenty-five billion pieces of on-line information including current and historical consolidated trade, quote, and clearance data. ISIS contains pertinent information on all orders entered through the NYSE's automated delivery system, as well as data relating to program trading on the exchange. In addition, ISIS produces an audit trail, which is a sequential reconstruction of trading in each stock, identifying the time of trade, the buying and selling member firms, the floor brokers who represented the order involved, and whether the trade was for a member firm's proprietary account.

Surveillance analysts review, among other things, price continuity, market depth, and specialists' trading activity including the extent of participation and degree to which such dealings are stabilizing. SEC rule 11b-1 allows an exchange to have a specialist system if it adopts various rules. Among other things, an exchange's rules must (1) establish "adequate capital requirements" for specialists; (2) impose limits on specialists' trading, including restrictions limiting specialists' trading as far as practicable to these dealings reasonably necessary to maintain a fair and orderly market; and (3) provide procedures for the effective and systematic surveillance of the activities of specialists.

Over and above the capital requirements, the limitations on dealing effectively require that specialists trade as passively as possible (negative obligation) and only when there is a gap between buyers and sellers (affirmative obligation). Specifically, a specialist's affirmative obligation refers to the maintenance of a "fair and orderly market" in the stocks in which he or she is registered. This implies the maintenance of price continuity with reasonable depth and the minimizing of temporary disparities between supply and demand through dealing to a reasonable extent from his or her own account. A specialist's negative obligation refers to the requirement that all purchases and sales by the specialist meet the test of "reasonable necessity" (NYSE Rule 104.10). In the context of the affirmative and negative obligations, there are strict limits on the manner in which specialists can liquidate their positions, special rules governing participation in openings, reporting requirements on all trading activity, and strict controls on preventing the misuse of information when a specialist's unit is affiliated with a member organization conducting a public business.

With respect to surveillance of specialists' trades, the Exchange requires electronic submission of information regarding all dealer trading activity, as well as dealer position information. Such data are integrated for analytical purposes with ISIS. A large number of reviews relating to specialist performance in individual stocks are conducted during the course of a year, supplemented by reviews resulting from inquiries received by the Exchange from the general public, retail investors, institutions, broker-dealers, listed companies, and government agencies. In addition, on a quarterly basis, the Exchange administers the specialist performance evaluation questionnaire (SPEQ), which is completed by floor brokers sufficiently in contact with a specialist unit to be able to fairly evaluate its performance. Specialist unit performance is also reviewed regarding the timeliness of specialists' interactions with orders and administrative messages received through the Exchange's automated order routing system, as well as the timeliness of specialists' openings of stocks. Auctions are overseen not only by specialists but also by floor officials, experienced market professionals who must approve all transactions at specified amounts away from the last sale for a stock trading at less than $20, and $2 for a stock trading at $20 or more (NYSE Constitution, Rule 79A).

Regulation of Broker-Dealers

The duties of registered brokers and dealers are different from those of exchanges. The chief aim of the SEC's regulation of broker-dealers is to protect their customers. The SEC defines a "broker" as any person "engaged in the business of effecting transactions in securities for the accounts of others, but does not include a bank." They are required to register with the SEC and with an SRO by which they are supervised. Broker-dealers do not have special responsibilities for enforcing the SEA, but must agree to abide by federal securities law. Thus, the business practices of NYSE or NASD broker-dealers are supervised by the New York Stock Exchange and the National Association of Securities Dealers, respectively. Often brokers and dealers are members of several exchanges, which results in duplicate supervision. Those that also are active in the futures markets must register with the National Futures Association (NFA) and abide by its requirements. These overlapping jurisdictions do result in much duplication, and some inconsistencies.

The requirements for exchange membership include a standard for capital adequacy, registration with the SEC, and completion of the necessary certification to operate as a broker-dealer. NYSE membership is further restricted to entities which pass a primary purpose test — 50 percent of their brokerage businesses are with the public. The Martin Report was written at the time of hearings preceding the 1975 Act Amendments (*The Securities Markets*, William McChesney Martin, Jr.) and took the position that the overriding concern was the concentration of economic power which might result from institutional membership. According to the report, concentration of power could lead to a market dominated by dealers dealing for their own account, which would tend toward the elimination of the agency relationship between broker and customer. An additional concern was that the interests of powerful groups would not be the same as those of the "general public investor."

Thus, by law, NYSE membership is restricted to broker-dealers. Additionally, Section 11(a) prohibits Exchange members from effecting transactions on national securities exchanges of which they are members for accounts managed by the member or its associated persons. Consistent with the concerns referred to above, the restriction was adopted in the mid-1970s due to concerns over institutional access to exchanges and the potential conflicts of interest resulting from allowing combinations of money management and brokerage functions. Money managers can use affiliated brokers to do everything other than actually executing a buy or sell order on the exchange floor for their managed accounts. Thus, Exchange members can effect transactions for managed accounts as long as independent brokers execute the trades on the Exchange floor. Section 11(a) has come under increasing pressure for repeal from the industry.

THE SEC'S MARKET 2000 REPORT

Motivation

Roughly twenty years after its last major studies of US equity markets,[20] which preceded the passage of the 1975 Amendments, in December 1991 the SEC announced that its Division of Market Regulation would undertake a major study of issues relating to the industrial structure of US equity markets. As a prelude to the Market 2000 Report, the Commission's July 1992 concept release asks for public comments on several issues related to market structure. In the introductory section of the concept release, the SEC refers to several market developments in the past twenty years that precipitate the study, including (1) the dramatic increase in equity market trading volume; (2) the growing importance of large institutional investors; (3) the proliferation of equity derivative products, including individual stock options, stock index options, and stock index futures; (4) the development of new equity trading strategies, such as program trading, index arbitrage, and indexation; (5) technological innovations that have facilitated order routing and execution; and (6) certain equity brokerage practices (e.g., growth in payment for order flow and the use of third-party soft dollars).

The concept release fails to document any adverse effects of these market developments on economic efficiency or investor welfare. The Commission recognizes that "to date, technological and competitive developments appear to have benefited investors by sharply reducing transaction costs" (SEC Release 34-30920, note 11, p. 8) and that "it does not appear that any of these issues poses an immediate threat to the quality of US equity markets" (SEC Release 34–30920, pp. 9–10). However, the SEC adopts the perspective that potential "problems" may be in their incipient stages and therefore may require regulatory attention.

Regulatory Approach Advocated in Market 2000

In January 1994, the SEC released the Market 2000 Report. The report contains specific proposals for the SEC under the headings transparency, fair treatment of investors, fair market competition, and open market access. A description and discussion of these proposals comes later in this section.

For the most part, the Report claims that competition has been effective in leading the market centers to greater efficiency. For instance, it states that "competition for equity market share has resulted in notable service improvements and efficiencies, and has forced the primary markets to respond to their users" (Market 2000, note 12, p. III–1). Nonetheless, the

Report anticipates that the SEC will continue to play a large role in regulating market structure. Perhaps the most fundamental purpose of the study is reflected in the following statement:

> ... the markets and users continue, however, to operate within the framework of a regulatory structure that was created 20 years ago under very different market conditions. Whether this structure still works is the primary focus of the Market 2000 study (Market 2000, p. 4).

The Division's answer is suggested by the following statement:

> ... the strength of the US equity markets are evidence of the effectiveness of the markets' and Commission's efforts since 1975, and the viability of the standards embodied in the 1975 Amendments. The challenge in 1975 was to correct a market structure that could not accommodate the increase in institutional activity or technological change. The Commission and Congress met that challenge with the 1975 Amendments. As a result, the markets now fulfil the needs of an ever-expanding universe of investors (Market 2000, p. 13).

By so associating the quality of markets with the involvement of the SEC, the Report reaffirms the 1975 Amendments and their mandate for the development of a national market system. This posture effectively keeps the SEC involved in market structure issues. For example, in the Report's conclusion, the Division states that its recommendations are "consistent with the Congressional intent expressed in the 1975 Amendments and reflects the market's evolution since that time" (Market 2000, p.32). It then cites a multitude of goals which its recommendations are designed to achieve.

> The Division believes that its recommendations will enable the Commission to carry out the goal of ensuring fair and transparent equity markets while providing for an environment where investor protection is enhanced and the needs of individuals and institutions are met. The recommended initiatives also address the competitive concerns expressed by the different market participants and significantly improve NASDAQ [National Association of Securities Dealers Automatic Quotation] (Market 2000).

In short, in crafting its recommendations, the Division attempts to juggle numerous goals imposed on the SEC by the 1975 Amendments. For reasons discussed later in this section, it is unlikely that the SEC has the information and incentives necessary to achieve a desirable balance between these goals. Furthermore, its substantial involvement in the regulation of market centers maintains the regulatory uncertainty that hangs over new, innovative trading systems and impedes the adjustment of SROs and PTSs to new ways of trading securities. For example, operations that do not conform with the SEC's vision of a national market system may be discouraged or even disallowed. As we discuss later in the section, this power to enforce or disallow is likely to damage the dynamic development of the US securities markets.

Analysis of the Market 2000 Report

A Framework for Examining Market 2000

Later in this section, we describe and comment on specific policy recommendations contained in the Report, but our first goal is to critique the report's absence of a conceptual framework to guide the SEC's regulation of market structure. In part, our analysis builds on points raised initially in Kleidon (1992).

Market centers as business enterprises

We adopt the perspective that self-regulatory organizations and proprietary trading systems are business enterprises that compete in the market for transaction services. There are several dimensions on which they compete, including the provision of (1) immediacy, (2) price discovery, (3) low price volatility, (4) liquidity, (5) transparency, and (6) transaction costs.[21] Some cater only to institutional investors (e.g., Arizona Stock Exchange, POSIT, Instinet), while others service both retail and institutional investors (e.g., NYSE). The production of transaction services is costly and requires (1) the development of rules and procedures to govern trading activity, (2) investments in trading facilities, and (3) a governance structure which allocates decision rights within the enterprise.[22]

A growing literature on the governance of firms suggests that governance structures matter and that the choice of governance structures conforms with rationality.[23] Most relevant for this paper is the relation between the instability of a firm's operating environment and its governance structure. In unstable environments, where rapid decision-making is desirable, firms are expected to develop accommodating governance structures that are less bureaucratic than those observed in more stable environments. For example, firms in the biotechnology industry are expected to select different governance structures (e.g., smaller boards of directors, higher insider holdings of equity) than their counterparts in the electric utility industry.

The special legal status of SROs mandates a highly bureaucratic governance structure for these enterprises, while their PTS counterparts are allowed to select from a larger menu of governance structures. The SROs are required by law to be nonprofit membership corporations which are quasi-governmental institutions. Since the 1934 Act, SROs are required to play an important role in the regulatory process and are subject to substantial oversight from both Congress and the SEC. For example, Section 19(b) of the 1934 Act requires SROs to file all proposed rule changes with the SEC. The SEC then publishes notice of proposed rule changes and awaits written comments from the public. The proposed rule changes do not become effective unless the SEC approves them and this can only occur after the notice period.

In contrast to the SROs, the PTSs are for-profit corporations, not membership organizations, and have more nimble governance structures. Perhaps most importantly, the PTSs are exempt from Section 19(b), which allows them to adapt their rules and procedures to changing market conditions. While these institutions also are subject to SEC regulation, it is less onerous than that governing SROs.

The Division recognizes the controversy over the disparate regulatory treatment of SROs and PTSs. Under the heading of "fair market competition," the Division states that "the SROs point out that PTSs may add new services or procedures to their systems instantaneously without governmental approval . . . The SROs believe that their competitors should be subject to the same review process as they are, or alternatively, that the SROs should be relieved from the review requirement" (Market 2000, p. 28). As we discuss later, the Division proposes to "level the playing field" somewhat by increasing record-keeping requirements for the PTSs and expediting the Section 19(b) review process for SROs for certain administrative proposals.

Because the 1934 Act and the 1975 Amendments require the SEC to play an important role in the governance of the SROs, these enterprises are burdened with bureaucratic, decision-making processes at a time when technological change and competitive forces are inducing substantial change in the industry. Whereas many large enterprises in other industries have substantially decentralized their organizations over the past several years, especially those experiencing large losses of market share and value (e.g., General Motors and IBM), the SROs are constrained in similarly adapting their organizational structures to a rapidly changing environment.

Jensen and Meckling (1992) provide a framework for examining the advantages and disadvantages of centralized versus decentralized decision-making in business enterprises. Where specific knowledge exists, defined as knowledge that is costly to transfer, an advantage of decentralization is that it co-locates decision rights with individuals at lower levels of the organization who possess knowledge about input prices, technology, customers' tastes, and so forth. This raises the likelihood that the "right" decisions are made. However, a disadvantage of decentralization is that the decision-makers may use the rights to maximize their own utility, rather than the value of their organizations. Hence, greater decentralization results in lower information costs, but higher agency costs, and greater centralization results in the opposite. One of the tasks faced by all organizations is to choose a governance structure that strikes an efficient balance between these two costs.

The SEC's involvement in the governance of SROs represents a high degree of centralized decision-making. Following Jensen and Meckling, one of the costs of this governance structure is that the Commission does not have the information and business expertise that managers of market centers are likely to possess. Hence, SEC involvement in the business decisions of market centers is likely to be costly, since the likelihood of value-reducing decisions increases. The bureaucratic regulatory procedures impose additional costs on market centers, both directly and indirectly through foregone (or less profitable) opportunities. These costs are likely to be higher in periods when both production functions and consumer preferences are changing rapidly, as they are today in the securities industry.

The benefit of centralized decision-making generally is that it may mitigate agency problems at lower levels of the organization. This presupposes the incentives of centralized decision-makers are more compatible with the owners' wishes than those of the lower-level decision-makers. In the case of SEC regulation of SROs, this is a suspect assumption. The "owner" in this case presumably is "the public." The implicit assumption behind SEC regulation is that the public interest would be ill-served if SROs were allowed to operate as for-profit enterprises, independent of SEC control. Regardless of whether the "natural monopoly" rationale for this position was once valid, it is certainly less true today.[24]

This is not to say there is no reason for regulating SROs and other market centers. As with firms in other industries, regulation can play a useful purpose in mitigating anticompetitive behavior and externalities. But direct regulation of business decisions, especially in a highly unstable environment, is likely to result in high costs, with little or no public benefit. The Division recognizes this somewhat in the report and proposes a streamlined 19(b) process for SROs. However, no conceptual justification is provided for continued SEC involvement in the governance of SROs. This is not a policy decision the SEC can make; it is a matter for the US Congress.

Oesterle, Winslow, and Anderson (1992) argue that the traditional organizational structure of the NYSE is stifling innovation and inhibiting the development of more effective equity markets. In response, Cochrane, McNamara, Shapiro and Simon (1993) point out that Oesterle, Winslow, and Anderson's proposal for restructuring the governance structure of the NYSE presently is illegal. They note that Section 6 of the 1934 Act mandates that only broker-dealers, or persons associated with broker-dealers, can be members of an exchange. Also, such members must be "fairly represented" in the selection of exchange directors, as well as in the administration of an exchange's affairs. These requirements effectively limit exchanges to be membership-controlled, not-for-profit corporations.

Cochrane et al. also note that Congress clearly intends the exchanges to be membership-controlled entities. While the law allows considerable flexibility in the governance structure of clearing agencies, it restricts the organizational structure of exchanges. This issue also has been addressed by the courts. For example, a 1990 ruling of the US Court of Appeals for the Seventh Circuit held that

> The Delta System cannot register as an exchange because the statute requires an exchange to be controlled by its participants, who must be registered brokers or individuals associated with such brokers.

The authors note that they "do not mean to imply that it would never be appropriate for a US exchange to operate as a for-profit corporation with governance separated from membership." What they demonstrate is that the possibility is "contrary to current US legal requirements and Congress expressed intent on how exchanges should be governed."

Since organizational structure matters for economic performance, the SEC and Congress should consider freeing SROs from this regulatory process and widening the choice of organizational forms they can adopt. Competition for order flow will reward market centers that choose appropriate governance structures and business decisions, while penalizing those which do not.

Defining competition

The Securities Exchange Act (SEA), which circumscribes the authority of the SEC, stresses the role of regulatory oversight as being in the "public interest."[25] In the SEA and the 1975 Amendments, the term "public interest" often is linked with the phrase "or the protection of investors and the maintenance of fair and orderly markets," as in Section 11(a) dealing with the "segregation and limitation of functions of members, brokers, and dealers."

> The Commission shall prescribe such rules and regulations as it deems necessary or appropriate in the public interest or for the protection of investors . . .

And in Paragraph 1095, mandating the establishment of a national market system.

> The Commission is directed, therefore having due regard for the public interest, the protection of investors, and the maintenance of fair and orderly markets, to use its authority under this title to facilitate the establishment of a national market system for securities.

Congress also regards the public interest as benefiting from a competitive environment. In Section 249 of the 1975 Amendments, Congress seeks to clarify the authority of the SEC "to take all necessary steps to bring . . . a national market system into existence . . . The objective would be to enhance competition and to allow economic forces, interacting within a fair regulatory field, to arrive at appropriate variations in practices and services."

Carrying out the Congressional mandate to promote competition between marketplaces is not without ambiguities for the SEC, since the term *competition* has many different meanings. As Bork (1978, p. 58) points out in a classic text on antitrust policy, the ambiguous meanings of "competition" often result "in the fruitless discourse of men talking past each other." Bork cites several definitions of competition that have been used in antitrust law, including (1) the presence of rivalry, (2) the absence of restraints by one firm over others, (3) the existence of a fragmented market consisting of many small firms, and (4) economically efficient resource allocation. Implicitly, the Division's report accepts the first two definitions of competition, which may not be consistent with economic efficiency and the interest of investors.

Economists usually refer to *competitive* outcomes as those which promote economic efficiency (i.e., the sum of producer and consumer surplus). Economic efficiency, in turn, has two components: allocative efficiency, which concerns the relation between price and marginal cost; and productive efficiency, which concerns the unit costs associated with the production of goods and services.[26] An analytical device that frames the frequent trade-off between the two types of efficiency is shown in Figure 3.1, which was developed by Williamson (1968) for the purpose of examining the welfare effects of mergers.

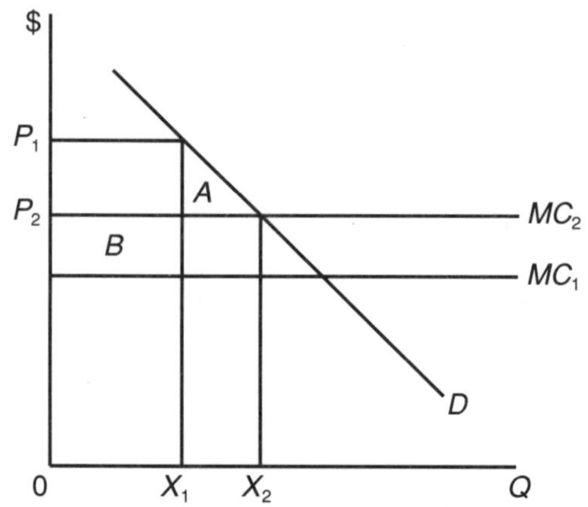

Figure 3.1 Efficiency Effects of a Monopoly that Restricts Output and Lowers Costs. Adapted from Bork (1978).

Figure 3.1 reveals the trade-off associated with market structures that provide firms with the ability to set price above marginal cost. The deadweight efficiency loss associated with this pricing policy is triangle *A*. This reflects the fact that profit-maximizing firms with *market power* will produce X_1 units of output and charge a price of P_1, even though the marginal cost of production is less than the marginal benefit to consumers over the output range from X_1 to X_2.

Triangle *A* represents a loss of allocative efficiency. However, "market power," the ability to set price above marginal cost, usually is obtained because a firm has lower unit costs of production. Without this, it is hard to imagine how the firm achieved its dominant market position in the first place. The efficiency gains associated with this market structure are rectangle *B*. This represents the fact that the unit costs of production over the output range from 0 to X_1 are lower for the firm with the price-setting ability than they are for other firms in the industry. This rectangle represents the gains in productive efficiency.

Figure 3.1 provides a simple conceptual framework for identifying the trade-offs associated with alternative market structures. Most importantly, the promotion of allocative efficiency, reducing the triangle, may come at the expense of reducing productive efficiency, reducing the rectangle. From an efficiency point of view, the objective should not be the maximization of allocative efficiency per se, but rather the maximization of producer and consumer surplus.

The Division's report ignores the *efficiency* definition of competition and instead seems to equate competition with the promotion of rivalry. For example, the Division implicitly adopts the rivalry definition to justify mandated market linkages, such as the Intermarket Trading System (ITS). In the concept release, the Division describes the ITS as "an important addition to the National Market System" (SEC Release 34-30920, note 10, p. 19) in part because it purportedly enhances the competitive position of regional exchanges compared with the NYSE. The release states that ITS has permitted "regional specialists to attract orders from other markets by providing superior quotations and facilitated their market-making by enabling them to lay off their risk positions more efficiently, and at lower cost, through offsetting transactions on primary markets" (SEC Release 34-30920, note 10, p.19).

Enhanced rivalry of the sort promoted by the Division often leads to greater efficiency, but is also can lead to less efficient outcomes, especially if subsidized by government regulation. An example often used in antitrust is the case of resale price maintenance, the practice whereby a manufacturer requires retailers to sell its product at a minimum or maximum retail price established by the manufacturer. One view is that this practice is intrinsically anticompetitive since it diminishes price rivalry in the retail market. An alternative view is that resale price maintenance can promote efficiency by discouraging socially wasteful price rivalry. This can be the case if a manufacturer wants retailers to invest in the advertising, promotion, and marketing of its products. Without resale price maintenance or another type of vertical restraint, retailers (e.g., department stores) would be reluctant to incur costs associated with the promotion of products, since other retailers (e.g., discount chains) could free ride off their promotion and undercut their prices because they have not incurred the costs of advertising, promotion, and marketing. This is one illustration of how the promotion of price rivalry may work contrary to economic efficiency.

In a similar way, mandated market linkages may promote rivalry between market centers, but they can also diminish economic efficiency. The primary market is analogous to the department store that incurs the cost of advertising, promotion, and marketing. Potentially, other market centers can free ride off the primary market's quotes and perhaps provide "superior" quotes since they have invested less in the facilities necessary for price discovery. If mandated linkages reduce the ability of primary markets to capture the returns on their investments in price discovery, they have less incentive to produce price discovery. Hence, the promotion of rivalry through mandated linkages may have the perverse effect of reducing the quality of transaction prices. In the context of Figure 3.1, mandated linkages may improve allocative efficiency but impair productive efficiency. We revisit this issue later in our discussion of transparency as it is dealt with in the Market 2000 Report.

The Division also takes a narrow view of competition in its discussion of contractual restraints that exchanges place on their members and listed companies. For example, the Division expresses concern about the effects of NYSE Rule 390 on competition, since it limits the ability of NYSE members to effect transactions off an exchange. Coase (1988, p. 9) has commented more generally on a tendency to view exchange rules as anticompetitive.

> . . . economists observing the regulations of the exchanges often assume that they represent an attempt to exercise monopoly power and aim to restrain competition. They ignore, or at any rate, fail to emphasize an alternative explanation for these regulations: that they exist in order to lower transaction costs and therefore to increase the volume of trade.

Exchange members may voluntarily agree to limit their behavior through rules like NYSE Rule 390, an off-board trading restriction, in order to enhance the efficiency of the exchange. Off-board trading restrictions can promote economic efficiency by mitigating the problems associated with fragmented order flow. By consolidating order flow, these restrictions are likely to sharpen price discovery, foster liquidity, and generally reduce the cost of providing trading services. In this regard, they may be inconsistent with a definition of competition that judges competition by the absence of restraints of one firm over another, but not inconsistent with an efficiency-based definition of competition.[27]

It is noteworthy that the order consolidation rules, which the Division views as anticompetitive, had their genesis before the NYSE became the dominant market for equity trading; these rules originated as part of the Buttonwood Agreement in the late eighteenth century. Since anticompetitive devices are self-defeating in competitive markets, it is unlikely the raison d'être of order consolidation rules is to deter competition. Furthermore, since the NYSE emerged as the dominant firm in a market initially characterized by many competitors, its dominance is likely derived from its superior ability in providing transaction services, otherwise how did it emerge as the dominant firm? To the extent that the rules governing trading in its market, such as order consolidation rules, account in part for its success, these rules should not be viewed as intrinsically anticompetitive.

It is unwise for the Division to regulate voluntary, *intrafirm* contractual agreements, such as NYSE Rule 390, in a market which it characterizes as "highly competitive." If the market is highly competitive, there cannot be any loss of allocative efficiency, since any attempt to set price above marginal cost would be self-defeating. Yet, a mandated abolition of Rule 390 risks a loss of productive efficiency. More generally, this perspective suggests the Division should limit its "antitrust" regulation to agreements between market centers to restrict output or collude on the pricing of their services. As seen in Figure 3.1, *interfirm* collusion results in a loss of allocative efficiency with no countervailing gain in productive efficiency.

Externalities, regulation, and property rights

The division's report identifies many purported "market failures" and recommends numerous corrective policy actions. However, as the burgeoning literature on the economics of regulation shows,[28] governments, as well as markets, often "fail" to achieve idealized outcomes. The Division's report commits the "nirvana" fallacy described initially by Demsetz (1969, pp. 1–2).

> The view that now pervades much public policy economics implicitly presents the relevant choice as between an ideal norm and an existing "imperfect" institutional arrangement. The nirvana approach differs considerably from a comparative approach in which the relevant choice is between real institutional arrangements . . . Whether the free enterprise solution can be improved upon by the substitution of the government or other nonprofit institutions . . . cannot be ascertained solely by examining the free enterprise solution. The political or nonprofit forces that are substituted for free enterprise must be analyzed and the outcome of the workings of these forces must be compared to the market solution before any such conclusions can be drawn.

In particular, there are costs associated with using government regulation to supplant market outcomes, including the costs associated with (1) collecting and analyzing information; (2) rent-seeking behavior, whereby interest groups compete for regulations that advance their economic interests, even though the regulations may impair efficiency; and (3) the creation of institutional or statutory rigidities that may not be easily modified later.

It is widely accepted that an appropriate role for government regulation is to mitigate the effects of externalities. Externalities, in the tradition of Pigou, are said to exist when there is a divergence between the private and social costs (or benefits) of one's behavior. Regulation or taxes often are prescribed as solutions to the externality problem. However, as Coase (1960) showed in a seminal article, a necessary condition for the persistence of externalities is the existence of transaction costs. Without transaction costs, economic agents will bargain to an efficient outcome. However, as a precondition to bargaining, property rights must be well defined. Hence, as an alternative to regulation and taxes, some externality "problems" can be resolved most efficiently by creating well-defined property rights, and allowing market forces to determine resource allocation.

The Division's report commits the nirvana fallacy by asserting that the optimal amount of transparency (i.e., the dissemination of real-time trade and price information) in securities markets can only be achieved through regulation. In fact, the Division's approach to transparency not only fails to appreciate there may be a property rights/contracting solution to the transparency problem, but regulation itself may actually create new externality problems.

As pointed out in Bronfman and Overdahl (1993) and Bronfman (1992), a 1984 SEC ruling, which determined the NASD's obligations to sell real-time information to Instinet, effectively allowed the NASD to charge no more than its costs for the collection and dissemination of quotation data.[29] This policy was consistent with the Congressional sentiment at the time that exchanges should be treated as public utilities. Congress was less concerned with compensating the producers of information and more concerned with assuring that all securities information processors distribute and publish the information on *fair and reasonable terms*. This ruling has had the effect of restricting the freedom of a market center to price its product. Consistent with public utility regulation, the SEC ruling encouraged cost-based pricing regulation in the dissemination of real-time trade information, since the law regards the transaction prices produced by exchanges as being in the public domain.

The present regulatory policy towards transparency contrasts sharply with a property-rights-based approach which previously existed. Mulherin, Netter, and Overdahl (1991) and Bronfman and Overdahl (1993) trace how the rights to trade and quote information in financial markets evolved in the nineteenth century after the advent of the telegraph. The telegraph facilitated free riding by "bucket shops" off the prices discovered in primary markets, which set off legal disputes concerning the ownership rights to information about securities and future prices. These disputes culminated in a 1905 decision in which the Supreme Court ruled that information about trades is the property of the exchanges on which the trades occur.[30] Once the ownership rights to this information were defined, exchanges were free to sell these rights to vendors and other market centers at freely negotiated prices. Hence, determining how much real-time information should be disseminated need not be a problem for the SEC, provided rights to this information are well defined.[31] However, by viewing this information as being in the "public interest," and subjecting exchanges to cost-based pricing in the dissemination of this information, the SEC has created a public-goods-like problem where one need not exist.

A disadvantage of a regulatory solution to the transparency problem is that the Division adopts the view that transparency is an unambiguous good, and ignores its associated costs.[32] One disadvantage of mandating greater transparency can be seen by observing order flow between international securities markets with different levels of transparency. For example, the Securities and Investments Board in London requires only that firm quotes be displayed on the Stock Exchange Automatic Quotation (SEAQ) system screens. Transaction prices and volume information are released, but with a lag, currently as long as five business days for the largest trades. Because the London market is a dealer market, NYSE members who route their orders to London when the NYSE is closed do not run afoul of NYSE Rule 390. The London International Stock Exchange (ISE) thus competes directly with the NYSE for order flow and the resulting trading volume. Competition arises, in part, because of differences in the microstructure of the market centers. The willingness of dealers in London to put large amounts of capital at risk allows large traders to minimize the market impact of their orders, and thus reduces an implicit cost of trading. Because the dealers take large positions to accommodate these traders, the exchanges differ significantly in terms of the level of transparency. A dealer who has a large inventory (long or short) will want to be able to unwind the position before the trade is publicly revealed. However, these differences in the levels of transparency create problems for the NYSE.

In addition to the cost imposed on the NYSE because of these differences in transparency and the loss of order flow to London, the asymmetry means that the more opaque exchange, London, has better information. While market professionals in London can monitor the prices set on the NYSE, the NYSE is less aware of market activity in London. At least some portion of the costs that the opaque market imposes on the retail market could be recovered if the "transparent" NYSE could charge appropriately for the contemporaneous dissemination of its market data.

By regulating both the level of transparency and the price at which the information can be sold, Congress, through the SEC, has prevented market-based contracting solutions to informational problems between competing exchanges, necessitating more complicated regulations.[33] By precluding a market solution, the dual regulation of the level of transparency and the price at which the information can be sold has created a public-goods-type problem; the regulators now face the problem of how to regulate the proprietary trading systems, several of which free ride off the price discovery of the NYSE.

Critique of Market 2000

Earlier we critiqued the Division's report for lacking a conceptual framework to govern its policy recommendations on issues pertaining to the governance of SROs and PTSs, competition, and externalities. Now we describe and comment on specific recommendations made by the Division under the report's four headings: transparency, fair treatment of investors, fair competition, and open market access.

Transparency

Reports recommendations — The Market 2000 Report (Study IV, Transparency) defines transparency as the "extent to which trading information (i.e., information regarding quotations, price, and volume of transactions) is made publicly available promptly after either the entry of a quotation or completion of a transaction" (Market 2000, note 12, p. IV–1). It notes that

> The Division (of Market Regulation) believes that transparency plays a fundamental role in the fairness and efficiency of secondary markets. Transparency ensures that stock prices fully reflect information and lowers trading costs by improving investors' ability to assess overall supply and demand. It also contributes to the fairness of the markets by offering all investors timely access to market information . . . The high level of transparency in the US markets today can be attributed largely to Commission action that resulted in the creation of a consolidated quotation system, the consolidated tape, and last-sale reporting for NASDAQ securities (Market 2000, note 12, p. 17).

One of the Report's conclusions is that the Division believes the Commission must lead the markets again to enhance transparency (Market 2000, note 12). The Division's recommendations in this area focus on the disclosure of customer interest within a given market, the exposure of customer orders across markets, narrowing the minimum spread variation, and public reporting of after-hours trades and of overseas trades of US equities. We expand on these recommendations briefly below then include some comments of our own immediately after.

The Division recommends the SROs to consider whether to encourage the display of all limit orders in listed stocks priced better than the best intermarket quotes (unless the ultimate customer expressly requests an order not be displayed). The Division also recommends the NASD to consider whether to encourage the display of limit orders in NASDAQ stocks when the orders are at prices better than the best NASDAQ quotes (unless the ultimate customer expressly requests an order not to be displayed).

The Division recommends the SROs to develop proposals to reduce the minimum price variation (tick size) lower than the current $0.125, suggesting either one-sixteenth, or the adoption of a decimal pricing system similar to foreign equity markets and the derivative markets. The Report draws support for its recommendation from the fact that much of the trading in stocks on PTSs is done in stocks quoted in eighths, by parties that trade inside the quotes at one-sixteenth or finer.

The Report also raises concerns about the limited information available for trading on SelectNet, a screen-based trading system on NASDAQ workstations, offered to NASD members to facilitate negotiation of securities transactions through computer automation. SelectNet orders are not always disseminated over all NASDAQ terminals. Instead, market-makers using SelectNet may display orders selectively to other market-makers or may broadcast orders to other market-makers or to all NASD members. In other words, under the current system, discretion is left to the market-maker as to how he or she wants to negotiate the order. The Division also recognizes that mandatory display of all SelectNet orders could discourage the use of SelectNet for larger orders. According to the Report, this is a factor for the NASD to consider in determining how best to increase disclosure.

Trading that takes place in US markets during regular hours is captured by public trade reporting. However, a growing amount of trading is occurring after regular trading hours and in foreign markets and therefore escapes public reporting requirements. The Report recommends that SROs develop a transaction reporting system to capture trades in US equities executed outside regular trading hours.

Both the NYSE and the General Accounting Office have recommended that the Commission reconsider an order exposure rule, and the Report encourages the NYSE together with other SROs to coordinate the development of an order exposure rule for Commission consideration. In developing such a rule, the Report notes that order exposure rules may change the pricing of market-maker services. If market-makers earn less income because they expose orders and execute fewer trades at the quotes, they can be expected to charge higher commissions. While customers may be no better off financially, the Report suggests that the markets as a whole may improve because of greater information on the flow of trading interest.

Authors' critique — We wish to consider the Division's suggested rule-makings in the area of market transparency in the spirit of our comments earlier in the section. Several of the Division's recommendations can be viewed as attempts to redistribute the property rights to information. For example, the Division's recommendations can be interpreted as suggesting the property rights to an order be reassigned from SROs to customers. The Division leaves to the markets the determination of the precise terms and conditions for the display of limit orders, recognizing there may be customers who do not want their orders exposed. This recommendation appears to encourage private contracting as a means of resolving problems related to customer orders.

On the other hand, the rulings suggest some hesitation about the effectiveness of competition in the industry. The Report notes

> . . . the successful capture of NASDAQ volume by PTSs, which do display customer limit orders, demonstrates the appeal of limit order book display. Because access to PTSs is limited, as a practical matter, to institutions, retail investors cannot use PTSs to display limit orders (Market 2000, note 12, p. 18).

Two factors are worth noting: (1) competition among market centers may well lead the NASD to respond out of self-interest even in the absence of SEC rule-making; and (2) SEC regulations prevent retail investors from using the PTSs. We also question whether the recommendations encouraging eventual decimalization of stock prices are wise, given that this is largely a business decision which should be governed by competition among market centers. If decimalization is desired by the customers of an exchange, and it is cost-effective to provide it, the exchanges will have strong private incentives to adopt decimalization without prodding or rule-making from the SEC.

SEC rule-making with respect to making markets transparent maintains the correctness and value of its position. However, the question of why this "unambiguous good" is not being adequately supplied deserves attention. If institutions prefer the anonymity of foreign markets, US markets are perhaps better able than the SEC to assess the trade-offs associated with greater transparency.

Lastly, the order exposure rule raises concerns similar to our earlier cautions about expansion of the ITS; that is, that linkage may reduce a market center's ability to capture a return on its investment in price discovery. Similarly, if one of the dimensions along which competition takes place between market centers is in attempts to capture order flow, an order exposure rule can reduce the number of dimensions along which competition can occur. The impact of the rule on property rights also needs to be addressed. For example, if the NYSE develops a centralized facility, it will capture order flow from other market centers. From this perspective, a consolidated limit order book may have the effect of weakening the competitive thrust from other market centers. Among other questions that should be addressed, will participation be mandated or voluntary and will it be left to the wishes of customers?

Fair treatment of investors

Report's recommendations — A broker-dealer has a duty to seek to obtain the best execution for its customer orders — that is, to obtain the most favorable terms under the circumstances for a customer's transaction — one of the cornerstones of market integrity. The rapid increase in payment for order flow, soft dollar practices, the use of automatic routing procedures, and the use of price improvement are addressed in the Report. Some of the suggestions on transparency discussed above are in part designed to reduce payment for order flow by narrowing spreads. In the main, the Report relies on greater disclosure to customers of these practices and of improved monitoring of execution quality by broker-dealers.

Authors' critique — We return once again to the involvement of the SEC in this level of operation if securities markets are viewed as business enterprises. On the one hand, the markets may have very little incentive to disclose practices that may have the appearance of harming individual customers. On the other hand, the empirical evidence is mixed. Evidence reported below suggests there may be some loss to investors from the payment for order flow but the total dollars involved are relatively small compared to the total dollar volume of trade. Lee (1993) finds that for NYSE-listed securities, the price obtained on similar adjacent trades can differ by location of execution. In particular, the results for 1988 and 1989 suggest that Cincinnati, Midwest, and the NYSE executions are generally more favorable to the initiator of the trade than executions on the other exchanges. The average price difference between the NYSE and the matched off-board trades is between 0.7 cent and one cent per share. In total dollars, the aggregate excess cost for off-board trades is estimated at between \$13 million and \$18 million for 1988 and between \$36 million and \$47 million for 1989. Lee notes that while investors appear to pay more for off-board executions, brokers who receive order flow inducements might indirectly pass on these savings through lower commission fees.

The Report also points out that a broker-dealer's duty to seek to obtain the best execution of customer orders derives from the common law agency duty of loyalty, which obligates an agent to act exclusively in the principal's best interest. This has been incorporated into case law and Commission decisions under the federal securities laws. Failure to exercise reasonable diligence to obtain best execution or provide sufficient disclosure in the absence of obtaining best execution has resulted in violations of the antifraud provisions of federal securities laws. As noted earlier in the report, the Commission has not promulgated a separate best execution rule or explicitly defined best execution. Self-regulatory organizations have prescribed rules or provided interpretive guidance concerning their members' duty to obtain best execution of customers orders.

Nissen (1991) notes that in response to the need to define a broker's fiduciary duties in a principled manner, the courts increasingly have turned to contract law principles. Rather than imposing new broad fiduciary duties on all brokers, courts have looked at the contract between customers and brokers as the source for the broker's duties. Under this theory, a broker's fiduciary duties depend upon what he undertook to do for the customer, and therefore they may be different for different brokers. Rather than rely upon regulation, the Division would be wise to let this matter be governed by contract law and competition among brokerage firms.

Fair market competition

Report's recommendations — The Report notes that the alternative markets and services for equity trading have developed in response to investors' desires to utilize prices discovered in primary markets. The primary markets derive benefits from their primary status (e.g., listing fees, majority of the order flow, membership, and information fees), and they also bear many of the regulatory costs. Therefore, the Report considers whether the primary markets are saddled by burdens that affect their competitiveness. While resistant to suggestions that the exchanges deserve compensation for their provision of price discovery, the Report suggests that fair market competition can be promoted by fairly allocating regulatory responsibilities among the various market centers. Specifically, the Report considers the surveillance and order handling responsibilities for third market trading (issues of self-dealing and safeguards against fragmentation), additional record-keeping and reporting requirement for PTSs, transaction fees for NASDAQ securities, and the process of reviewing SRO rule or system changes.

The Report also suggests that the Commission amend Rule 19b-4 to accelerate review of routine administrative and procedural modifications. Modifications that present restrictive or anticompetitive concerns or raise investor protection issues should still be considered in detail after a notice and comment period. While lowering the burden on the exchanges is clearly the goal, the Report is unclear about which areas of exchange governance do not require a notice and comment period. Arguably, almost any change in procedures can have potential implications for investor protection at some level.

Authors' critique — On a more general level than these specific recommendations is the issue of whether a "level playing field" is an appropriate basis for regulating market structure. The determination of the appropriate level of regulation is a concern shared by a number of financial market regulators. Among the criteria that have been proposed are (1) an "institutional approach" followed by the SEC which regulates exchanges differently than broker-dealers, even if they perform similar functions; (2) a functional approach advocated by the Commission des Opérations de Bourse in France (i.e., all systems should be regulated equally if they perform the same functions); (3) that the regulatory scheme is a function of the market microstructure (Bronfman and Lawton, 1993); and (4) that the trading public is the key determinant of the appropriate regulatory regime (the basis of exemptive authority granted to the Commodity Futures Trading Commission under the 1992 Futures Trading Practices Act). In opposition to many of these is the argument for a "level playing field" so that regulation does not impose differential costs on market centers and put some at a competitive disadvantage relative to others.

For instance, SROs have certain statutory obligations not imposed on alternative trading systems; that is, proprietary trading systems (the Arizona Stock Exchange) and systems regulated as broker-dealers (POSIT and Instinet) operate under a different regulatory regime. For example, in addition to the responsibility of assuring that the federal securities laws are not violated, the exchanges have to file proposed rule changes for approval by the Commission. Specifically, Section 19(b)(2) states that no changes in the rules of any SRO may become effective until the SEC finds it to be consistent with the registration requirements for the organization and purposes of the 1934 Act. This often requires a period for public comment as well.

There are historical parallels between the debates now and at the time of the 1975 amendments. For example, during hearings on the structure, operation, and regulation of the securities markets that took place in December 1971, the US Department of Justice stated that the issue was whether to have a regulated monopoly or whether to allow the forces of competition to make the most of basic economic allocations (pp. 3134–56). The Martin Report also referred to "unequal regulation" with respect to (1) specialists, (2) institutional membership on various exchanges, (3) the use of reciprocal commission splitting arrangements, (4) Rule 394 off-board trading by members of the NYSE, (5) requirements to print all executions on the tape, and (6) restrictions on short sales of odd lots. Prepared on behalf of the Martin Report Committee, the statement of Vice President Richard A. Wescott of Mid-America Inc. refers to "unequal regulations."

> The existence of unequal regulation grant(s) a competitive advantage to certain groups within the industry . . . Such regulation as exists is unequal in that it imposes different duties and responsibilities on participants . . . We do not want to imply that the regulation of regional exchanges or the National Association of Securities Dealers is inadequate. Such regulation as exists is unequal.

And in the context of the 1975 Amendments, the Report from the Senate Committee on Banking, Housing, and Urban Affairs stated

> The subject of equal regulation has been a matter of considerable controversy . . . In the Committee's view, equal regulation is appropriate only if the phrase is understood to mean that persons enjoying similar privileges, performing similar functions, and having the potential for similar market impact are treated equally . . . that the Commission regulate comparably those market makers and specialists enjoying the same opportunities, having the same market power, and subject to the same conflicts of interest.

Former Chief Counsel Donald M. Fueuerstein of the Institutional Investor Study argued[34]

> To the extent that public customers are unsophisticated, as are most individual

investors, the protection of agency representation is important . . . On the other hand, sophisticated investors, such as institutions, are able to fend for themselves.

The issue can be restated in efficiency terms. Efficient regulation takes into account both the costs and benefits of its rule-making. As analyzed in Albrecht, Bronfman, and Messenheimer (1994), the efficient level of regulation will differ according to the peculiarities of the trading system and the sophistication of the trading public. The same level of regulation will not provide the same benefits in a market predominantly of institutions as in a market predominantly of retail investors. Similarly, a market structure that relies on intermediaries to execute customers' orders will require a different level of oversight than one where trades take place between principals.

Open market access

Report's recommendations — The Report observes that "as competition for order flow increases, it is likely that the different marketplaces will act in ways that may restrict the activities of their competitors. Past experience has shown that competitive interests can cause an SRO to take actions to disadvantage competitors, while cloaking these actions with regulatory purposes." The Report also notes that certain exchange rules are keeping participants from accessing all markets and suggests they should be modified, including NYSE Rule 390 concerning off-board trading of NYSE-listed securities (to enable the after-hours trading of listed securities by NYSE members); NYSE Rule 500 and American Stock Exchange Rule 18 concerning delisting requirements. It also suggests an extension of the ITS-CAES link to include securities not covered by Rule 19c-3 under the 1934 Act.

Authors' critique — Earlier in the section, we suggest that all market centers should be viewed as business enterprises. From this perspective, an enterprise forms contracts deemed advantageous for the efficient functioning and performance of the business. The particular organizational form that has evolved into the present structure of the NYSE has clearly served the Exchange well. While Rule 390 may appear to have anticompetitive aspects, in its present form, it is limited to the trading of NYSE members' proprietary trades. Although the SEC has limited its recommendations to after-hours trading, the basis for its interference in the internal affairs of an exchange, which by its own admission operates in a highly competitive environment, is unclear.

It is worth noting that the Division's suggestion for modifying NYSE Rule 500 and American Stock Exchange Rule 18 is inconsistent with an earlier SEC position that competition for listings was quite robust. The position concerned a controversy in the 1980s over SROs' rules governing dual class recapitalizations, in which listed companies recapitalize from one class of common stock (with one share, one vote) to multiple classes of common stock with different voting rights. Some argue that these recapitalizations are highly effective takeover defenses, since they effectively transfer corporate control from outside investors to corporate managers. While these transactions violated the NYSE's "one share, one vote" rule, they were permissible on both the AMEX and NASDAQ.

During the hostile takeover wave of the 1980s, many NYSE-listed companies threatened to delist from the NYSE and relist on the AMEX or NASDAQ in order to adopt this purported takeover defense, unless the NYSE changed its listing standards to allow multiple classes of common stock with different voting rights. The SEC adopted a rule (which was later struck down by the courts) to curtail dual-class recapitalizations, on grounds that competition for listings between the NYSE, AMEX, and NASDAQ was resulting in a "race to the bottom" that could result in undesirable transfers of corporate control. This position seems to acknowledge that delisting requirements are not as onerous as the Division portrays in the Market 2000 Report.

CONCLUSION

Much of the force for change in US equity markets today is driven by the changing demands of institutional investors and technological innovations which have facilitated the entry of new market centers such as the Arizona Stock Exchange, POSIT, and Instinet. Both of these factors account, at least in part, for a substantial change in the industrial organization of US equity markets in recent years. This change has been characterized most prominently by a large decline in the share of equity trading accounted for by the New York Stock Exchange.

The Division of Market Regulation's Market 2000 Report addresses an appropriate question. Is the existing regulatory structure suitable for today's equity markets? Unfortunately, its response consists of proposals for more disclosure, changes in rules and procedures of SROs, and enhanced market linkages. On balance, the Division envisions the SEC as being actively involved in regulating market structure as the year 2000 approaches.

With the remarkable changes in the securities industry, we question the wisdom of continued SEC involvement in the management of the business decisions of market centers and competition between market centers. The increased contestability of the securities industry greatly weakens the natural monopoly rationale that exists for much of the SEC's role in regulating market structure. Furthermore, the SEC's continued involvement in the governance of self-regulatory organizations (and to a lesser extent, the proprietary trading systems) imposes a highly bureaucratic structure on these enterprises at a time of rapid technological change in the industry. Given the natural risk aversion of regulators, this is likely to impede innovation and work contrary to the public interest.

The SEC recently reaffirmed its position that the rules and procedures of market centers should be subject to federal regulation, not left to market forces. In a December 28, 1993 comment letter to the Commodity Futures Trading Commission (CFTC) relating to petitions from futures exchanges for exemptions from some regulations, the SEC wrote that such exemptions would leave the exchanges' "surveillance and enforcement programs solely to their business judgement. This is contrary to the system of self-regulation in the financial markets. Self-regulatory organizations should have ongoing regulatory responsibilities that are overseen by the CFTC, and not merely business discretion in this area." In contrast to our arguments for a smaller SEC role in the governance of SROs, the SEC continues to advocate a rather large role.

Given its Congressional mandate, the SEC's position on these issues is not surprising. However, Congress ought to reconsider whether there remains a legitimate role for the SEC to play in regulating market structure. The 1934 Act and the 1975 Amendments provide the SEC with a mandate to regulate market structure. Given these constraints, it is not surprising the Division's report goes out of its way to emphasize that its recommendations promote the multiple goals laid out in the 1975 Amendments. Rather than focusing on the SEC's proposals, which are likely to remain incremental, we encourage a new debate about the appropriateness of the Congressional mandate, and especially, the 1975 Amendments.

ENDNOTES

1. The NYSE provides continuous trading in which a specialist firm is required to maintain "fair and orderly" markets in listed stocks. It is structured as an agency auction in which specialists act as both brokers (i.e., agents for other traders) and dealers (i.e., principals who trade in and out of their inventories of stocks). More than two thousand companies, including most large US companies, have their stock listed on the NYSE.
2. The five principal regional stock exchanges in the US are Boston, Chicago (formerly the Midwest), Cincinnati, Pacific, and Philadelphia. Except for the Cincinnati Stock Exchange, all the regional exchanges provide continuous auction markets and employ the specialist system. Since 1978, the Cincinnati Stock Exchange has provided a computerized trading system in which orders can be entered, matched, and executed. Most of the trading volume in stocks on regional exchanges is accounted for by stocks that are listed on both the regional exchanges and the NYSE. Relatively few stocks are listed exclusively on regional exchanges.
3. The American Stock Exchange (AMEX) also provides continuous market trading

and employs a specialist system. More than 1,000 stocks or stock-related securities are traded on the AMEX. In recent years, trading of derivative products has accounted for most AMEX revenues.

4. In contrast to the exchanges, the over-the-counter (OTC) market is a dealer market. For each stock traded in the OTC market, dealers continuously quote prices at which they are willing to buy and sell a certain amount of stock. They act as principals, trading in and out of their inventory. In contrast to the specialist system, there must be at least two and are as many as 40–50 dealers who choose to make market in OTC stocks. Whereas exchanges (except for Cincinnati) have floors where centralized trading occurs, dealers in the OTC market are connected via computer terminals.

   The OTC market in the US consists of the National Association of Securities Dealers Automated Quotation (NASDAQ) and pink sheets markets. The stock issues of larger companies trade in the NASDAQ market. Within the NASDAQ market, two types of stocks trade: (1) more than twenty-five hundred national market system (NMS) stocks, which represent the largest NASDAQ stocks, and (2) more than fifteen hundred regular NASDAQ stocks. The stock issues of more than forty-five thousand smaller companies trade in the less liquid pink sheets market, named after the daily publication, *Pink Sheets*, which contains the nonbinding price indications of dealers. Within the pink sheets market, more than four thousand stocks trade in the OTC bulletin board, an automated market in which dealers list firm quotations.
5. Proprietary trading systems are electronic trading systems operated for a profit as opposed to the nonprofit structure of exchange markets like the NYSE. The major proprietary trading systems are Instinet and POSIT, owned by broker-dealers, and the Arizona Stock Exchange, which is owned by Steven Wunsch.
6. Nonintermediated markets refer to direct trades between two traders.
7. Overseas, US stocks principally trade on the stock exchanges of Tokyo and London.
8. For example, by one estimate the proportion of the dollar value of trading volume accounted for by the NYSE fell from 72.3 percent in 1982 to 57.9 percent in 1992 (Shapiro 1993). The data probably understate the decline in NYSE market share since they only include trading volume on the NYSE, regional exchanges, and the OTC market. The data exclude trading volume in overseas markets, proprietary trading systems, the pink sheets market, and the so-called fourth market (i.e., the nonintermediated market in which institutions trade with each other).
9. See Blume, Siegel and Rottenberg (1993).
10. Letter from Richard C. Breeden to Edward J. Markey, July 11, 1991.
11. See Securities and Exchange Commission (1992). The Administrative Procedures Act requires independent regulatory agencies to publish rule proposals in the Federal Register and allow a period for public comments before the rules can be adopted. After collecting and examining the public comments, regulatory agencies are then allowed to adopt, modify, or rescind proposed rules. The SEC's July 1992 release does not contain rule proposals. Instead, it is a "concept" release, which alerts the public that the commission is "undertaking a study of the structure of the US equity markets and of the regulatory environment in which these markets operate (p. 1)." This release does not contain rule proposals but instead invites the public to provide "any viewpoints and information on the structural issues that face the US equity markets today, as well as data supporting the viewpoints expressed (p. 1)."
12. For a discussion of contestable markets, see Baumol, Panzar, and Willig (1988).

13. For a discussion of the regulatory implications of greater contestability in the local telephone market, see Baumol and Sidak (1993).
14. These include the Divisions of Corporate Finance, Enforcement, Investment Management, and Market Regulation. In addition, the SEC has three major policy offices, including the Offices of the Chief Accountant, Economic Analysis, and General Counsel.
15. United States Securities and Exchange Commission Annual Report (1990), p. 25.
16. See, for example, Weingast (1984) and Weingast and Moran (1983).
17. See SEC Release No. 34-27445 (November 16, 1989) and SEC Release No. 34-29185 (May 15, 1991). Self-regulatory organizations in the US securities industry include the NYSE, AMEX, NASD, the regional stock exchanges, and the Chicago Board Options Exchange (CBOE).
18. See the NYSE's Floor Official Manual, published by Market Surveillance. The manual provides a description of specialist responsibilities and defines in detail the character of specialist dealings.
19. The material on enforcement and surveillance discussed below by the NYSE draws heavily on information provided by Doherty, Okun, Korostoff and Noji (1991), and Cochrane, McNamara, Shapiro and Simon (1993).
20. The SEC conducted three studies on the structure of US equity markets in the early 1970s. See Securities and Exchange Commission (1971, 1972, 1973).
21. These dimensions are discussed in more detail in the Chapter that follows.
22. The perspective that market centers are business enterprises is developed in more detail in Mulherin, Netter, and Overdahl (1991).
23. See, for example, the special issue of the *Journal of Financial Economics, Symposium on The Structure and Governance of Enterprise*, Parts I and II, September 1990.
24. It is worth noting that in 1971, the Congressional debates were filled with discussions that individual investors would become ill-served with the growing institutionalization of the markets. In fact, the NYSE faces stiff competition from electronic trading services which have designed their trading systems to service retail investors. This development was not anticipated in the 1971 debates.
25. The term *public interest* gained prominence in nineteenth century Supreme Court decisions that addressed the issue in the context of rulings that delineated bounds for regulation. *Munn v. Illinois* (1877) is a landmark decision which sets limits on property rights when the public interest is involved. At the time, virtually all of Midwestern grain flowed through Chicago, the "gateway of commerce." Nine firms owned all of Chicago's grain elevators and met periodically to fix storage rates. In 1871, the Illinois legislature passed a law fixing the rates firms could charge. Munn and Scott, owners of one of the firms, ignored the law and were sued for failing to comply. Upholding the state of Illinois, Chief Justice Waite argued " . . . we find that when private property is affected with a public interest it ceases to be juris private only . . . Property does become clothed with a public interest when used in a manner to make it of public consequence, and affect the community at large. When, therefore, one devotes his property to a use in which the public has an interest, he, in effect, grants to the public an interest in that use, and must submit to be controlled by the public for the common good.'
26. These terms are coined by Bork, note 24, page 91. Frank Knight recognized these two components of efficiency in 1933: "From a social point of view, this process may be viewed under two aspects, (a) the assignment or allocation of the available productive forces and materials among the various lines of industry, and (b) the effective coordination of the various means of production in each industry

into such groupings as will produce the greatest result." (*The Economic Organization*, University of Chicago Press, 1933).

27. The effect may be similar to that discussed above with respect to market linkages, that is, if dynamics are considered as well, by infringing on the property right of the established firm, incentives are reduced for investment over the longer term.
28. Seminal work in this area includes Buchanan and Tullock (1962); Stigler (1971); and Peltzman (1976). Also, for a discussion of different nonmarket failures, see Wolf (1979).
29. This SEC ruling is dated April 17, 1984; it appeared in the *Federal Register*, Vol. 49, No. 80, April 21, 1984. The SEC ruled that the only costs that were relevant in determining the fees for the sale of this information are the costs incurred by the NASD in collecting the information and passing it onto vendors.
30. *Board of Trade of the City of Chicago v. Christie Grain and Stock Company*, (1905) 198 U.W. 236. In deciding on the Board of Trade's behalf, Justice Holmes wrote that "the plaintiff's collection of quotations is entitled to the protection of the law."
31. The Report (p. 25) takes on Bronfman and Overdahl's arguments that primary markets be compensated for the provision of price discovery by appropriate fees for price and quote information. The report takes the position that this argument ignores the substantial revenues and benefits that the primary markets currently receive, and that such a position would force regulation into rate-making procedures.
32. The discussion on the disadvantages of mandating a level of transparency which follows is drawn largely from Bronfman and Overdahl (1993).
33. For example, the SEC has approved lower levels of transparency for the after-hours crossing session on the NYSE, in part to help the exchange recapture some portion of the order flow that has migrated to London. And the proposed rule-making in the Market 2000 Report recommends eliminating this exception to its position on transparency.
34. US Senate Committee on Banking, Housing and Urban Affairs, Hearings on the Structure, Operation, and Regulation of the Securities Markets, December 1, 1971, p. 2973.

REFERENCES

Albrecht, W., Bronfman, C. and Messenheimer, H. (1994) 'Regulatory regimes: the interdependence of rules and regulatory structure' in A. Lo, (ed.) *Industrial Organization and Regulation of the Securities Industry*, NBER Conference Volume. Chicago, University of Chicago Press, forthcoming 1995.

Baumol, W.J., Panzar, J.C. and Willig, R.D. (1988) *Contestable Markets and the Theory of Industrial Structure*. New York, Harcourt Brace Jovanovich.

Baumol, W.J. and Sidak, J.G. (1993) *Toward Competition in Local Telephony*. Cambridge, Mass., MIT Press.

Becker, B. and Angstadt, J. (1994) 'Market 2000: a work in progress' in R.A. Schwartz, (ed.) *Global Equity Markets: Technological, Competitive, and Regulatory Challenges*. Homewood, Ill., Irwin, forthcoming.

Blume, M.E., Siegel, J.E. and Rottenberg, D. (1993) *Revolution on Wall Street: The Rise and Decline of the New York Stock Exchange*. New York, W.W. Norton, p. 253.

Bork, R.H. (1978) *The Antitrust Paradox*. New York, Basic Books.

Bronfman, C. (1992) 'If it ain't broke, don't regulate it' in K. Lhen and R. Kamphuis, (eds.) *Modernizing US Securities Regulation*. Homewood, Ill., Irwin.

Bronfman, C. and Overdahl, J.A. (1993) 'Would the invisible hand produce transparent markets?' *Commodity Futures Trading Commission Working Paper.*

Bronfman, C. and Lawton, J. (1993) 'Market structure and regulatory cost: the effect of a single price auction.' *Commodity Futures Trading Commission Working Paper.*

Buchanan, J. and Tullock, G. (1962) *The Calculus of Consent.* Ann Arbor, Mich., University of Michigan Press.

Coase, R.H. (1960) 'The problem of social cost.' *Journal of Law and Economics*, **3**, 1–44.

———. (1988) *The Firm, the Market, and the Law*. Chicago, University of Chicago Press.

Cochrane, J.L., McNamara, B., Shapiro, J.E. and Simon, M.J. (1993) 'The structure and regulation of the New York Stock Exchange.' *Journal of Corporation Law*, Spring, 1992, 57–77.

Demsetz, H. (1969) 'Information and efficiency: another viewpoint,' *Journal of Law and Economics*, April, 1–22.

Division of Market Regulation, US Securities and Exchange Commission. (1994) *Market 2000: An Examination of Current Equity Market Developments*, January.

Jensen, M.C. and Meckling, W.H. (1992) 'Specific and general knowledge, and organizational structure' in L. Werin, (ed.) *Contract Economics*. Oxford, UK, Blackwell.

Khademian, A.M. (1992) *The SEC and Capital Market Regulation*, The University of Pittsburgh.

Kleidon, A.W. (1992) 'Market 2000' in K. Lehn and R. Kamphuis, (eds.) *Modernizing US Securities Regulations*, Homewood, Ill., Irwin.

Lee, C.M.C. (1993) 'Market integration and price execution for NYSE-listed securities.' *Journal of Finance*, July, 1009–1038.

Mulherin, J.H., Netter, J.M. and Overdahl, J.A. (1991) 'Prices are property: the organization of financial exchanges from a transaction cost perspective.' *Journal of Law and Economics*, October, 591–645.

Nissen, W.J. (1991) 'Defining the scope of a broker's fiduciary duty with contract law principles.' *Commodities Law Letter*, December, 28–30.

Oesterle, D., Winslow, D.A. and Anderson, S.C. (1992) 'The New York Stock Exchange and its out-moded specialist system: can the exchange innovate to survive?' *Journal of Corporation Law*, Winter, 223–311.

Peltzman, S. (1976) 'Toward a more general theory of regulation.' *Journal of Law and Economics*, August, 211–240.

Securities and Exchange Commission. (1971) *HR Document No. 64*, 92d Congress, 1st Session, Part 1.

———. (1972) *Statement on the Future Structure of the Securities Markets*, FR5286.

———. (1973) *Policy Statement on the Structure of a Central Market System*, March 29, reprinted in *Securities Regulation and Law Reporter* (BNA), No. 196 at d-1, April 4, 1973.

———. (1992). *Release 34-30920*, July 18.

Shapiro, J.E. (1993) 'Recent competitive developments in US equity markets.' *NYSE Working Paper 93-02*, May, p. 1.

Stigler, G.J. (1971) 'The theory of economic regulation.' *Bell Journal of Economics and Management Science*, Spring, 3–21.

Weingast, B.R. (1984) 'The Congressional bureaucratic system: a principal-agent perspective.' *Public Choice*, 147–192.

Weingast, B.R. and Moran, M. (1983) 'Bureaucratic discretion or Congressional control? Regulatory rule-making by the Federal Trade Commission.' *Journal of Political Economy*, **91**, 765–800.
Williamson, O. (1968) 'Economies as an antitrust defense: the welfare tradeoffs.' *American Economic Review*, **58**, 18–36.
Wolf, C., Jr. (1979) 'A theory of nonmarket failure: framework for implementation analysis.' *Journal of Law and Economics*, April, 107–140.

4
US Securities Markets Regulation: Market Structure

ROBERT A. SCHWARTZ*

Chapter 3 reviews the regulatory structure of the US equity market, and assesses competition and regulation as two forces that may be relied on to increase the efficiency of the market. In this chapter we turn to market structure itself. Our purpose is to highlight certain key considerations and to raise questions about issues that, with varying degrees of intensity, have been grappled with by market regulators over the past two decades: minimization of transaction costs, accuracy of price discovery, level of transparency, consolidation of order flow, provision of liquidity, level of transitory price volatility, provision of transactional immediacy to buy-side participants, and regulatory simplicity.

The first section deals with the market structure issues. The second section considers certain actual and potential developments in market structure: the advent of electronic trading, electronic call market trading, and the supply of supplemental liquidity. The possibility that change is being unduly impeded by current industry and regulatory structure is also considered. The third section is a conclusion.

*I thank Corinne Bronfman, Kenneth Lehn, Laura Garbuz and Benn Steil for their inputs into the production of this paper, which is also to be published in the *Financial Review* of the Ministry of Finance, Japan. Their assistance is much appreciated. Parts of this paper have been adapted from Schwartz (1993, 1994) and Economides and Schwartz (1995).

International Financial Market Regulation. Edited by B. Steil

MARKET STRUCTURE ISSUES

Transaction Costs

Market participants are classified as either buy-side traders (investors, both retail and institutional, who buy marketability services)[1] or sell-side traders (broker/dealer intermediaries who sell marketability services). On the buy side, between 75 and 80 percent of NYSE average daily volume is currently estimated to be institutional trading.[2] Can buy-side participants in general, and institutional investors in particular, trade in a liquid, transparent environment, with immediacy, without destabilizing the markets, at low cost? Let us begin by putting the size of transaction costs in proper perspective.

Transaction costs are thought by some to be on the order of eighths or quarters of a point, an amount that is not appreciable relative to share prices. However, costs may be higher and they are indeed substantial relative to an annual return that might be realized from equity investments. To see the effect of transaction costs, consider the following. If trading is costless, the expected return for a stock bought at $30 and held for one year is 10 percent if the expected price for the end of the year is $33. Now assume commissions of 6 cents a share for institutions and 50 cents a share for retail investors; a bid–ask spread of one-eighth of a point (the minimum tick size); and a market impact of one-eighth of a point for institutions and zero for retail customers.[3] One-way (buy or sell) transaction costs are

	Institutional Customer	Retail Customer
Commissions ($)	0.060	0.500
Bid–ask spread ($)	0.063	0.063
Market impact ($)	0.125	0.000
Total costs ($)	0.248	0.563

With these costs, the prices and expected returns for a one-year holding period are

	Institutional Customer	Retail Customer
Purchase price ($)	30.25	30.56
Expected selling price ($)	32.75	32.44
Expected return (%)	8.28	6.13
Costs as fraction of selling price (%)	0.83	1.88
Reduction in expected returns (%)	17.20	38.70

As a percentage of price, the costs represent slightly under 1 percent for institutional traders and slightly under 2 percent for retail traders, seemingly small amounts. However, expected returns are lowered from 10 percent to

8.28 percent (a 17 percent reduction) for the institutional trader, and to 6.13 percent (a 39 percent reduction) for the retail trader. The percentage reduction in that part of the expected return that is a compensation for risk-taking (the risk premium) is even greater. For instance, if the risk-free rate is 3 percent, the risk premium without transaction costs is 7 percent, and the reduction in the risk premium is 25 percent for an institutional trader and 55 percent for a retail trader.

Clearly, transaction costs have an appreciable impact on returns. To a large extent, costs to some traders, primarily buy-side participants, are returns to others, primarily sell-side participants.[4] However, if some participants choose not to trade because of the cost, transaction costs do not have a zero sum effect. For those participants who do not trade, a welfare loss exists because individual portfolios are not being properly balanced. In the discussion that follows, we presume the objective of market design and regulation is to reduce transaction costs as much as possible.

Price Discovery

Price discovery refers to the dynamic processes by which equilibrium values are found in the marketplace. Until recently, relatively little consideration has been given to price discovery in the market structure and regulatory debates, even though it is a complex, imperfect process. This is no doubt largely attributable to the fact that equilibrium values are not observable. Thus deviations from equilibria are not clearly apparent to participants, and their existence has been acknowledged by only some academic researchers. We next suggest why price discovery errors exist in a competitive securities market.

Let two fund managers consider a stock for inclusion in their portfolio, with the first assessing it at \$25 a share and the second assessing it at \$23 a share.[5] Because of the difference in their assessments, a profitable trade could be arranged between the two fund managers. How many shares should they trade? The first fund manager could go infinitely long if the second were to go infinitely short, and vice versa. However, neither would do so because risk and hence the risk-appropriate discount rate would increase as the dollar values of their holdings (both long and short) rose. Consequently, many asset managers set position limits that they will not exceed. More to the point, a relatively sophisticated manager might buy (sell) incremental amounts at incrementally lower (higher) prices. For example, hold up to 100,000 shares at a price of \$25, up to 200,000 shares at \$24, and so on. When share holdings are so adjusted, an asset manager's demand curve to hold shares is downward sloping.[6]

For the case just described, if the two asset managers were to seek a trade with each other in isolation, price indeterminacy would exist (as in any bilateral monopoly situation). However, if all investors in an atomistically competitive environment were to submit complete, downward-sloping demand curves to the market, price determination would be straightforward: an official or a computer would simply aggregate all buy and sell orders and find the value that equates the aggregate desire to buy with the aggregate desire to sell. But, as we discuss below with respect to transparency, it is never in the best interests of a trader to reveal completely his or her buy or sell intentions to the market, because telling the market exactly what one would like to trade at each possible price would result in the consumer surplus returns to trading being lost totally (also see Schwartz, 1991).

Traders generally submit one order either to buy or to sell to the market. The order is specified with regard to the trader's demand to hold shares, expectation of the prices at which shares might trade in the current period, and current shareholdings. Exactly what order to place (price and quantity) and when to place it, is itself a strategic decision. Ho, Schwartz, and Whitcomb (1985) and Bronfman and Schwartz (1993) show that, because of the decisions traders make, market-determined prices will generally differ from equilibrium values.[7] Honda and Schwartz (1994) show that departures from equilibrium values can be self-sustaining over short intervals.

Increasingly, the importance and difficulty of achieving accurate price discovery is being recognized by practitioners. If accurate assessments of each of the implicit costs of trading could be obtained, it may be observed that price discovery errors are the largest. While bid–asks spreads and market impact costs are on the order of one eighth or one-quarter of a point, price discovery errors could be on the order of a dollar or more.

Transparency

Transparency has received a great deal of attention in discussions concerning market structure and regulation. However, we suggest that the term has been considered too narrowly. Transparency is typically taken to mean that quote (pre-trade) and last sale (post-trade) information are widely available on a real-time basis.[8] The quality of pretrade information is impaired when market-makers widen their quotes, understate the number of shares they would be willing to trade at the quotes, and then give within the spread transactions of larger size, as commonly occurs on the London Stock Exchange's automatic quotation system (SEAQ).

When a trade is realized, information is produced concerning the particulars of the transaction (price, quantity, and time). Thus, a completed trade may be viewed as a joint product: the trade itself and information. In a continuous market, the produced information is of no benefit to the transacting parties, but, because of the complexity of price discovery, is of considerable value to others who may be transacting in the near future. The quality of post-trade information is impaired when trades are not reported quickly to the market, as is the case for large orders in London's SEAQ market, US trades that are made in after-hours proprietary systems such as Instinet's crossing network and the Arizona Stock Exchange, US trades made abroad (largely in London), and *sold sales* (exchange trades that are reported late on the tape).

Although not widely discussed, transparency should also include buy-side participants disclosing their orders after their investment decisions have been made. Unfortunately, revealing information before a trade can be detrimental to the participant seeking to trade because a stock's price will commonly rise (fall) in the market when it becomes known that a large buy (sell) order is in the offing. Consequently, participants in a continuous market attempt to hide information about their orders and seek to execute their trades as quickly as possible once their intentions to trade have become known to others. An important issue concerning market architecture is whether a system can be designed that will make institutional investors more willing to reveal their orders.

Consolidation of the Order Flow

Order flow consolidation has also received a great deal of attention. However, it too has been considered too narrowly. For the most part, spatial but not temporal consolidation has been focused on. However, for a trade to be realized, buyers and sellers must meet in two dimensions — place and time. Consolidating orders makes it easier for counterparties to a trade to find each other and to transact at reasonable prices with minimal sell-side intervention. Orders can be consolidated spatially (geographically) and temporally (over time). To date, attention has focused almost exclusively on spatial consolidation. Temporal consolidation would also facilitate order handling for the institutions, and enable better integration of institutional and retail order flow.

The set of participants who meet to trade can be viewed as a network. When a transactions network includes a larger number of participants, counterparties can more easily find each other in time and in place, and transaction prices are expected to be in closer alignment with underlying equilibrium values. Because the size of a transactions network contributes positively to the value of the good that is being produced, a securities market may be said to exhibit "positive network externalities."[9,10] Positive externalities in a trading network explain why order flow attracts order flow; and they give a large market center such as the New York Stock Exchange (NYSE) a strong competitive advantage.

Order flow can fragment spatially in a continuous market if satellite markets offer faster execution for lower commissions while freeriding on the price discovery and other services provided by a major market center, as was suggested by Bloch and Schwartz (1978).[11] Prices can be pirated with relative ease in a continuous market because trading takes place while prices are being set. A trade in the continuous market establishes a price, and the posting of quotes gives the price continuing validation until new quotes and/or a new transaction price are set. Hence, a price established on the NYSE, for example, can become the benchmark against which other orders can be executed elsewhere. These off-board trades do not contribute to price discovery and are of no benefit to those participants who have actively participated in price discovery by posting quotes on the market.

Liquidity

Institutional order flow is characteristically lumpy and may be one-sided (buyers only or sellers only), especially when a market is under stress. Market-makers dampen excess volatility caused by temporary buy/sell imbalances by adding liquidity to the market. Can the market-makers provide sufficient liquidity? Can institutions provide liquidity to themselves? Are other innovations in market structure needed?

The liquidity of a market is of paramount importance, and the concern is generally felt that natural buyers and sellers cannot supply adequate liquidity to themselves. For this reason, dealers have been thought of as fulfilling the economic role of providing liquidity to a market. We suggest the potential importance of a third source of supplemental liquidity — the listed companies whose shares are traded.

The listed corporations are one of the most important constituents of the securities markets. Although the possibility has been given scant attention, these players too should be actively involved in market-making. The listed companies benefit primarily because greater liquidity would lower their costs of equity capital.[12] Listed companies would further benefit because they themselves are investors through their pension funds, postretirement medical plans and other corporate sponsored funds.

Liquidity, price stability, and the price discovery aspects of market-making involve public goods type externalities from the viewpoint of individual participants. These beneficial attributes are not externalities for the listed companies, however, to the extent that the companies represent shareholders in aggregate. The "internalization" of an externality provides an economic reason for the listed companies to commit capital to market-making if they so choose. The concern about formally involving listed companies in market-making is that they might exploit the opportunity to manipulate their share prices. However, the manipulation problem can be dealt with by having liquidity orders entered according to a prescribed procedure, and by using a third-party fiduciary to operate the corporate programs.[13]

Volatility

Microstructure effects cause intraday price movements to be excessively volatile. That is, transaction prices in the short run bounce between the bid and the ask; rise and fall with the market impact of large buy and sell orders; and swing around equilibrium values as eager buyers in aggregate outweigh eager sellers, or as eager sellers outweigh eager buyers. How strong is the effect? Hasbrouck and Schwartz (1988) assess the excess short-period volatility that characterizes a continuous market. The essence of their model can be summarized as follows.

Under random walk, an exact relationship exists between measurement interval length and returns variance. If one-day returns variance is x, a T-day returns variance is Tx.[14] Alternatively stated, T times the variance of one-day returns divided by T-day returns variance would equal unity under random walk. However, if short-run volatility is inflated, the ratio will be greater than unity. Hasbrouck and Schwartz analyzed the ratio of scaled variances using half-hour returns and two-day returns for a sample of NYSE, AMEX, and NASDAQ/NMS stocks, for forty-two trading days in March/April 1988.[15] The distribution of the scaled variance ratio for each of the market centers is shown in Table 8.1.

Table 8.1 Distribution of the Scaled Variance Ratio of Half-hour to Two-day Returns for AMEX, NYSE, and NASDAQ/NMS Firms

	Number of Issues	Percentage of Firms Having the Given Variance Ratio		
		<1	1.0–2.0	>2.0
AMEX	200	30	47	23
NYSE	1209	24	49	27
NASDAQ/NMS	651	7	33	60

Clearly, in all three market centers, short-run price volatility is in excess of that expected under random walk. Only 30 percent of AMEX, 24 percent of NYSE, and 7 percent of NASDAQ/NMS firms had variance ratios less than unity and, as shown in the right-hand column, short-run volatility is more than twice what it would be in a random walk environment for 23 percent of AMEX firms, 27 percent of NYSE firms, and 60 percent of NASDAQ/NMS firms. Cross-sectional regressions run by Hasbrouck and Schwartz indicate that only a part of the increased half-hour returns variance is attributable to the bid–ask bounce. We suggest that market impact and price discovery errors are also significant factors.

Immediacy

It has been widely assumed that traders want to be able to transact immediately, and our securities trading systems are based on the principle of continuous trading. In this regard, dealers and specialists, as suppliers of immediacy, have been considered essential to the operations of the market. These assumptions should also be questioned. Far too much importance has been attached to providing immediacy, and the costs associated with the privilege of transacting whenever a participant chooses during a trading session have not been properly understood. Most critically, an alternative to not trading in the continuous market has, for the most part, not been made available to participants (see call market trading below).

Some investors choose not to pay the price for immediacy.[16] They include passive investors, limit order traders, and other informationless traders for whom lower transaction costs are more important than immediacy. For instance, mutual funds may trade certain amounts each day, not because of the receipt of news, but because of redemptions or other cash flow needs. This does not mean that the funds must be able to trade at any given moment during the day.

In fact, the continuous market may actually make it more difficult for institutional investors to execute large orders at reasonable cost by the end of a trading day. Data collected by the Plexus Group indicate that 40 percent of the orders given to buy-side trading desks are greater than a stock's average daily trading volume.[17] Orders of this size cannot be traded quickly in the continuous market because the provision of immediacy causes the order flow to fragment temporally.

Regulatory Simplicity

The structure of a market affects the difficulty of regulating it. In call market trading (discussed below), orders are cumulated for execution in a multilateral trade, at a single time and at a single price (the value that clears all crossing orders, and, in so doing, maximizes the number of shares that transact). The procedure facilitates market surveillance and mitigates the incentive for front-running, along with economizing on post-trade clearance and settlement costs.

The continuous market, on the other hand, is an inherently complex environment to operate in and to regulate.[18] Symptomatic of the difficulty, exchange specialists commonly stop orders and do not display all limit orders to the market. Knotty regulatory issues range from the desirability of maintaining an order focusing rule such as NYSE Rule 390, to practices such as front-running[19] and payment for order flow.[20] In part, the problems are attributable to the fact that, in a continuous trading environment, trading and price discovery are concomitant processes. The alternative is to batch orders, determine the clearing price, and then clear all of the batched orders that cross at this price.

The fundamental question concerning regulatory simplicity is the extent to which a regulatory authority — the Securities and Exchange Commission (SEC) in the US — should be actively involved in resolving market structure issues. The Securities Acts Amendments of 1975 mandated the development of a national market system (NMS) and effectively thrust the SEC into the business of directly managing market design. In the nearly two decades that followed, the SEC has played an active role in the development of the intermarket trading system (ITS),[21] the Consolidated Tape Association (CTA) and the consolidated quotations system (CQS); in forcing the partial removal of the NYSE's order consolidation Rule 390,[22] and in allowing a carefully controlled emergence of the proprietary trading systems. Now, the SEC and others have questioned the desirability of the agency's activist role.[23] In its July 1992 request for public comment, the SEC's Division of Market Regulation stated

> The Division is not trying to dictate what the structure of the equity markets should be in the year 2000. That determination should be made by the markets and their participants as a result of competition. However, that competition should not be skewed by inequitable regulation or allocation of self-regulatory costs, beyond that which is necessary for the protection of investors. (SEC Release 34-30920, p. 14).

We underscore the importance of this point. Regulation can have complex, unintended effects (Bronfman, 1994).

No clear regulatory constraint on the PTSs is proposed in the Market 2000 Report itself, and the SEC's involvement with market structure issues appears relatively modest. The reason for not pushing regulation further into market structure issues is suggested by Brandon Becker in his letter of transmission for the report. "The Division concludes that the equity markets operate efficiently within the existing regulatory structure. Accordingly, radical reform of how equity trading is conducted or regulated is not necessary." The report claims that competition has been effective in leading the markets to greater efficiency. For instance, it states, "Competition for equity market share has resulted in notable service improvements and efficiencies, and has forced the primary markets to respond to their users" (Market 2000 Report, p. III–1). Nevertheless, one of the most fundamental purposes of the report is reflected in the following statement: "The markets and users continue, however, to operate within the framework of a regulatory structure that was created 20 years ago under very different market conditions. Whether this structure still works is the primary focus of the Market 2000 Study" (Market 2000 Report, p. 4). And an answer is suggested by the following statement:

> The strength of the US equity markets are evidence of the effectiveness of the markets' and Commission's efforts since 1975, and the viability of the standards

> embodied in the 1975 Amendments. The challenge in 1975 was to correct a market structure that could not accommodate the increase in institutional activity or technological change. The Commission and Congress met that challenge with the 1975 Amendments. As a result, the markets now fulfill the needs of an ever-expanding universe of investors (Market 2000 Report, p. 13).

By so associating the quality of markets with the involvement of the regulatory authority, the report endorses the Securities Acts Amendments of 1975 and their mandate for the development of a national market system (NMS). Despite the Commission's laudatory words about competition, this posture effectively keeps the SEC involved in market structure issues. Unfortunately, this in turn maintains the regulatory uncertainty that hangs over new, innovative trading systems. An operation that does not conform with the SEC's vision of an NMS may be disallowed. In the longer run, this power to enforce or to disallow could damage the dynamic development of the US securities markets.

CHANGES IN MARKET STRUCTURE

Having discussed the issues involved in market design, we next consider the potential for structural change that is now emerging in the industry. In this section, we give particular attention to call market trading, an approach that is itself starting to make its impact in the marketplace. Our purpose is to illustrate one possibility for structural change — the introduction of call market trading — that might appreciably increase the efficiency of the equity markets. We also draw attention to an impediment to change.

The Advent of Electronic Trading

Remarkable change, brought about by technology, deregulation, and the introduction of new financial instruments, has characterized the securities industry since the early 1970s. Three powerful forces are now causing the change to accelerate. First, trading and markets are rapidly becoming more global. Second, buy-side participants, primarily the mutual and pension funds, are becoming far more aware of the extent to which trading costs impair portfolio performance, and fund managers are increasingly demanding better market performance. Third, new trading systems are attracting the attention of an appreciable number of buy-side participants; increasingly, these systems are exerting competitive pressure on traditional sell-side broker/dealer firms and market centers.

The computer, of course, has long since found its way onto trading floors and trading desks, and the pros and cons of electronic trading have been debated for a good twenty years (see, for example, Peake, Mendelson, and

Williams (1976)). For the most part, however, the computer has been used for order routing and information dissemination, not trade execution. Clearly, a large-scale integration of computerized trading into an agency/auction market such as the NYSE, or a competitive dealer market such as NASDAQ, would have a profound effect on these market centers. It would also have major implications for the profitability of the brokerage houses and dealer firms that are their members.

Technological inertia, the vested interests of sell-side participants, and the very complexity of trading itself account for the slow pace of the computer's adoption. But the impediments are starting to be overcome. Electronic information systems enable quantitative investment/trading programs to be run profitably if — and only if — transaction costs are kept low.[24] The computer has allowed trade data to be captured and analyzed, and the analysis has revealed the cost of trading, not just to the quantitative managers, but to buy-side participants in general. And, the reality is sinking in that, with computer technology, natural buyers and natural sellers can find and trade with each other without the intervention of intermediaries. Increasingly, major buy side participants are pressuring the market centers to improve the efficiency of their operations, and increasingly, we presume, the pressure will be effective.

One of the most notable developments within the US is the emergence of the proprietary trading systems (PTS). Though still small, the PTSs are also beginning to exert substantial pressure on the traditional market centers. These systems include Instinet's electronic continuous market and crossing network, the Investment Technology Group's POSIT (an electronic crossing network), and the Arizona Stock Exchange's (AZX) electronic call market.

The PTSs are owned by equity shareholders. As such, they are not membership associations, as is the NYSE, where members own seats. The profit incentive of their owners provides an incentive for the proprietary trading systems to listen to the needs of their customers, the buy-side participants, with a different receptivity than do the seat holders of the major market centers.

Electronic Call Market Trading

POSIT, Instinet's crossing network, and AZX each batch orders for multilateral execution at a single time at a single price. Only AZX, however, is an electronic call market that provides price discovery. The electronic call market has attractive properties for buy-side participants. It also simplifies market structure for the regulators. We next briefly consider this approach to trading with regard to immediacy, the use of electronic technology, order handling, transparency, consolidation of order flow, and the free riding problem.

Immediacy. A perceived limitation of call market trading is that it does not allow for continuous access to the market. As discussed above, it has been widely believed that traders demand transactional immediacy, and our securities trading systems are for the most part based on the principle of continuous trading. Moreover, dealers and specialists, as suppliers of immediacy, have been considered essential to the operations of the market. However, the demand for immediacy is in part endogenous to the continuous market, and institutional participants, because of the size of their orders, cannot always trade with immediacy in any event. Thus an alternative to trading with immediacy should be made available. This would effectively enable the unbundling of two services: a trade itself, and the "immediacy" of the trade. This could be accomplished by integrating call market trading with continuous trading in a major market center such as the NYSE or NASDAQ. Specifically, the call could be held three times a day: to open the market, at noon, and to close the market.

Use of electronic technology. Nonelectronic calls do not fully exploit the potential of call market trading. With computerization, participants can see the order flow and interact with the call on a real-time basis, entering their orders while the computer broadcasts the orders and indicated clearing prices. At the moment of the call, the computer finds the single price for each stock that clears the market, and market clearing prices for all issues can be determined simultaneously. Thus, in a call market, the computer serves important informational and computational functions.

Order handling. Commission costs can be lower in call market trading because order handling is facilitated in that environment. Execution costs can be lower as well. Because orders are bunched together for simultaneous execution at a common clearing price, the bid–ask spread does not exist, large orders have less market impact, and large traders are less apt to have their orders front-run. The risk of orders being front-run is further reduced if public traders are given direct access to the call. Because all orders execute at a common clearing price, participants can put limit prices on their orders without extending a free option to others or risking being "picked off" (as long as enough participants are present at the call).[25]

Transparency. Each individual, while preferring that the market be transparent, is reluctant to disclose his or her own order, because there are strong advantages to letting others be the providers of liquidity and suppliers of information. Participants who place their orders early provide information and liquidity to those who place their orders closer to the time of the call. Once enough orders have been placed, the call provides a particularly transparent and orderly environment.

The problem of getting participants to reveal their orders early in call market trading can be handled in several ways. Participants can enter orders with the contingency that their orders not be disclosed to the market until counterpart orders of sufficient size have also been placed.[26] Early order disclosure can also be encouraged in call market trading by using time priorities and by charging lower commissions for orders that have been placed earlier in the entry period that precedes a call. For example, AZX's electronic call uses time priority rules and time-dependent commission rates for this purpose.[27]

Consolidation of order flow. Order flow is necessarily fragmented temporally in continuous market trading. Moreover, order flow can fragment spatially in a continuous environment as satellite markets offer fast execution and charge low commissions while free riding on the price discovery and other services provided by a major market center, as was suggested by Bloch and Schwartz (1978). The problems of fragmentation may be eliminated with call market trading. Introducing a call into a continuous market will naturally focus orders at specific points in time. And, because trading in a call market results in all orders collectively determining the price, it reduces the possibility of free riding on price discovery: before the call, the indicated clearing price is only tentative; after the call, the clearing price has rapidly diminishing validity. Because orders are less apt to fragment spatially, the need for an order-focusing rule, such as NYSE Rule 390, is obviated.

The free-riding problem. Prices can be pirated with relative ease in a continuous market because trading takes place while prices are being set. A trade in the continuous market establishes a price, and the posting of quotes gives the price continuing validation until new quotes and/or a new transaction price are set. Hence, prices established on the NYSE can become the benchmarks against which orders can be executed on the regional exchanges or through proprietary trading systems. These off-board trades do not contribute to price discovery and are of no benefit to those participants who have actively participated in price discovery by posting quotes on the market. On the contrary, free riding diminishes the extent to which the positive network externalities of a trading network can be realized.

The Supply of Supplemental Liquidity

The introduction of an electronic call market into an agency/auction market, such as the NYSE, or a dealer market, such as NASDAQ, would have a further advantage. It would present an environment within which appreciable capital could be committed to providing supplemental liquidity and stability to the market. Stabilization trades cannot be effectively made in a continuous market because they could retard the adjustment to a new equilibrium and, in so doing, benefit some traders unjustifiably. For example, suppose a stock's equilibrium price falls from 50½ to 49½. Further suppose that a liquidity-providing order of a given size has been entered at 50. In the continuous market, the order would execute at 50, while in the call it would execute at 49½. There is no reason to enable some public trader to sell at 50 when the new equilibrium price is 49½, and a transaction at 50 would be misleading for the market and costly for the stabilizer.

In a call market, clearing prices simultaneously reflect all orders, including those entered for liquidity-providing purposes, and all orders transact at the same price. Price discovery and the provision of supplemental liquidity are effectively integrated in the call. As discussed above, the listed companies themselves should be the source of the supplemental liquidity.

Is Change Being Impeded?

If seemingly desirable changes in market structure are not being made, one would question whether change is being unduly resisted by the industry. An example of the difficulty of changing trading arrangements on the floor of the NYSE is the introduction of the electronic display book at the specialists posts.[28] The Market 2000 report suggests that the Exchange should move from one-eighth pricing to one-sixteenth pricing or decimal pricing, not something the exchange is likely to accept readily. Is this because of technical difficulties, or because market makers as a group benefit when a larger minimum allowable price change sets a higher floor that a competitively determined bid–ask spread cannot be driven below?

A major impediment to certain structural changes may be the interests of sell-side intermediaries who have become increasingly proficient at finding their profits in the inefficiencies of the continuous market. Sell-side institutions, by their membership votes and budgetary power, exert extensive control over market structure decisions made by market centers such as NYSE and NASDAQ. As noted above, a membership association's incentive is to maximize the price of a seat, not the value of shareholder equity. The price of a seat reflects the value of access privileges given to members. Herein lies a conflict: an innovation that might decrease the cost of trading shares for the membership organization (for instance, a more efficient order-handling procedure) could lower the value of a seat (if that system reduced the need to use broker/dealer intermediaries).[29] Consequently, structural arrangements exist in the securities industry that shield the profitable operations of broker/dealer firms as a group. The bottom line is, the needs of buy-side participants may not be being adequately met at the current time.

In the long run, one would expect that a more efficient way of handling trading would make its way into the marketplace and gain market share. In the long run, less efficient markets will either adjust or lose major market share. But in the short run, impediments may inefficiently retard the process. Of particular concern is that the regulatory authority itself will not be an impediment. If it is, the long run may indeed be a long time in arriving.

CONCLUSION

We have considered key market structure issues that the SEC has been concerned with since the Securities Acts Amendments of 1975 effectively thrust the commission into an active involvement with market design. The issues are the minimization of transaction costs, the accuracy of price discovery, the level of transparency, consolidation of the order flow, liquidity, the level of transitory price volatility, the provision of transactional immediacy to buy-side participants, and regulatory simplicity.

The most fundamental questions about market operations are (1) whether or not the market centers are operating with reasonable efficiency from the perspective of buy-side participants, and (2) whether or not competition and innovation are being unduly stymied by sell-side participants and/or regulatory authorities. By many standards, the US markets are highly efficient. Nevertheless, significant inefficiencies persist, and one should question whether this is partly because they offer profitable opportunities to sell-side broker/dealer firms.

Given that inefficiencies exist, what function should a regulatory authority perform with regard to market structure issues? It could seek to reduce trading costs (e.g., by requiring a change from one-eighth pricing to decimal pricing); to make a market more transparent (e.g., by requiring the display of all public limit orders); to insure the consolidation of orders (e.g., by supporting NYSE Rule 390); or to encourage greater competition (e.g., by requiring the removal of NYSE Rule 390). Alternatively, the regulatory authority could explicitly distance itself, as much as possible, from ruling on market structure issues and let competition be the force that drives the markets toward greater efficiency.

It is one thing to argue for competition in the abstract, and another to adhere to a truly competitive stance in relation to specific issues. For instance, consider the challenges involved when another market attracts order flow away from a major market center such as the NYSE. The exchange has certain options. It could make adjustments in its trading system, or it could seek regulatory support in requiring order flow consolidation.[30] Assume the NYSE seeks regulatory support — it pressures the SEC to keep Rule 390, disallow payment for order flow, and constrain the development of the proprietary trading systems — and does not innovate with regard to its own trading system. How should the SEC respond?

A standard regulatory approach would be to consider the arguments concerning each issue and to decide the preferred market structure "by committee." Alternatively, the agency could let the market decide. This would mean (1) allow Rule 390 to stand because the NYSE, as a competitive player in the market, believes it to be in its best self-interest to impose an order-focusing rule on its members; (2) allow payment for order flow; and (3) allow the proprietary trading systems to operate without undue regulatory restriction because alternative trading technologies put competitive pressure on a major market center to innovate.

The "competition alternative" may be difficult to select, especially because externality arguments concerning payment for order flow are valid. However, regulation itself can have complex, unintended effects. With the intricacies of both competition and regulation more fully perceived, the opinion has been broadly voiced that the regulators should rein in their desire to control market structure.[31] Given the competition that now exists and the advances in market structure that sophisticated technology will no doubt enable in the future, designing market structure by the regulatory process is more apt to impair the efficiency of competition, than it is to bring us trading systems that will better service the needs of buy-side participants.

The SEC has produced a considerable amount of information about the industry as a result of its investigations and analyses (for instance, the Market 2000 Report). Perhaps in this way the commission can perform its most valuable service. Simply asking the questions, identifying the problems, and presenting the evidence is valuable. A lack of transparency, insufficient order flow consolidation, generally high transaction costs, undue resistance to structural change, and so on, should be documented. Perhaps these are, to some extent, manifestations of a more fundamental problem — sell-side intermediaries find their profits in relatively opaque, fragmented markets. All participants might then assemble the information in whatever form they themselves determine is most desirable. All said and done, trading services will be provided in the manner that sell-side participants find most profitable, and buy-side traders will direct their orders to those markets that give them the best service. Ultimately, if participants have sufficient knowledge about the intricacies of the markets, competition will make the markets more efficient.

ENDNOTES

1. Marketability services include order handling, the provision of liquidity, trade execution, and post-trade clearance and settlement.
2. See Becker and Angstadt (1994).

3. One-eighth of a point, the minimum size of a nonzero execution cost, may appreciably understate the magnitude of this cost for a large trader.
4. See Stoll (1994).
5. The assessment could be done using, for instance, the dividend discount model (DDM). The DDM equation is

$$\text{Share price} = \frac{\text{Next period dividend}}{\text{Discount rate} - \text{Growth rate}}$$

Thus if an annual dividend of 45.5 cents per share has just been paid, the risk appropriate discount rate is 12 percent, and the expected growth rate is 10 percent, share price would be $25. Lowering the expected growth rate by 20 basis points to 9.8 percent gives a share value of $22.7.
6. See Ho, Schwartz, and Whitcomb (1985) and Bronfman and Schwartz (1993) for a formal derivation of an investor's downward sloping demand to hold shares of a risky asset. A downward-sloping curve is meaningful in an environment where price changes are not caused by informational change alone. Prices change with the receipt of orders that reflect participants' individual reassessments of existing information, liquidity needs, and/or desires to rebalance their portfolios. Thus, for the investor who does not change his or her beliefs concerning the expected future value of a stock, a price decline in the market that results in a cheaper purchase implies an increased expected return to a long position, and equivalently, a price rise that enables a better sale implies an increased expected return to a short position. The increased return associated with the price change compensates the investor for the greater risk of a larger position (long or short). With downward-sloping demand, the possibility that a large block of shares may be sold (i.e., a corporation might have shares 'on the shelf' because of a Rule 415 offering, or it might be known that a large investor is seeking to liquidate a large block of shares) exerts downward pressure on price, as the shares are said to be "hanging over" the market. Similarly, an announced corporate buy back may put upward pressure on share prices.
7. A price discovery error can be considered an aggregate market impact effect. That is, transaction prices will exceed equilibrium values if buyers, in aggregate, are more eager than sellers, and will be below equilibrium values if sellers, in aggregate, are more eager than buyers. See Bronfman and Schwartz (1993).
8. See Bradley (1994), Domowitz (1994), and Hasbrouck (1994).
9. Markets with *network externalities* have received increasing attention in the industrial organization literature in recent years. The approach has yielded new insights in telecommunications, electricity networks, and other high technology industries. Applications are not limited to traditional "network" industries, but also include industries that use compatible components such as IBM-compatible software and hardware, picture phones and fax machines. See Rohlfs (1974), Farrell and Saloner (1985), Katz and Shapiro (1985), and Economides (1989).
10. See Economides and Siow (1988), Economides and Heisler (1993), and Economides and Schwartz (1995).
11. Note that Bloch and Schwartz's (1978) analysis of how the order flow can fragment in the absence of an order-focusing rule applies to the continuous market.
12. See Amihud and Mendelson (1988).
13. See Schwartz (1988, 1991), and Jacquillat, Schwartz, and Hamon (1994).
14. The linear relationship holds for returns expressed as a rate per T and measured as the log of price relatives.

15. For the sample period, the trading day extended from 10:00 A.M. to 4:00 P.M. (six hours). Thus the half-hour returns variance was multiplied by 24 to assess the scaled variance ratio based on half-hour and two-day returns.
16. Economides and Schwartz (1994) have used a questionnaire to assess buy-side traders' demand for immediacy.
17. Wagner and Edwards (1993).
18. See Harris (1994).
19. Front-running is the practice of brokers using knowledge of public customers' buy and sell orders to trade ahead of the customers.
20. Payment for order flow is the practice of market makers compensating brokers for directing customer orders to them.
21. The Intermarket Trading System is an electronic execution and linkage system that displays quotes for exchange listed securities to market makers on national and regional exchanges and in the over-the-counter (OTC) market.
22. NYSE Rule 390 prohibits NYSE member firms from entering into principal executions in exchange listed securities away from an exchange floor. The scope of the rule was narrowed in July 1980, when the SEC instituted Rule 19c-3, which allows exchange members to make off-board markets for issues listed after April 26, 1979.
23. Many of the comment letters submitted in response to the release have urged that competition, not legislative interference, be relied on to drive the markets toward greater efficiency.
24. See Fisher (1994).
25. See Copeland and Galai (1983) for a discussion of the option value of a limit order in a continuous market.
26. Although a contingent order is not revealed to other traders until its conditions have been satisfied, it has, most importantly, been entered into the system. Because the system knows of contingent orders on both sides of the book, trades will be made that might otherwise not have been found.
27. Economides and Heisler (1993) discuss the fee schedule in a call market.
28. Allen and Zarembo (1989) describe the history of how the display book was developed into a full-blown production system at the NYSE.
29. See Oesterle, Winslow, and Anderson (1992).
30. For instance, we have argued above that appreciable order flow could be recaptured by the exchange in the absence of an order focusing rule if it were to introduce an electronic call market into its system because free riding on price discovery is more difficult in a call market than in a continuous market environment. Also see Schwartz (1993) and Schwartz and Economides (1995).
31. See Lehn (1994).

REFERENCES

Allen, A.E. and Zarembo, L. (1989) 'The display book: the NYSE specialists' electronic work station' in H.C. Lucas, Jr. and R.A. Schwartz, (eds.) *The Challenge of Information Technology for the Securities Markets: Liquidity, Volatility & Global Trading*. Homewood, Ill., Irwin.

Amihud, Y. and Mendelson, H. (1988) 'Liquidity and asset prices: financial management implications.' *Financial Management*, 5–15.

Becker, B. and Angstadt, J. (1994) 'Market 2000: a work in progress' in R.A.

Schwartz, (ed.) *Global Equity Markets: Technological, Competitive and Regulatory Challenges*. Homewood, Ill., Irwin, forthcoming.
Bloch, E. and Schwartz, R.A. (1978) 'The great debate over NYSE Rule 390.' *The Journal of Portfolio Management*, Fall, 5–8.
Bradley, H. (1994) 'Market 2000 — the user's perspective' in R.A. Schwartz, (ed.) *Global Equity Markets: Technological, Competitive and Regulatory Challenges*. Homewood, Ill., Irwin, forthcoming.
Bronfman, C. (1994) 'In the public interest? Reassessing the regulatory role in the financial markets' in R.A. Schwartz, (ed.) *Global Equity Markets: Technological, Competitive and Regulatory Challenges*. Homewood, Ill., Irwin, forthcoming.
Bronfman, C. and Schwartz, R.A. (1993) *Price Discovery Noise*. New York University working paper.
Copeland, T. and Galai, D. (1983) 'Information effects on the bid–ask spreads.' *The Journal of Finance*, 1457–69.
Domowitz, I. (1994) 'Financial market automation and the investment services directive' in R.A. Schwartz, (ed.) *Global Equity Markets: Technological, Competitive and Regulatory Challenges*. Homewood, Ill., Irwin, forthcoming.
Economides, N. (1989) 'Desirability of compatibility in the absence of network externalities.' *American Economic Review*, **78**, 108–121.
Economides, N. and Heisler, J. (1993) 'Fee structure in electronic call markets,' mimeo.
Economides, N. and Schwartz, R.A. (1994) 'Making the trade: equity trading practices and market structure — 1994,' a survey of US Institutional Equity Traders conducted by Institutional Investor for its TraderForum Research Service.
———. (1995) *Journal of Portfolio Management*, Winter, forthcoming.
Economides, N. and Siow, A. (1988) 'The division of markets is limited by the extent of liquidity.' *American Economic Review*, **78**, 108–121.
Farrell, J. and Saloner, G. (1985) 'Standardization, compatibility, and innovation.' *Rand Journal of Economics*, **16**, 70–83.
Fisher, E. (1994) 'Is market fragmentation bad?' in R.A. Schwartz, (ed.) *Global Equity Markets: Technological, Competitive and Regulatory Challenges*. Homewood, Ill., Irwin, forthcoming.
Handa, P. and Schwartz, R.A. (1994) *Dynamic Price Discovery*. New York University working paper.
Harris, L. (1994) 'Consolidation, fragmentation, segmentation and regulation' in R.A. Schwartz, (ed.) *Global Equity Markets: Technological, Competitive and Regulatory Challenges*. Homewood, Ill., Irwin, forthcoming.
Hasbrouck, J. (1994) 'Trade and quote transparency: principles and prospects for the year 2000' in R.A. Schwartz, (ed.) *Global Equity Markets: Technological, Competitive and Regulatory Challenges*. Homewood, Ill., Irwin, forthcoming.
Hasbrouck, J. and Schwartz, R.A. (1988) 'Liquidity and execution costs in equity markets.' *Journal of Portfolio Management*, Spring, 10–16.
Ho, T., Schwartz, R.A. and Whitcomb, D.K. (1985). 'The trading decision and market clearing under transaction price uncertainty.' *Journal of Finance*, March, 21–42.
Jacquillat, B., Schwartz, R.A. and Hamon, J. (1994) 'A program to increase the liquidity of shares in the French equity market' in R.A. Schwartz, (ed.) *Global Equity Markets: Technological, Competitive and Regulatory Challenges*. Homewood, Ill., Irwin, forthcoming.
Katz, M. and Shapiro, C. (1985) 'Network externalities, competition and compatibility.' *American Economic Review*, **75**, 424–440.
Lehn, K. (1994) 'The market for marketplaces: reflections on the SEC's Market 2000

Report' in R.A. Schwartz, (ed.) *Global Equity Markets: Technological, Competitive and Regulatory Challenges*. Homewood, Ill., Irwin, forthcoming.

Oesterle, D., Winslow, D. and Anderson, S. (1992) 'The New York Stock Exchange and its out moded specialist system: can the exchange innovate to survive?' *The Journal of Corporation Law*, Winter, 223–310.

Peake, J., Mendelson, M. and Williams, R.T., Jr. (1976) 'The national book system: an electronically assisted auction market.' *Proceedings of the National Market Advisory Board of the Securities and Exchange Commission*, April 30.

Rohlfs, J. (1974) 'A theory of interdependent demand for a communications service.' *Bell Journal of Economics*, **5**, 16–37.

Schwartz, R.A. (1988) 'A proposal to stabilize stock prices.' *The Journal of Portfolio Management*, Fall, 4–11.

———. (1991) *Reshaping the Equity Markets: A Guide for the 1990s*. New York, Harper Business, reissued by Business One Irwin, 1993.

———. (1993) 'Competition and efficiency' in K. Lehn and R. Kamphuis, (eds.) *Modernizing US Securities Regulation: Economic and Legal Perspectives*. Homewood, Ill., Business One Irwin.

———. (1994) 'Addressing the needs of buy-side traders' in R.A. Schwartz, (ed.) *Global Equity Markets: Technological, Competitive and Regulatory Challenges*. Homewood, Ill., Irwin, forthcoming.

Stoll, H. (1994) 'The importance of transaction costs' in R.A. Schwartz, (ed.) *Global Equity Markets: Technological, Competitive and Regulatory Challenges*. Homewood, Ill., Irwin, forthcoming.

Wagner, W. and Edwards, M. (1993) 'Best execution.' *Financial Analysts Journal*, January/February, 65–71.

5
EC Banking Regulation

JEAN DERMINE*

At a meeting of the Council of Ministers held in Milan in 1985, the European Commission proposed a detailed timetable for the complete integration of the European markets by January 1993. The aim was to dismantle the technological, regulatory, and fiscal barriers which prevented the free flow of goods, capital, and persons in the European Community (EC). As concerns banking and financial services, a major issue arises as to whether regulation and supervision must be handled by a unique European authority, or whether it can be delegated to independent national central banks and supervisory bodies. After trying in vain to harmonize national banking regulations over twenty years, the European Commission adopted the principle of the single banking license, home-country control, and the opening of borders with minimal harmonization of regulations. Each country will recognize the competence of foreign authorities to regulate and supervise their own banks. In December 1991 at the Maastricht meeting in the Netherlands, the heads of state or government signed a draft treaty on economic union; it provides for the creation of a European System of Central Banks, a European central bank, and a common currency by 1999 at the latest. The treaty, which became European law on November 1, 1993, recognizes explicitly the principle of decentralization of regulation and supervision.

The issues raised in this chapter go far beyond the creation of a European market. They concern international trade in financial services. At a time when the North American Free Trade Agreement (NAFTA) proposes to

*The author is grateful to the editor, Dr. Benn Steil, for his many insightful comments.

International Financial Market Regulation. Edited by B. Steil

integrate further the economies of Canada, Mexico, and the US, and when financial services will be the object of further discussion in the new World Trade Organization, it is useful to make a critical review of the approach adopted for the integration of banking markets in the European Community.

The chapter is structured as follows: first a description of the European banking industry and the early effects of financial integration, second an overview of European banking legislation, and third a critical assessment of the regulatory and supervisory framework. There are four conclusions.

1. Early evidence on the effects of European financial integration demonstrates that the banking industry is undergoing a major restructuring driven by lower interest rates, competitive deregulation, and taxation. This process is just beginning in some countries, such as France and the UK.
2. More work remains to be done to achieve open and stable markets. In particular, host-country prudential supervision is warranted in two cases: to prevent systemic risks in domestic markets, and to protect one class of customers of financial services, the "uninformed." The implication is that supervision of international banks (subsidiaries and branches) should be organized jointly by authorities of the home and host countries.
3. As domestic regulators will be responsible for controlling the ownership of banks (public or private), and the degree of market power in their domestic market, a European authority must ensure that banks do not exploit domestic rents to subsidize their international activities.
4. The achievement of an internal banking market should not lead to tax evasion. Substantial work remains to be done to prevent inefficient competitive moves to reduce taxation of income on capital.

EUROPEAN BANKING STRUCTURE

The EC banking industry contains 2183 commercial banks and 2478 savings or mutual banks. As is indicated in Table 5.1, it is still a fragmented market with leading financial institutions having a substantial market share in their domestic market (84 percent in the Netherlands, 77 percent in Denmark). But at EC level the five largest institutions control only 14 percent of the market. In Europe, banks play a major role in the financial system with a ratio of total assets to GDP of 1.7, compared to 0.8 in the US, and 2.8 in Japan. Financial services represent a major source of employment and exports for several countries. As is documented in Table 5.2, the share of the labor force occupied in banking, insurance, or real estate has grown substantially over the last ten years, reaching more than 10 percent in the UK. Table 5.3 reports the results of a recent study by the Organization of Economic Cooperation and Development (OECD)[1] on the relative

Table 5.1 Summary Statistics on Selected National Banking Systems

	Belgium	Denmark	France	FRG	Greece	Ireland	Italy
No. of commercial banks	85	76	404	299	34	33	267
No. of savings and mutual banks	29	165	421	594*	4	2	813
Assets of commercial banks (billion Ecu)	239	93	771	518	39	20	588
Assets of other depository institutions (billion Ecu)	41	NA	412	1,085	19	14	246
GDP (billion Ecu)	141	92	869	1,072	49	27	783
Total assets/GDP	2.0	1.0	1.9	2.4	1.2	1.3	1.1
Population (millions)	10	5	56	62	10	4	58
Market share of five largest institutions (%)	58	77	43	26	63	45	53
Ecu rate (domestic currency per Ecu)	43.40	8.05	7.02	2.07	179.00	0.77	1,510.00

	Luxembourg	Netherlands	Portugal	Spain	UK	EEC	USA	Japan	Switzerland
No. of commercial banks	166	89	29	145	556	2,183	12,689	145†	236
No. of savings and mutual banks	49	53	1	188	163	2,478	3,323	1,080	214
Assets of commercial banks (billion Ecu)	239	345	45	400	1,745	5,003	2,754	4,183	399
Assets of other depository institutions (billion Ecu)	NA	223	NA	175	283	2,497	1,033	3,100	382
GDP (billion Ecu)	5	203	39	343	764	4,387	5,720	2,623	170
Total assets/GDP	44	2.8	1.1	1.7	2.7	1.7	0.8	2.8	4.6
Population (millions)	0.4	14.8	10.5	38.9	57.2	326.0	247.0	123.5	5.5
Market share of five largest institutions (%)	26	84	56	39	29	14	14	25	60
Ecu rate (domestic currency per Ecu)	43.4	2.33	173	130.2	0.67		1.1	152	1.8

*Does not include 3,225 cooperative credit institutions.
†Includes city and regional banks.
NA: Not available
Source: Dermine (1993b).

Table 5.2 Percentage of Labor Force in Banking, Insurance, or Real Estate

	1980	1989
Belgium	6.2	8.6
France	7.5	9.6
Germany	NA	7.9
Switzerland	NA	10.5
UK	8.2	12.7
US	8.4	11.3

NA: Not available.
Source: OECD (1991).

Table 5.3 Trade in Financial Services as a Percentage of Exports and Imports of Goods and Services*

	1988	1991		1988	1991
Belgium			Switzerland		
Exports	1.17	2.60	Exports	3.00	3.80
Imports	0.74	1.70	Imports	NA	NA
France			United Kingdom		
Exports	1.50	5.7	Exports	2.40	3.20
Imports	1.70	6.3	Imports	0.09	0.20
Germany			United States		
Exports	0.74	0.96	Exports	3.80	4.70
Imports	0.12	0.33	Imports	1.70	2.30

NA: Not available
*The data include commissions and fees received or paid related to the following transactions: foreign exchange, international payments, management of cash balances, factoring, operations in securities, asset management, fiduciary funds, guarantees and endorsements, financial leasing, counselling on takeovers or mergers, participation in barter arrangements.
Source: OECD (1993).

Table 5.4 Sector Distribution of the Hundred Largest EC Banks

Sector	Number of Banks Ranked Among the Hundred Largest	Market Share Among the Hundred Largest Banks (Percent of Assets)
Public	42	37.9
Cooperative	9	11.0
Mutual	5	1.5
Private	44	49.6

Source: Revell (1989).

Table 5.5 Interest Margins and Operating Expenses of Commercial Banks

Percent	Belgium	Denmark	France	FRG	Italy
Percent average margin on demand deposits*					
1980–1985	11.2	16.2	11.7	6.5	4.3
1987–1992	8.7	9.0	9.7	7.2	NA
Percent average margin on savings deposits*					
1980–1985	5.6	8.9	4.3	2.8	3.4
1987–1992	3.9	7.0	5.2	2.2	NA
Population per branch	1,816	1,677	2,189	1,564	3,800
Percent operating expenses per asset†	2.6	2.8	3.2	2.5	3.0
Operating expenses as percentage of gross margin	0.66	0.65	0.65	0.65	0.63

*Current short-term rate minus interest rate paid on deposits.
†Excludes interbank assets; expenses on noninterbank is calculated as total expenses minus (interbank assets × 0.125 percent).

	Luxembourg	Netherlands	Portugal	Spain	UK	US	Japan	Switzerland
Percent average margin on demand deposits*								
1980–1985	NA	5.6	NA	14.5	10.8	9.0	5.6	4.8
1987–1992	NA	6.8	NA	6.0	7.0	7.5	5.4	6.8
Percent average margin on savings deposits*								
1980–1985	NA	2.8	NA	10.7	2.5	1.0	3.8	1.3
1987–1992	NA	4.7	NA	9.0	2.0	1.0	2.0	2.6
Population per branch	NA	2,000	6,031	1,127	NA	NA	8,700‡	1,622
Percent operating expenses per asset†	1.0	2.5	2.5	3.5	4.2	3.5	1.0	2.0
Operating expenses as percentage of gross margin	0.41	0.65	0.47	0.60	0.65	0.61	0.61	0.55

*Current short-term rate minus interest rate paid on deposits.
†Excludes interbank assets; expenses on noninterbank is calculated as total expenses minus (interbank assets × 0.125 percent).
‡Does not include 22,000 branches of postal savings banks.
NA: not available.

importance of financial services in international trade. The figures, which refer to the share of fees and commissions in trade (excluding interest revenue), show sharp differences across countries; France leads with 5.7 percent share of goods and services export linked to commissions and fees.

As is documented in Table 5.4, the type of ownership of banks in Europe is diverse. Out of the hundred largest credit institutions, only forty-four are privately owned. In principle, this raises substantial issues of fair competition between private and public institutions. So far to my knowledge, no empirical studies have critically examined the issue, nor has any case been brought to the attention of the European Commission or the European Court of Justice.[2] Moreover, the public ownership issue could disappear with the large privatization programs under way in several countries.

The need for a restructuring of the banking industry arises from the breakdown of anticompetitive market practices. Over the last twenty years, banks from Belgium, Denmark, France, and Spain have benefited from regulations or gentlemen's agreements on interest rates paid on retail deposits. As Table 5.5 shows, interest margins on demand deposits reached 11 percent on average in Belgium and France over the period 1980–1985.

In contrast, spreads were much smaller in Germany and the Netherlands. The major reason for the divergence in spreads was that the market (interbank) interest rate was much higher in some countries than in others, allowing banks from the former group to realize major benefits from deposit rate control and pricing arrangements. Interestingly enough, in the more recent period 1987–1992, one observes a clear pattern of convergence. Interest rate margins are going down in Belgium, France, Denmark, and Spain, but they are going up in the Netherlands and Germany. The convergence of spreads is a direct effect of the convergence of short term interest rates brought on by the European Monetary System (EMS) and the abolition of controls on capital flows. The reduction of interest margins observed in many European countries is a first shock to bank profitability.

Besides the lowering of margins on retail deposits, major shocks have resulted from the competitive deregulation process undertaken by national regulators attempting to enhance the attractiveness of their home market. Two examples concern the reduction of taxes on interest income, and the deregulation of money markets. The case of Belgium, documented in Table 5.6, is symptomatic. Banks in that country used to benefit from tax-free low-cost savings deposits, *carnet de dépôts*, which were highly competitive with respect to other financial instruments subject to a 25 percent tax rate. In April 1991, the minister of finance lowered the tax rate on interest income to 10 percent to reduce capital outflows to the neighboring country of Luxembourg. As a result, the tax differential between savings deposits and other instruments was reduced, and Belgian banks have seen the low-cost fraction of their funding base reduced from 49 percent to 34 percent in less than two years.

Table 5.6 Structure of Bank Liabilities in Belgium, Interbank Excluded (B Fr billions)

	Deposits			Savings Bonds*	Total	Savings and Demand Deposits as Percent of Total
	Savings Accounts	Demand Deposits	Term Deposits			
1986	607.3	450.9	677.6	447.6	2,183.4	48
1987	690.6	476.1	769.8	455.4	2,391.9	49
1988	766.6	517.7	805.0	465.0	2,554.3	50
1989	862.3	572.9	982.2	526.0	2,943.4	49
1990	757.5	581.2	1,229.3	673.3	3,241.3	41
1991	707.6	604.7	1,423.8	794.3	3,533.4	37
1992	667.3	588.0	1,500.0	889.3	3,644.6	34

*Known as *bons de caisse*, these are three-year to five-year maturity deposits.
Source: Commission Bancaire et Financière, 1993.

Another example of the effects of deregulation can be seen in the money markets. In France, money market funds, *Sicav de Trésorerie* created in the early 1980s, have increased from 8 percent of money supply (M2) in 1985 to 45 percent in 1992. The commercial paper market, created in 1986, already represents 18 percent of short-term bank lending to business firms.

The creation of competitive financial products is forcing banks to reduce their costly branch networks. This is often achieved by domestic mergers between the largest banks. Table 5.7 documents the major mergers that have taken place in Denmark, the Netherlands, Spain, and Italy. As is quite apparent, countries such as France and the UK have not thus far experienced

Table 5.7 Domestic Mergers in Europe

Belgium	1992	CGER-AG Credit Communal
Denmark	1990	Den Danske Bank
		Unibank (Privatbanken, Sparekassen, Andelsbanken)
Italy	1992	Banca di Roma (Banco di Roma, Cassa di Risparmio di Roma, Banco di Santo Spirito)
		IMI-Cariplo
		San Paolo-Crediop
Netherlands	1990	ABN-AMRO
	1991	NMB-PostBank-ING
Spain	1988	BBV (Banco de Vizcaya-Banco de Bilbao)
	1989	Caja de Barcelona-La Caixa
	1992	Banco Central-Banco Hispano
Switzerland	1993	CS-Volksbank

Table 5.8 Percentage Market Share of Banks in Life Insurance Market

Germany	3.9
Spain	74
France	37
Italy	<5
Netherlands	10
UK	40

Source: Association Belge des Banques (1993).

a major restructuring of their banking industry. In addition to domestic mergers, there has been a major expansion into life insurance to exploit more completely the distribution capacity of branch networks. Table 5.8 documents the significant penetration of banks into life insurance in Spain, France, and the UK.

Competitive deregulation and taxation have thus far had a much greater effect on the structure and performance of national banking markets than market penetration by foreign institutions. As Table 5.9 documents, the market share of foreign institutions in domestic markets has not changed much over the years, whether in an open market such as the UK, or in a fairly closed market such as Germany.

Table 5.9 Market Share of Foreign Institutions as a Percentage of Total Assets

	1986	1989
Germany	4.27	4.61
Belgium	46	47
France	10.9	13.0
Italy	2.45	2.9
UK	62.2	59.1
Japan	2.12	1.4
US	17.9	21.4

Sources: Goldberg (1992), Swary and Topf (1992).

These are the early results in banking systems preparing for more competition. They raise substantial issues of fair competition. Indeed, since individual countries are responsible for the type of ownership (private or public) and the degree of concentration on their domestic markets, there is a possibility that some countries will try to create national "champions" to compete on world markets. One needs a European authority to ensure that banks do not subsidize their international activities with oligopolistic rents earned on the domestic markets.[3] One could argue that oligopolistic rents will disappear in the presence of free entry. However, some industrial organization scholars, such a Vives (1991), take the view that retail banking does not fit the model of "contestable markets." In a contestable market, potential competitors discipline established firms since these are vulnerable to hit-and-run entry. In retail banking, fixed costs incurred in branching, the creation of networks, like ATM systems, the presence of switching costs for consumers, and reputation effects could be effective barriers to entry. Only time will reveal the significance of these barriers, which, in view of the degree of concentration existing in some domestic markets, should be monitored closely.

In the next section, I review the major parts of the EC's legislative process. This will be followed by an economic assessment of the regulatory and supervisory framework.

THE EC APPROACH TO INTERNATIONAL INTEGRATION

The actions taken by the European Commission and the Council of Ministers can be divided into three time periods: deregulation of entry into domestic markets from 1957 to 1973, various attempts toward harmonization of regulations from 1973 to 1983, and the recent directives regarding the single banking license, home-country control, mutual recognition, and freedom of cross-border services.[4]

Deregulating Entry (1957–1973)

The objective of the 1957 Treaty of Rome was the transformation of highly segmented national markets into a single common market. This objective was achieved through two types of measures: the recognition of the right of establishment, and the coordination of legislation wherever necessary. In June 1973, the Council adopted Directive 73/183/EEC *The Abolition of Restrictions on Freedom of Establishment and Freedom to Provide Services for Self-Employed Activities of Banks and other Financial Institutions.* This directive applies the national treatment principle which ensures the equal regulatory and supervisory treatment of all firms operating in one country. It is explicitly recognized that subsidiaries of banks whose parents are chartered in nonmember countries are to be recognized as EC undertakings in every way. Although in 1973 entry restrictions could not be discriminatory, the objective of the initial treaty was still far from being met. International competition through the supply of cross-border services was severely restricted by regulations on capital flows. Furthermore, there was no coordination of banking supervision, so that banks operating in different countries could be subject to different rules. This additional burden would raise the costs of operating internationally. This led to the second phase of attempts to harmonize regulations.

Harmonization of Banking Regulations (1973–1983)

Progress in harmonization came in 1977 with the adoption of the First Banking Directive on *The Coordination of Laws, Regulations and Administrative Provisions Relating to the Taking Up and Pursuit of Credit Institutions (Directive 77/780/EEC)*. The Directive establishes the principle of home-country control. Responsibility for the supervision of credit institutions operating in two or more member countries will gradually be shifted from the host to the home country of the parent bank. The 1977 directive is a first step towards harmonization of regulations. It is a general program which, without providing any specific regulation, calls for further directives. Directives on *Supervision of Credit Institutions on a Consolidated Basis (Directive 83/350/EEC)*, *Uniform Format for Bank Accounts (Directive 86/635/EEC)*, and *Consumer Protection (Directive 87/102/EEC)* were adopted by 1987. The First Banking Directive initiated work on winding up and liquidation and on the mortgage market. After the 1977 directive, the European banking markets were still fragmented for the following reasons:

- A bank wishing to operate in another country still had to be authorized by the supervisors of that country.
- A foreign bank remained subject to supervision by the host country and its range of activities could be constrained by host country laws.
- In most countries, branches had to be provided with earmarked capital as if they were new banks.
- Finally, the supply of international services was severely impaired by restrictions on capital flows. For instance, the 1984 exports of financial services represented only 2 percent of output in France and Germany, while foreign institutions in these countries had market shares of 16 percent and 4 percent respectively.

The inability to agree on a common set of regulations prompted a new approach towards European integration.

The Completion of the Internal Market (1983–1992)

While most international agreements have used the national treatment principle, which ensures the equal treatment of all firms operating in one country, the European Commission has used a powerful method of integration — home-country control with very minimal immediate harmonization of national regulations.

In the context of banking, the 1985 White Paper calls for a single banking license, home country control, and mutual recognition.[5] These principles are incorporated in the Second Banking Directive. All credit institutions authorized in an EC country will be able to establish branches or supply cross-border financial services in the other countries without further authorization, provided the bank is authorised to provide such services in the home state. These services include:

- Acceptance of deposits and other repayable funds from the public.
- Lending, including consumer credit, mortgage credit, factoring, with or without recourse, and financing of commercial transactions (including forfeiting).
- Financial leasing.
- Money transmission services.
- Issuing and administering means of payment (e.g. credit cards, travellers' checks, and bankers' drafts).
- Guarantees and commitments.
- Trading for own account or for account of customers in
  - (a) money market instruments (checks, bills, certificates of deposit, etc.)
  - (b) foreign exchange
  - (c) financial futures and options
  - (d) foreign exchange and interest rate derivative instruments
  - (e) transferable securities
- Participation in securities issues and the provision of services related to such issues.
- Advice to undertakings on capital structure, industrial strategy and related questions, and advice and services relating to mergers and the purchase of undertakings.
- Money broking
- Portfolio management and advice.
- Safekeeping and administration of securities.
- Credit reference services.
- Safe custody services.

The banking model adopted by the EC is the universal banking model. It permits banks to undertake investment banking activities and leaves it to national regulators to control financial conglomerates, the ownership structure of banks, and their relationship with industry. For instance, it is known that the Bank of England does not favor the ownership of banks by industrial groups, while this is allowed in France and Belgium. The Second Banking Directive calls for home-country control on solvency.[6] This extends to the bank itself, its foreign and national subsidiaries which have to be consolidated for supervisory purposes, and its foreign branches. As concerns the latter, the host state retains the right to regulate a foreign bank's activities in the host state to the extent only that such regulation is necessary for the protection of the "public interest." Thus the manner in which a bank markets its services and deals with customers can be regulated by the host state. The host state may also intervene in those matters which have been expressly reserved to it; notably liquidity, monetary policy, and advertising. A bank constituted in a member state has the right to open a subsidiary in another member state on the same conditions as nationals of the latter state. The establishment of a subsidiary bank will be subject to the control of the country in which it is established since that is the "home" state.

To address a need for a minimal harmonization of regulations, the Second Banking Directive calls for initial capital of at least Ecu 5 million, harmonized capital adequacy standards and large exposure rules and supervisory control of banks' permanent participation in the nonfinancial sector.[7] The 1989 *Solvency Ratio Directive (Directive 89/647/EEC)* establishes a Community-wide rule that bank's own funds must be at least 8 percent of its risk-adjusted assets and off-balance-sheet transactions. Own funds have been defined by the 1989 *Own Funds Directive (Directive 89/299/EEC)* and risk-adjusted assets and off-balance-sheet transaction are defined by the *Solvency Ratio Directive.* The total of a bank's qualifying participations (basically shareholdings of 10 percent or more) in undertakings which are not banks, financial institutions, or undertakings engaged in ancillary services such as leasing, factoring, management of unit trusts, or data processing, may not exceed 60 percent of the bank's own funds. Moreover, no single qualifying participation may exceed 15 percent of the bank's own funds. A directive on the *Monitoring and Control of Large Exposure (Directive 92/121)* states that, since January 1994, a limit of 40 percent of capital will be imposed for exposures to a single client, which will be reduced over time to 25 percent. The aggregate amount of large exposures (those exceeding 10 percent of capital) may not exceed 800 percent of such capital.

A supportive piece of legislation is the 1988 *Directive on Liberalization of Capital Flows (Directive 88/361/EEC)*. However, that directive contains a safeguard clause authorizing member states to take necessary measures in the event of balance of payments problems.[8]

A draft directive on deposit guarantee schemes (Draft directive COM (92) 188) was accepted by the Council of Ministers in September 1993 (qualified majority with opposition only by Germany). It aims to adapt the current deposit insurance mechanisms which are summarized in Table 5.10.

The draft directive provides for mandatory insurance for all EC financial institutions. The coverage per depositor is a minimum of Ecu 20,000 ($23,000), (Ecu 15,000 until 1999), with a franchise[9] of maximum 10 percent.

Table 5.10 Deposit Insurance Systems in Selected Countries

	Coverage (Domestic Currency)	Coverage (Ecu)
Belgium	BFr 500,000	12,100
Denmark	DKr 250,000	32,470
France	FFr 400,000	60,000
Germany	30% of equity per deposit	
Ireland	I£ 10,000	12,350
Italy	L 1 billion (100% for the first 200 million and 75% for next 800)	536,400 (100% for first 107,000 and 75% for next 428,000)
Luxembourg	Lux Fr 500,000	12,100
Netherlands	Fl 40,000	18,800
Spain	Pta 1,500,000	9,765
UK	75% of deposits (ceiling of £15,000)	75% of deposits (ceiling of 19,350)
Greece	No system	
Portugal	No system	
Japan	¥ 10,000,000	80,000
US	$100,000	85,000

The principle of home country control would apply; that is the insurance system of the parent bank would cover the deposits collected by domestic and foreign branches. The depositor will be informed, and publicity will be controlled to prevent abuse. This is the principle, against which two very important exceptions stand. In the case where the home coverage is too large compared with the host coverage (e.g., a French bank operating in Belgium), the coverage of foreign branches cannot exceed that of the host country to prevent "unfair" competition. In the case where the home coverage is lower than that of the host country, the foreign branch will have the right to obtain supplementary insurance from the host state. Finally, for the branches of non-EC banks, the host country will decide whether or not they must join an insurance system, with the provision that depositors will be informed about the magnitude of the coverage.

The integration of investment services (investment banking) proceeds in a very similar manner. From January 1996 onwards, directives for investment services in the securities field and for capital adequacy provide for a single license, home country regulation and control on shareholders, capital adequacy standards, and compliance with prudential rules. A major difference with the Second Banking Directive is that substantial powers are given to host authorities concerning the design of conduct of business rules. These include share registration and new issues procedures, securities prospectuses, investor protection, insider trading and related market practices.[10]

The issue of reciprocity has received considerable attention in nonmember countries. Two concerns have to be distinguished: the denial of national treatment, and effective market access comparable to that which the Community grants to third countries. Article 9(4) of the Second Banking Directive deals with the situation where there is discrimination against Community financial institutions, compared with their domestic counterparts in a third country. In this case, the directive provides for the initiation of discussion with the option to suspend new banking licenses for institutions from the third country. In the second case — comparable access — Article 9(3) provides for negotiation with the country without the suspension of the right of establishment. Although a recent report, *Treatment of European Financial Institutions in Third Countries* (European Commission 1992a), recognizes the existence of discriminatory treatment in some countries, it recommends negotiating in the framework of the new World Trade Organization. Moreover, it makes no reference to a temporary suspension of authorization.

The December 1991 Maastricht Treaty on economic and monetary union has confirmed the Single Market program. Although the primary objective of the European System of Central Banks (ESCB) shall be to maintain price stability, there are explicit references to regulation and supervision.

> The European System of Central Banks shall contribute to the smooth conduct of policies pursued by the competent authorities relating to the prudential supervision of credit institutions and the stability of the financial system . . . The national Central Banks are an integral part of the ESCB and shall act in accordance with the guidelines and instructions of the European Central Bank (ECB) . . . The ECB may offer advice to and be consulted by the Council, the Commission and the competent authorities of the Member States in the scope and implementation of Community legislation relating to the prudential supervision of credit institutions and to the stability of the financial system . . . The ECB may fulfil specific tasks concerning policies relating to the prudential supervision of credit institutions and other financial institutions with the exception of insurance undertakings (European Commission 1992b).

Although the exact rules governing the functioning of the new system have yet to be worked out, the treaty is explicit on the principle of decentralization and allocation of regulatory and supervisory powers to national central banks. It is only in very special circumstances and with unanimity in the European Council that the European Central Bank will be allowed to regulate or supervise financial institutions. On October 12, 1993 the last obstacle to ratification was lifted with a ruling by the German Constitutional Court, and the Maastricht Treaty has officially been in effect since November 1, 1993.

Finally, it should be recognized that the single banking market will go beyond the twelve members of the European Union. On May 13, 1992, the countries of the European Free Trade Association (EFTA),[11] with the exception of Switzerland, joined the European Economic Area (EEA). This implies that the EEA countries accept the European banking legislation on the single banking license, home-country control, mutual recognition, and acceptance of the common regulations.

ECONOMIC EVALUATION OF EC LEGISLATION

The economics literature has identified several potential market failures which explain the need for banking regulations. The objective in this section is to review the nature of these market failures and to see whether the current European regulatory and supervisory framework is adequate.

With respect to banking services, three independent explanations have been advanced for the existence of potential market failure: imperfect (asymmetric) information which prevents the proper functioning of unregulated private markets, the potential for bank runs and the related fear of systemic crisis, and trade policy issues. Furthermore, the freedom of capital flows raises the issue of tax evasion.

Imperfect (Asymmetric) Information and Consumer Protection

The analysis which follows explains why there is a need to protect consumers of financial services. This leads directly to a discussion of the principles of home-country control and mutual recognition. Indeed, these rules imply that banking services offered to nationals of a particular country by a branch of a foreign bank are regulated by another country with, possibly, an inadequate degree of protection.

The first and most important case of asymmetric information concerns the imperfect knowledge about the solvency of a banking firm. Depositors find it costly to evaluate the solvency of their bank. Additional sources of asymmetric information concern the potentially fraudulent character of management, the nature of the legal contract (for instance, the exact nature of a loan covenant), and problems related to conflicts of interest between different departments in a bank. For instance, a mergers and acquisitions advisor should not inform a fund manager about the likelihood of a transaction, otherwise the fund manager will purchase securities of the "target" firm, the price of shares will increase, and the acquisition will be made more expensive.

The economics literature[12] recognizes that market failure can be created by the inability of consumers to properly evaluate the quality of a product. It distinguishes between three types of goods: *search goods*, whose quality is apparent before purchase; *experience goods*, whose quality is apparent after consumption; and *trust goods*, whose quality is not always apparent even after consumption. An inefficiency may arise because the quality of a service is not valued properly by the market and reflected in higher prices. This leads to insufficient incentives for firms to produce quality. Regulation (such as minimum qualifications in the legal or medical professions) is a way to ensure a minimum level of quality. In the context of banking, quality refers in part to the degree of solvency of an institution. When depositors are uninformed, there are fewer incentives to limit the riskiness of the assets of a financial institution or its degree of financial leverage (deposit-to-equity ratio). According to finance theory,[13] whenever depositors are not properly informed, bank shareholders benefit from an increase in risk. With perfect information, depositors would react by demanding a higher rate of interest to offset the transfer going to shareholders. With imperfect (asymmetric) information, this would be difficult, raising a well-defined and well-documented moral hazard problem.[14] However, the existence of imperfect information per se does not yet justify public intervention. It has to be shown that private mechanisms cannot succeed.

A natural solution to the imperfect information problem is the provision of information and regulation of disclosure. However, the evaluation of bank risks is a costly activity which could create a free-rider problem. Individually, each consumer may prefer not to engage in information search and analysis on the assumption that other investors will do it. In such a situation the provision of private information is too low. Moreover, since information once produced is available to consumers at a very low transfer cost, the evaluation of banks need not be undertaken by each depositor but could be delegated to a public agency or a private rating firm. Furthermore, since small account holders may find it expensive to interpret the rating and/or since they care only about risk-free deposits, two alternatives could be developed. The first is to have deposit insurance. The second is to create risk-free institutions, which invest all deposits in risk-free securities (the so-called "narrow bank" proposal). Depositors would have the choice between institutions offering a higher expected but risky return and those providing quasi-risk-free deposits. It would appear that the evaluation of risks is not inherently more difficult in banking than in other industries. It is quite likely that a large fraction of depositors desire risk-free deposits, but these could be provided by the markets.

In addition to the disclosure and evaluation of information, there are two alternative private ways to reduce the imperfect information problem are reputation and warranty provided by the industry. Firms who care for reputation, the value of their franchise, and long-run profits have an incentive to build an internal control system to reduce risks and fraud. However, a tradeoff will exist between (potentially high) shortterm fraudulent profit and the benefits of longterm reputation. An alternative is for a firm or an industry to provide a guarantee on the quality of the services offered. For instance, the private deposit insurance organized by the industry guarantees clients against potential losses. Peer monitoring or industry self-regulation prevent deviant behavior.

This analysis has shown that the information problem can be solved privately in the market by disclosure, information gathering, reputation, and insurance. But when there is evidence that the market cannot discriminate among firms,[15] there is a case for government to regulate entry and ensure a minimum quality, as in the medical and legal professions. The argument is that regulation is necessary to maintain a minimum desired level of quality. In this context, a question arises as to whether this should be done privately or quasi-privately as in the UK with the self-regulatory organization (SROs), or whether it should be public. The benefits of flexibility and industry expertise provided by private self-regulation have to be balanced against the risk of capture by the SROs, whose members have an obvious incentive to limit entry and competition. As there is currently no empirical evidence in favor of one system or another, I suggest letting the national regulatory structures compete.[16]

The possibility of competitive deregulation raises immediately the question of the need to harmonize regulations at the international level. This issue is particularly relevant in Europe, since, according to the home-country principle, nationals from one particular country will be offered services from institutions supervised in another country. The answer is again related to imperfect information. Competition among national regulators or private clubs is desirable whenever the parties can evaluate the quality of regulatory systems. For instance, competition among regulators in Tokyo, Paris, Frankfurt, London, and New York will shape the development of local stock exchanges, and the outcomes will be optimal if participants can discriminate among different regulatory systems. Harmonization of rules to ensure minimum quality would be necessary only if the market could not discriminate. This suggests that the degree of international harmonization could vary for different activities and classes of investor — the informed and the uninformed. An alternative to the harmonization of prudential regulations is to grant some supervisory powers to the host state whenever it is felt that investors are not adequately protected by foreign regulation or supervision. This is precisely the approach adopted by the European Commission, which leaves to each host country the right to control foreign branches for reasons of "public interest." No doubt, these interventions by the host state will be challenged at the European Court of Justice, which will have to define the notion of public interest.

To summarize, the economics literature identifies a first market failure, imperfect information. This creates a need to protect the "uninformed" investors. Since the home country principle implies that services offered by a branch of a foreign bank will be regulated by another country, there is the possibility that the degree of protection could be inadequate. The public interest criterion allows the host country to intervene in such a case.

Bank Runs and Systemic Risks

The second market failure is the potential for bank runs and systemic crisis. Banks are special because the financial contract that emerges — illiquid loans funded by short-term deposits — creates a potential market failure and a need for public intervention. The financial contract creates the risk that depositors run to withdraw their funds. A run can be triggered by bad news about the value of bank assets or by any unexplained fear.[17] In both cases, there may be a loss since illiquid assets will be sold at a discount. Moreover, a bank failure could eventually trigger a signal on the solvency of other banks, leading to a systemic crisis. Here, a distinction should be drawn between a "domino effect" and systemic crisis.

A domino effect exists if the failure of one bank would directly endanger the solvency of other banks. However, this risk is substantially reduced since banks are systematically collecting and controlling their counterparty exposure through, for instance, netting arrangements. A pure case of systemic run could occur if, lacking information, there is a run by depositors on all banks.

This market failure explains banking regulations and the establishment of safety nets to guarantee the stability of banking markets. They have taken the form of deposit insurance and lender-of-last-resort interventions. Deposit insurance funds in Europe are unlikely to contribute much to reducing systemic risk because they cover small deposits only. Runs are likely to be initiated by large firms or financial institutions. Therefore, lender-of-last-resort interventions by central banks remain the most efficient tool to avoid bank runs and systemic crisis.

The safety net with deposit insurance or a lender of last resort creates an additional problem in the European Union. It concerns the potential liability of the lender of last resort and the deposit insurance agency.

As lenders of last resort will be concerned primarily with their domestic markets and banks operating domestically,[18] it is legitimate that they keep some supervisory power over all institutions (branches and subsidiaries) operating domestically. That is, host-country regulation could apply to limit the risks taken by financial institutions and the exposure of the domestic central bank in cases of bailing out.[19] A first alternative to host-country control is to harmonize completely the solvency standards of different countries, but experience has shown that it would be very difficult to reach an agreement on harmonization of regulations and supervisory practices. Moreover, I do not believe that centralized regulation is necessary, or even desirable. Competition between national regulators should produce efficient standards and prevent regulatory capture by those under regulation, as has happened so often in banking over the last sixty years. It thus seems reasonable to let domestic supervisors keep some host supervisory powers over international banks (subsidiaries and branches) having substantial funding at risk in their own country.

Similarly, the national deposit insurance systems create their own problems. Since the insurance coverage is different across countries, deposit insurance could be destabilizing if investors were to chase the best coverage. Moreover, the deposit insurance systems currently in place cover the deposits of domestic and foreign banks operating locally. This creates an accountability problem. Indeed, any insurance activities require the monitoring of risks taken by the insurer, but the principle of home-country supervision would not allow the control of the foreign branches by the domestic lender of last resort or the deposit insurance agency. The problem is well illustrated by the January 1992 winding-up order made for the Bank of Credit and Commerce International (BCCI), a bank chartered in Luxembourg with significant activities in the UK. It automatically created a liability for the British Deposit Protection Board. This important case led to the review of deposit insurance systems in Europe.

The motivation for the 1993 deposit guarantee draft directive is illustrative, as it incorporates several of the arguments discussed previously.

> . . . deposit protection is as essential as prudential rules for the completion of the single market ... the cost to credit institutions of participating in a guarantee scheme bears no relation to the cost that would result from a massive withdrawal of bank deposits not only from a credit institution in difficulties but also from healthy institutions following a loss of depositor confidence (Draft Directive COM (92) 188).

This proposal creates two problems. The first, well illustrated by the German opposition to the draft directive, is that foreign banks could join the German scheme, but the German deposit insurance system would have no power to monitor the risks taken by branches of foreign institutions. There is an accountability problem, as mentioned earlier. The second problem is that deposit insurance further reduces private incentives for monitoring the solvency of banks. The creation of risk-free deposits could be organized by the market (the "narrow bank" proposal), or preferably insured deposits could be classed as "first-order" claims. The uninsured deposits, bearing larger losses in the case of bank failure, would have additional incentives to monitor the solvency of financial institutions.

The analysis of the second type of market failure, bank runs and systemic crises, leads to the following conclusion. Since domestic central banks will be primarily concerned with the stability of their domestic markets, they should have the right to control the solvency of banks (subsidiaries and branches) operating in their domestic market. Since in many cases, solvency would depend on the solvency of an entire group, I recommend joint supervision by authorities of the home and host countries. The case for sole home-country supervision is weak as long as sovereign countries are responsible for the stability of their own markets.

Fair Trade

Two issues will be distinguished. The first relates to the implicit guarantee given by central banks. The second refers to the possibility of cross-border subsidization.

Public safety nets or deposit insurance systems can provide an implicit subsidy that can alter competition. For instance, deposit financing can reduce the cost of funding loans, not only because of the tax deductibility of interest payments, but also because of the implicit guarantee given by the lender of last resort. To foster stability and create a level playing field, the Basle Committee on Banking Supervision and the European Commission have enforced minimal capital requirements and lending limits on large exposure. From the point of view of competition, the harmonization of prudential regulations is warranted when the objective is to create a level playing field. But harmonization should be limited only to that objective. For instance, the current effort to harmonize the regulation of interest rate risk and foreign exchange exposures does not appear desirable because they do not provide a clear competitive advantage to banks (Dermine 1993a). Quite often, the identification of a regulatory subsidy will be difficult. For instance, do links between banks and industrial groups provide a competitive advantage which is subsidized by the central bank who takes a greater risk? There is no case for harmonization as long as the existence of a subsidy yielding a competitive advantage cannot be demonstrated. Such a case was clear in the context of loan funding and capital adequacy. It is much debatable in the context of the links between banks and industrial groups.

The second issue is the possibility that oligopolistic home markets could generate rents used to subsidize foreign activities. The issue arises because of the fear that some countries could allow concentration in their domestic banking markets. The trade policies in the Netherlands and the UK are quite different. The UK Office of Fair Trading prevents excessive concentration in the domestic market, while the Dutch authorities have allowed substantial concentration in their domestic market.

Taxation of Capital Income

To enhance the attractiveness of their home market, various countries have reduced the taxation of income on capital, at least relative to the taxation of labor income. From a fiscal policy perspective, it would seem that the

Table 5.11 External Position of Banks *vis-à-vis* to the Nonbank Sector ($ billions)

	1989	1992
Austria	10.9	8.9
Belgium	27.1	41.1
Luxembourg	77.2	121.6
Denmark	4.1	4.1
Finland	3.5	1.0
France	32.1	49.1
Germany	39.2	73.3
Ireland	4.4	4.9
Italy	9.1	9.2
Netherlands	31.9	42.2
Norway	1.4	1.3
Spain	20.4	29.3
Sweden	9.5	9.2
Switzerland	178.4	208.7
UK	266.4	313.7
Caribbean Centres	204.5	231.1

These statistics could underestimate the external position of banks to the extent that fiduciary deposits are not reported.
Source: BIS (1992).

creation of a single EC banking market should not affect the relative taxation of labor and capital income. Obviously, this will not be the case as long as there is no harmonization of taxation, or sharing of information by tax authorities. Table 5.11 reports the external liabilities of national banks with respect to the nonbank sector.

Even acknowledging the expertise of some banking centers, it would appear that the volume of deposits housed in a few small countries is abnormally large. Proposals for a common withholding tax on interest revenue have been rejected so far by Luxembourg and the UK with the argument that the Euromarket would be transferred to a non-EC country (Association Belge des Banques 1989). An alternative proposal to lift bank secrecy would arouse similar concern. Lifting bank secrecy would allow the fiscal authority of one member state to obtain information about bank deposits in another Member State. Within the US, the federal tax authorities are able to obtain this type of information. To reduce the size of potential capital outflows, I recommend the lifting of bank secrecy for EC investors only. Investors from a non-EC country, not being affected by the proposal, would find EC financial markets quite attractive. As concerns some EC investors, they might wish to transfer bank accounts to a non-EC country. This is a risk that should be taken, especially as the rules could be reversed if necessary.

CONCLUSION

The purpose of this chapter has been to analyze the EC's internal banking market. While most international agreements have used the national treatment principle and kept domestic authorization and supervision, the European Commission has used a powerful innovative method of integration: opening markets with a single banking license, home-country control, mutual recognition, and very minimal harmonization. There are four policy conclusions.

1. Early evidence on the effects of European financial integration demonstrates that the banking industry is undergoing a major restructuring driven by lower interest rates, competitive deregulation, and taxation. In a few countries, such as France and the UK, the process is only just starting.
2. A review of the economics of banking regulation calls for further work to improve the stability of European banking systems. The literature has identified three potential sources of market failure calling for national regulations: imperfect information, bank runs, and fair trade. The first source of market failure is the traditional need to protect investors. I have argued that domestic regulation of quality is only warranted in those cases where investors cannot evaluate the quality of a product. As for information disclosure, competition between public or private regulators and the creation of risk-free funds will be satisfactory in many situations; different products and classes of investors will require different regulatory treatment. An exception to the home country principle in the Second Banking Directive allows host-country control for reasons of public interest. This exception is justified as long as it applies to the uninformed investor. A second market failure calling for regulation and harmonization comes from the need to provide a safety net for liquid deposits and the legitimate need to limit moral hazard and risk-taking by banks. From this angle, host country regulation of branches of foreign banks is justified to limit the exposure of the domestic lender of last resort. Moreover, I recommend modifying the deposit insurance scheme recently adopted by the European Council of Ministers. Insured deposits should be made a first-order claim so as to increase monitoring incentives for uninsured deposits.
3. From the perspective of the "fair level playing field," the international harmonization of regulations is only necessary to limit implicit public subsidies which create a competitive advantage. Moreover, as domestic regulators will be responsible for controlling the ownership of banks (public or private), and the degree of market power in their domestic market, a European authority must ensure that banks do not exploit

domestic rents to subsidize their international activities.

4. The achievement of an internal banking market should not lead to tax evasion. Substantial work remains to be done to prevent inefficient competitive moves to reduce taxation of income on capital.

ENDNOTES

1. See OECD (1993).
2. In 1991, Peter Lilley, then UK trade and industry secretary, tried to block the acquisition by Credit Lyonnais of Woodchester Investment, an Irish-based finance company with interests in Britain. He argued the acquisition of a private firm by a nationalized French bank was "nationalization through the back door." The UK Monopolies and Merger Commission concluded there was no justification for blocking the deal on competitive grounds.
3. An alternative is to refer all mergers to a single European authority, but this would run against the principle of decentralization, very much in favor in Europe. Since September 21, 1990, the European Commission can only investigate mergers involving large firms operating in several countries.
4. References on EC integration include Benink (1993) and Foster (1991).
5. The principles of home-country regulation and mutual recognition have been inspired by the famous case of Cassis de Dijon, *EC Commission vs. Germany*, 205/84, ECR 3755 (1987). In this case, the European Court of Justice found that Germany could not prohibit the import of liquor that was lawfully produced and sold in France solely because the alcohol content was too low for it to be deemed liqueur under German law. See also Directive 89/646/EEC.
6. As discussed in Norton (1991), the EC directives have basic ideas in common with the Basle Concordat (June 1993) on guidelines for consolidated supervision, and the division of supervisory responsibilities between the home and host states.
7. See Dermine (1990, 1993b). Compliance with these regulations will be enforced by national banking supervisors.
8. The June 1988 capital directive (Article 3) provides for the temporary implementation of capital controls. In the case of large speculative movements, the Commission after consultation with the Committee of Central Banks Governors can authorize capital controls. In very urgent cases, a country can implement them, but must notify the Commission. After consultation with the Committee of Central Bank Governors, authorization to pursue capital controls can be given for a period not exceeding six months.
9. The fraction of the deposit that would not be covered by deposit insurance.
10. See Dale (1992).
11. EFTA includes Austria, Finland, Iceland, Liechtenstein, Norway, Sweden, and Switzerland.
12. See Kay and Vickers (1986).
13. Merton (1977). The underlying intuition is that an increase in risk (variance of asset return) allows the shareholders of a firm to reap potentially large gains, while limiting the downside risk to zero because of the limited liability characteristic of shares.
14. See Lawrence White's application of moral hazard to the American S & L industry (White 1991).
15. Evidence is a strong word. In most cases, there will be a sociopolitical belief in

the need to protect consumers.

16. An additional argument for competition between national regulatory structures is the incomplete understanding of "general equilibrium" costs incurred. With the exception of a paper by Santomero and Watson (1977), most scholars have used partial equilibrium models to analyze the effects of regulation.
17. Calomiris and Gorton (1991) argue that most of the bank runs are linked to a decrease in value of bank assets.
18. It is well known that the Bank of Italy did not intervene to prevent the collapse of the holding of Luxembourg-based Banco Ambrosiano because it created little disturbance on the Italian financial markets.
19. Bailing out would occur if the failure of a branch of a foreign bank led to a run on domestic banks.

REFERENCES

Association Belge des Banques. (1989) *Harmonisation Européenne de la Fiscalité Mobilière,* Brussels.

———. (1993) *La Distribution des Produits d'Assurance par les Banques.*

Benink H. (1993) *Financial Integration in Europe.* Dordrecht, Kluwer.

BIS. (1983) *The Revised Basle Concordat, Principles for the Supervision of Banks' Foreign Establishments*, Basle.

———. (1992) *Recent Developments in International Interbank Relations,* Basle.

Calomiris, C. and Gorton G. (1990) 'The origins of banking panics, models, facts and banking regulations.' Wharton School, mimeo.

Commission Bancaire et Financière. (1993) *Statistiques,* Brussels.

Dale, R. (1992) *International Banking Deregulation.* Oxford, Basil Blackwell.

Dermine, J. (1990) The specialization of financial intermediaries, the EC model. *Journal of Common Market Studies.* **28**, 219–233.

———. (1993a) 'The evaluation of interest rate risk, some warnings about the Basle proposal.' *Finanzmarkt und Portfolio Management.* **7**, 141–149.

———. ed. (1993b) *European Banking in the 1990s*. Oxford, Basil Blackwell.

European Commission. (1992a) *Traitement Réservé dans les Pays Tiers aux Etablissements de Crédit et aux Enterprises d'Assurance de la Communauté,* Brussels.

———. (1992b) *Traité sur L'Union Européenne,* Brussels.

Foster, N. (1991) *EEC Legislation*. London, Blackstone Press.

Goldberg, L. (1992) The competitive impact of foreign commercial banks in the USA, in Gilbert, (ed.) *The Changing Market in Financial Services*. Boston, Kluwer.

Kay, J. and Vickers, J. (1988) 'Regulatory reform in Britain.' *Economic Policy.* **7**, 286–351.

Merton, R. (1977) 'An analytic derivation of the costs of deposit insurance and loan guarantees.' *Journal of Banking and Finance* **1**, 3–11.

Norton, J. (1991) 'The EC banking directives and international banking regulation,' in R. Cranston, (ed.) *The Single Market and the Law of Banking*. London, Lloyd's of London Press.

OECD (1991) *Labour Force Statistics,* Paris.

———. (1993) *Trade in Financial Services, Financial Market Trends*, June.

Revell, J. (1989) 'Bank preparations for 1992, some clues and some queries.' *Revue de la Banque,* March.

Santomero, A. and Watson, R. (1977) 'Determining an optimal capital standard for the banking industry.' *Journal of Finance.* **32**, 1267–1282.

Swary and Topf. (1992) *Global Financial Deregulation*. Oxford, Basil Blackwell.

Vives, X. (1991) 'Banking competition and European integration,' in A. Giovanini and C. Mayer, (eds.) *European Financial Integration*, Cambridge, Cambridge University Press.

White, L. (1991) *The S & L Debacle: Public Policy Lessons for Bank and Thrift Regulation.* Oxford, Oxford University Press.

6
EC Securities Markets Regulations

BRIAN SCOTT-QUINN

The securities markets of Europe have long been viewed as fragmented. In this respect, they have been contrasted unfavorably with the "integrated" financial markets of the US and, to a lesser extent, Japan. Concern with fragmentation in Europe arose principally from a belief that it hindered the efficient allocation of capital and thus held back economic growth in Europe in comparison with the US and Japan. The emphasis given to creating a "unified" capital market in Europe in the early years of the Community was based on the demands of industrialists for financing opportunities in European industry. They saw what was available to their competitors in the US and Japan and they wanted something similar for themselves.

Fragmentation of markets, whether in goods and services or capital, damages the prospects for economic growth. This belief is fundamental to the framework for the economic development of the European Community laid out in the 1957 Treaty of Rome.[1] The Treaty provides for the free movement of goods, persons, services, and capital within the Community with an initial focus on establishing a customs union. The customs union was achieved in 1968. In 1979 the European Monetary System (EMS) was established, designed to lead to a reduction in the volatility of inter-Member-State exchange rates hence greater unification of goods and services markets in the Community.[2] But nowhere in the Treaty of Rome is there any mention of unification of capital markets as a goal. Instead, the Treaty limits itself to requiring Member States "to progressively abolish between themselves all

International Financial Market Regulation. Edited by B. Steil

restrictions on the movement of capital," with the proviso that this was only to the extent necessary "to ensure the proper functioning of the common market." While the obligations on Member States reduced the fragmentation of markets in goods and services (including markets in financial services) in the twenty years following the signing of the Treaty of Rome, in no sense had a "single market in goods and (financial) services" developed.

By the early 1980s it was clear that economic growth in Europe was falling behind growth in Japan and the United States. Many in Europe held the view that recovery from the recession of the 1970s was being held back by the failure to create the single market that had been an objective of the Treaty of Rome. The European Commission took the view in the early 1980s that modifications to the Treaty of Rome would be required to achieve this objective on an acceptable time scale.

In order to prepare a basis for these modifications, the Commissioner responsible for the internal market prepared *Completing the Internal Market*, a White Paper published in 1985.[3] This identified three hundred pieces of legislation that would have to be adopted by the EC, and implemented in national law in each Member State, in order to remove restrictions that were seen to be preventing the development of a single market. In respect of financial services, the objectives were

- The complete liberalization of capital movements
- The unification of national markets for financial services
- The establishment of a common regulatory structure for financial institutions

What was just as important as the measures themselves was a timetable for their introduction that required the whole program to be in place by the end of 1992. The White Paper was adopted by the Council of Ministers of the EC and became the basis for the Single European Act, an amendment to the Treaty of Rome. The Act was adopted in 1986 and, by 1987, had been ratified by the national parliament of every Member State.

In addition to the measures designed to lead to a single market, the preamble to the Act referred specifically to monetary union as an EC goal to be "progressively realised." However, in a concession to both the UK and Germany, not strongly in favor of monetary union, this was not among the 1992 priorities laid down by the Act as legally binding. Monetary union, which many believe is essential to complete the single market, arose again as an issue at the 1991 Maastricht summit.[4] At this summit it was agreed to introduce a single European currency by 1999. However events since Maastricht have reduced the probability of a single European currency being achieved by this date.

Today, beyond the objective of creating a Community-wide capital market in which European issuers can raise capital and investors can acquire investment products, the Commission has (informally) stated that one of its aims is "... to ensure that the Community has a sufficiently efficient marketplace to be able to compete on equal terms with the markets of the US and the Pacific Basin. Potentially the Community's securities market could rival or even overtake those other markets, once its component parts are welded into an integrated whole."[5] It is clear from this statement that the Commission views securities market products as potentially an important element of trade between the Community and third countries.

It is likely that this view arises, in part, from the success that one Member State — the UK — has had as a provider of international financial services and as an entrepôt for global capital. Even before 1973 (the date when the UK acceded to the Community), it had a well-functioning international capital market well able to compete with the international markets in New York. The success of the UK arose, initially, for historical reasons, rooted in its merchandise trading culture and its associated financing needs. In more recent times the nature of its securities market infrastructure has given it some competitive advantages. The UK's global competitive advantage in financial services has been perceived by individual EC members and by the European Commission as something worthy of emulating. Achieving this would clearly help to attain the Commission's objective of "competing on equal terms with the markets of the US and the Pacific Basin."

NATIONAL MARKET REGULATION IN THE EC AND MARKET INTEGRATION

An understanding of why European markets have traditionally been so fragmented can be gained by examining the differences between the social, political, and economic structure, securities market infrastructure, and regulatory frameworks in different Member States. The social, political, and economic differences cannot be covered here in detail, but most relevant is that the majority of the twelve Member States of the European Community have their own language (or languages), currency, legal system, and accounting rules. In contrast, in the US, each of the fifty states uses a common language, currency, legal system, and set of accounting rules. In addition to these factors, the degree of state ownership of both industry and the banking system, the extent of universal banking, and the relative importance of individual versus institutional participation in the stock market vary country by country within the Community. Finally, the structure of the securities industry and the type of market mechanism used (in particular the extent of market-making in the equity market) vary substantially. All these factors inhibit the development of a single securities market in the EC directly comparable with that in the US.

In addition to the above differences, each of the twelve Member States has, and for the foreseeable future will continue to have, its own securities market legislation, statutory regulatory bodies, self-regulatory organizations, and compliance mechanisms. This leads to variations across the Community in the balance between centralized regulation and regionally based regulation, between self-regulation and statutory regulation, and the extent to which certain practices are permitted or prohibited. We examine below the regulatory and market structures in a number of EC countries. The country sections below (apart from the UK) are based on information in Linklater and Paines' *Securities Regulation in the Single Market.*

United Kingdom

The UK stock market capitalization bears a higher ratio to GNP than in any of the Continental countries. The UK also has separate banking and securities sectors, generally a feature of countries with well-developed securities markets. But, unlike the US, the UK separation is based on custom, not legislation.

In contrast to much of Continental Europe, where the value of government securities exceeds that of the corporate sector, UK company securities have a value around four times that of the government sector. In consequence, institutional investors in the UK holding domestic portfolios have traditionally held a much higher proportion of equities in those portfolios relative to debt securities than Continental institutional investors. UK stock exchange transactions are also dominated by institutional investors to a much greater extent than in Continental markets, despite the attempt by the Thatcher governments since 1979 to encourage private ownership of equity shares, in particular privatization issues. As a consequence, the average size of transaction on the UK market is higher than on most Continental exchanges.

The UK was the first country in the EC to reform its markets and its regulatory framework. Historically, the investment market had been governed by a combination of some statutory legislation and much self-regulation. The statutory framework included the Companies Acts and the Prevention of Fraud (Investments) Act of 1958. The stock exchange, however, was viewed as a professional body which should operate on the basis of "my word is my bond." Although this framework had been considered satisfactory up to the mid-1970s, subsequent investment frauds resulted in the government taking the view that a system based more on statute law was required.

The Financial Services Act, passed by Parliament in 1986, came into force in 1988. This Act changed the framework of regulation of markets in the UK from one which had been principally self-regulatory to one with a strong statutory basis. While not eliminating self-regulation, it created a new body, the Securities and Investment Board (SIB), with a wide range of statutory powers. Although a statutory body, the SIB is funded by the industry. The SIB, in turn, delegates many powers to a number of self-regulatory bodies which, in the case of wholesale securities markets is the Securities and Futures Authority (SFA). This body regulates those firms participating at the wholesale level in equities, bonds (including Eurobonds) and futures and option products. All persons dealing with the public in securities have to pass a qualifying examination and be registered with the SFA. The SFA also provides the Conduct of Business Rules that have to be followed by its member firms. Regulation in the UK is functionally based; the Bank of England regulates credit and the SFA regulates the wholesale securities market. However, since many financial firms are involved in both credit and securities activities, the UK employs a lead-regulator approach under which one regulator has overall responsibility for companies involved in both types of business.

The restructuring of the mechanisms used in the equity market was sparked by an investor complaint in 1978 about fixed commissions, which led ultimately to the reform of 1986, known as Big Bang. This introduced negotiable commissions, dual capacity transacting (i.e., as broker and dealer), corporate ownership of broker-dealers and permission for foreign companies to acquire UK broker-dealers. While the initial complaint had been only about fixed commissions, it was shortly to become clear that the sclerotic structure of the industry was causing it to lose market share. Initially this loss was in its share of business in non-UK equities. UK interest in foreign equities had increased sharply subsequent to the abolition of exchange controls in the UK in 1979, and much of the subsequent capital outflow was invested in foreign equities through foreign, in particular US, securities houses. UK institutional investors who developed working relationships with US securities houses found that they could also transact in UK domestic equities in New York through these houses without having to pay such large "fixed" commissions. The ability to do this had, in turn, resulted from the New York Stock Exchange moving to negotiated commissions in May 1975 (Mayday) and from the improvement in transatlantic telecommunications since that time.

The radical nature of the change in the structure of the stock exchange was, at least in part, due to the Thatcher government's concern with the complacency of the industry and its intolerance of a major British industry losing world market share, particularly in its domestic product. The rapid growth of the Eurobond market in London, dominated by foreign securities houses, pointed up the importance of allowing, and indeed encouraging, foreign-owned firms to base themselves in the UK if London was to continue to prosper as a global financial center.

Prior to Big Bang, the UK market functioned as a dealer market, with the jobbers (as dealers were called) making two-way prices to brokers on the floor of the exchange. Since Big Bang, the UK has moved to a competing dealer market structure, with broker-dealers based in their offices offering competing quotations through Stock Exchange Automated Quotation (SEAQ), a screen-based quote dissemination system. In addition to SEAQ, the UK also has a quotation system (and rule book) for international equities known as SEAQ International (SEAQI). It is SEAQI, offering liquidity through competing dealers, that has provided intense competition in institutional-sized deals for many of the order-driven domestic markets of Continental Europe. Exact percentages of business lost by Continental European exchanges to the London SEAQI system are disputed. However, a recent study for the London Stock Exchange by Davis (1993) concluded that during 1993 the turnover of DAX stocks has on average been 13 percent of turnover on the German domestic market. However, for some bond markets the percentage of business lost to London has been much higher, with some estimates as high as 60 percent for institutional-sized deals. Interestingly, the Exchange also acknowledges that market-making firms are less likely to close out positions in London than on the Frankfurt floor or on the Inter-Bank Information System (IBIS), the German electronic order-matching system. Interlinking, says the exchange, ensures an efficient flow of information between the markets and in reality relations between the two markets are characterized by interdependence, not head-on competition. As we shall see, much of the reform in Continental Europe was initiated after Big Bang in the UK, as European stock exchanges, in their turn, began to see London as a threat to their domestic market.

France

The principal reform of the French stock market came into effect in 1988. Before then, the title of stockbroker (*agent de change*) was granted to individuals in the form of a lifetime appointment by the Minister of the Economy and Finance. To the extent that agents de change formed companies, they were generally thinly capitalized and were not permitted to engage in underwriting. Since the reform, stockbrokers are required to practice through companies known as *sociétés de bourse*. These companies are required to have more capital than previously, and most of them are now backed by major French or foreign financial institutions. These companies have a monopoly over almost all trading in, and direct or indirect transfers of, securities quoted in France.

The French market has always been centralized, and operated, traditionally, as a call market; i.e., a matching market where orders were batched for execution rather than being traded continuously. This system has now been replaced by a computer-assisted trading system (CATS) which provides a continuous electronic order-matching market. Without market-makers willing and able to bridge the time gap between buy and sell orders, such a market is unlikely to provide the liquidity required by institutional investors willing to transact without waiting and in large size. As institutional business grew within France, it became clear that the existing mechanism could not cope with such large orders. In 1989 the authorities introduced the *contrepartie* system, which seeks to maintain the central market with a single price while still allowing sociétés de bourse to carry out transactions for their own account at a price other than the bourse price. When undertaking such transactions, there are strict requirements including the obligation to take out any orders on the central market at the contrepartie price. This, therefore, gives any other investors in the market at that time the possibility of transacting at a better price. Although this system moves in the direction of a market-making system, it is still a poor compromise in terms of providing liquidity in size compared with the competing dealer system in London. Many French securities houses object to a system which prevents them operating like broker-dealers in London and New York. In the early 1990s, a report was produced within the securities industry (the Bacot Report), which recommended the introduction of market-making. Although the authorities have yet not acted on this report, we note later that changes in EC regulation may drive the authorities to permit market-making.

Regulation in France is institutionally based and thus, with exceptions such as the need to obtain a seat on the Matif S.A. (the French futures and options exchange), French financial institutions are generally authorized by, and report to, only one set of regulatory authorities. There is quite a complex network of regulatory agencies, all of which are statutory bodies under the general direction of the Ministry of the Economy and Finance. The Commission des Opérations de Bourse (COB) is responsible for investor protection. It establishes rules on matters such as public offers, prospectus requirements, use of privileged information, and so on. It authorizes portfolio managers, approves investment funds, and conducts hearings to enforce its own regulations. It can impose fines comparable to those in the criminal courts. Regulating the stock exchange and the sociétés de bourse is the Conseil des Bourses de Valeurs (CBV), which drafts the stock exchange rules, admits securities for listing, authorizes sociétés de bourse, establishes capital adequacy and conduct of business rules, and so on. Beneath this is the Société des Bourses Françaises (SBF), responsible for running the stock exchange and for prudential supervision of sociétés de bourse. Other regulators are responsible for banks, *maisons de titres*, and financial and commodity futures and option markets.

Germany

Germany has a long tradition of *Universalbanken*, without the separation of banking and securities activities mandated by law in the US and practiced by custom in the UK. As a consequence, investment firms with a distinct identity do not exist in substantial numbers in Germany. Foreign subsidiaries of investment or merchant banks would normally be licenced as banks even if they did not undertake credit activities, and thus would fall under the umbrella category of universal bank. The Banking Act defines the (nine) activities that constitute banking. Any business undertaking activities defined in the Act must be licenced by the Banking Supervisory Authority. Persons and institutions wishing to trade on an exchange must also be admitted by the board of governors of the exchange. Trading is governed by the Exchange Act (*Börsengesetz*).

While universal banking has long been the normal mode of operation in Germany, a more recent development has been the growth of financial conglomerates which, in addition to these business activities, may also include a mortgage bank, a real-estate broker and an insurance company. The range of activities of such *Allfinanzkonzerne* conglomerates is not restricted by the federal government or the Federal Banking Supervisory Authority, but their activities are regulated by both the Banking Supervisory Authority and, where appropriate, the Insurance Supervisory Authority.

Germany, unlike France, is a federation of states, each with considerable administrative autonomy. Each state has its own stock exchange, though for many years the Frankfurt exchange has been dominant. In order to compete more effectively, not only against London but against other European exchanges, Germany has created a German "Stock Exchange Company Limited" to organize the reform of the market and to link all the exchanges into a single mechanism. Although the old floor market still exists, the active market is rapidly moving across to the electronic matching market, IBIS. Under the Exchange Act, the supervision of all the exchanges is the responsibility of the government of the federal state in which the exchange is located and of the exchange's self-regulatory bodies. Governmental supervision is generally exercized by an exchange supervisory authority which forms part of the Ministry of Economics of the respective federal state. The government itself does not supervise and regulate the markets: having approved the rules of the self-regulatory bodies, it leaves them to undertake supervision.

Until 1994 there was no law governing insider dealing. Such a law was introduced in order to comply with an EC directive on insider dealing. Prior to this there were rules established in 1970 and amended in 1988 which were "binding by voluntary acceptance" and were widely accepted by banks and others trading on exchanges, and by company directors, managers, and employees. However, insider trading scandals in the early 1990s discredited this approach. The government included its insider-trading law in the new Securities Trading Act, discussed in a later section.

Spain

The Securities Market Act of 1988 was designed to restructure fundamentally the securities markets in Spain. The new structure reflects the increasing internationalization of the markets, and the consequent need to improve the dissemination of information and the speed at which transactions can be processed. In addition, the new structure provides a greater degree of supervision and investor protection, with a view to promoting domestic and international confidence in the market and its institutions.

The new structure has integrated the four existing stock exchanges in Spain. These are linked by the Stock Exchange Interconnection System, a computer system to which any subsequently authorized exchanges can be added. Securities are traded using a continuous electronic matching system (CATS), similar to the French market.

The exchanges are regulated by the Comision Nacional del Mercado de Valores (CNMV), a central supervisory authority modelled on the American Securities and Exchange Commission. CNMV is an independent public agency which supervises the activities of securities market participants and advises the government and the Ministry of Economy and Finance on matters within its area of competence. It is responsible for supervision and control of the primary and secondary markets, including the admission of securities to listing, supervising compliance with trading rules to ensure that prices are transparent, and ensuring compliance with conduct of business rules. The Ministry of Economy and Finance has an important regulatory role, since it authorizes securities companies, specifies accounting standards, administers sanctions and nominates some of the members of the board of the CNMV.

The players in the market are securities companies, which act as both principal and agent, and securities agencies which act only as agents. Most of the larger companies and agencies are owned by commercial banking groups with which they are consolidated for capital and accounting purposes. In addition, Spanish banks also have large shareholdings in major industrial companies through nonconsolidated holding companies. Such interlinking of banking and industry is believed to have been a factor in the 1994 collapse of a major Spanish bank, Banesto.

Italy

The Italian financial markets have traditionally been largely unregulated. However, as in other EC countries, the late 1980s saw a modernization of the regulatory framework. Italy has functional, rather than institutional, regulation:

thus a number of different authorities regulate and supervise the activities of institutions in the securities markets. As a result, the same institution may be subject to regulation and supervision by different authorities for its different activities. The ultimate regulatory powers lie with the Ministry of the Treasury and with the legislative power of parliament. In turn, the ministry delegates its powers in respect of the securities market to CONSOB (the Italian Securities Commission), and for banking activity to the Bank of Italy.

Recent attempts to modernize the Italian financial markets have involved a radical change in the regulation of financial intermediaries. Previously there were various categories of intermediaries, each entitled to perform only specific activities. These are now being replaced by the *Società de Intermediazione Mobiliare* (SIM), an investment firm which can obtain authorization in respect of all securities activities. To qualify for authorization, a SIM must satisfy requirements in respect of its legal form, capital adequacy, and management. A SIM must also be incorporated as an Italian company limited by shares with a registered office in Italy. This requirement is potentially in conflict with the EC regulatory framework, and has led to complaints to the Commission by non-Italian securities houses. The Commission is currently taking Italy to the European Court of Justice over this matter. But this conflict will probably be resolved well before the required deadline. SIMs are mostly owned by banks, a majority of which, in turn, are owned by the state. However, Italian banks have not in the past specialized in securities market services, and only a small proportion of their income is currently derived from such activities.

In 1991 Italy passed an insider-dealing law and the CONSOB has issued regulations setting the terms and conditions for disclosure to the public of information connected with listed companies which may be of relevance to investors.

Integration of EC Markets Prior to the Single European Act

We noted above that a number of countries in Europe had undertaken reforms in both the equity market structure and the regulatory framework in the period from 1986. Much of this reform was initiated in response to competitive pressures from other markets. Across Europe these reforms have produced equity market frameworks currently more compatible than pre-1986. European debt and derivative markets have also become much more integrated.

This has occurred as part of a much wider global integration of financial markets not directly related to the Single European Act. In particular, the international securities market (commonly known as the Eurobond market) has for a long time provided an integrated market open to major European corporate and sovereign borrowers. Over time, the distinction between Euro issues and domestic issues in a particular currency has been disappearing. A principal reason for this is that many of the distinctions resulted from domestic regulations or tax features that governments have abolished. They have done this in order to increase the demand for government securities from non-resident investors as a means of reducing their own cost of funding. These reforms have also reduced the differences in regulation and practice between different government bond markets.

Technology and innovation have driven much of the integration in the 1980s, principally through facilitating arbitrage in a way that was not possible in the 1970s. Not only has integration been occurring within the EC, but also between the EC and the rest of the world. As a result of technological developments, the concept of a country's domestic market is one that has been losing its meaning.[6] One reason for this has been the ability of securities houses and banks to offer financial services cross-border or to set up subsidiaries in other countries to create financial assets and sell financial products. Not only has there been relative freedom to do this within the EC (on the basis of rights of establishment and trade conferred under the Treaty of Rome), but between EC member states and third countries. A second reason has been the ability of swap markets to link domestic markets and synthesize domestic products even when these are protected by regulation and controls. A third has been the increase in tradable financial assets relative to nontraded bank assets in investor portfolios as a result of securitization. Such securitization leads to greater use of the securities market price discovery mechanism and more uniform pricing of risky assets across countries. A fourth is the ability of financial assets to be traded on a mechanism outside the country of the issuer of the asset, in addition to on a domestic stock exchange. This has resulted from the increasing sophistication and falling cost of electronic, as distinct from floor-based, securities exchange mechanisms.[7] A final reason has been the increase in the extent to which investors have diversified their portfolios across countries, and in so doing arbitraged away some of the price discrepancies between previously segmented markets. These factors were responsible for much of the integration sought by the 1985 White Paper, just as much as the regulatory developments we discuss in a later section.

THE EC APPROACH TO CREATING A SINGLE MARKET IN FINANCIAL SERVICES

> Unifying this market (of 320 million) presupposes that member States will agree on the abolition of barriers of all kinds, harmonization of rules, approximation of legislation and tax structures, strengthening of monetary co-operation and the necessary flanking measures to encourage European firms to work together.

These were the terms in which the Commission defined its task in respect of markets in goods, services, labor and capital in the program of the Commission for 1985 presented to the European Council in Brussels that year. In addition, the Commission asked the Council "to pledge itself to completion of a fully unified internal market by 1992 and to approve the necessary program together with a realistic and binding timetable."

The Commission developed its 1992 Program to remedy shortcomings in the fulfilment of a single market under the provisions of the Treaty of Rome. In respect of financial markets, its goal was to create the legislative framework that would allow greater integration of EC markets with the minimum sacrifice of the public policy interests of Member States in the areas of prudential rules, market stability, and consumer protection. One possibility was simply to continue to enforce the principle of national treatment, defined by the OECD as "treatment under host country laws, regulations and administrative practices . . . no less favorable than that accorded in like situations to domestic enterprises."[8] This principle is incorporated in Articles 52 and 59 of the Treaty of Rome as the right of establishment and the right to provide services in other Member States without being subject to any restrictions based on nationality. But recourse to the European Court of Justice has been required to give practical effect to some of these rights. Even if all the rights enshrined in the Treaty of Rome could be established, and this resulted in equality of treatment within the country, there would still be twelve national markets in the Community.

An alternative approach to national treatment would be "complete harmonization." This is the approach taken by the Commission in its first twenty-five years of existence. It involves all Member States agreeing a set of financial market regulations that would substitute for their existing national regulations. In theory, such an approach would create a legislative framework within which a single market in securities could develop. However, by the time the White Paper was being written it became clear that this approach was unsatisfactory. The White Paper notes, somewhat regretfully, "... experience has shown that the alternative of relying on a strategy based totally on harmonization would be over-regulatory, would take a long time to implement, would be inflexible and could stifle innovation."

The Commission's solution to the dilemma it faced, and the approach taken in the White Paper, has been to accept that each country has, and will continue to have, its own securities market regulation. This was an acceptance that there would continue to be "competition among rules" in the EC regulatory framework. However, in order to prevent these differences in rules creating barriers between Member States, the Commission has developed a principle known as mutual recognition, under which all Member States agree to recognize the validity of each other's laws, regulations, and standards and thereby facilitate free trade in goods and services without the need for prior harmonization. Thus Member States would not be able to invoke differences in national rules in order to restrict rights of establishment or rights to provide services.

Accepting "competition among rules" might be thought to be a result of the Commission's belief in the benefits of competition between regulatory frameworks. Much more credible, however, is Steil's belief.

> Reading the Commission's version of history in the White Paper, it is clear that the minimum harmonization principle is not seen simply as a necessary response to negative externalities deriving from free competition among rules, but rather that competition among rules is seen as a necessary but regrettable consequence of the Commission's legislative inability to achieve full harmonization (Steil 1993, p.18).

While the principle of mutual recognition clearly speeds the process of creating a unified market, each Member State has a different legal system, regulatory framework, and supervisory practices. It was necessary, therefore, to try to define what were the minimum essential elements of a regulatory framework that all Member States must comply with. Unfortunately, the Commission has not been explicit about how the determination of "essential" rules should be made. In practice, however, the determination of essentials among a group of nations is likely to proceed as much by horse-trading as by a rational consideration of de minimus requirements.

Once mutual recognition has been agreed as the governing principle for EC regulation, there follows a need for a rule to determine which country's regulatory framework applies in particular cases. The most logical rule is "home country control."[9] Under this approach, if national laws that have not been harmonized are accorded mutual recognition, home-country rules are accepted as those to be employed in the control of the activities of host-state branches and in cross-border provision of services. In consequence, the supervisors of host-state branches will be the home-state supervisors. Although this principle may be logical, in practice the Commission has weakened it by providing a let-out clause under which the host country also has a right to regulate to the extent necessary to "protect the public interest." At present, under this provision it has been agreed that host-state rules of conduct will apply to all firms. In practice, it remains to be seen to what extent host countries use their discretion in regard to host-country regulation not in the public interest, but as a competitive weapon against securities firms of other Member States.

The first major piece of EC legislation to apply the principle of mutual recognition was the Second Banking Coordination Directive (2BCD), which was adopted in December 1989 and implemented on January 1, 1993. This Directive had provisions to create what is commonly known as a "single passport," under which credit institutions incorporated in an EC Member State would be allowed to offer, in any Member State, a range of services listed in an Annex as activities subject to mutual recognition. While 2BCD is a Directive applying to credit institutions, the "passported" services include securities trading, underwriting securities issues, and portfolio management advice. Thus, since the implementation of 2BCD in January, 1993, universal banks have had the benefits of the single passport in respect of their securities market activities. As 2BCD does not apply to investment firms, they do not yet have such benefits and will need to wait until the Investment Services Directive (discussed below) is implemented by all Member States, at the latest, by January 1, 1996.

The White Paper, as well as dealing with measures required to achieve mutual recognition of national regulations and standards, considered the measures that were required to ensure greater liberalization of capital movements in the Community. The White Paper took the view that "decompartmentalization of financial markets would boost the economic development of the Community by promoting the optimum allocation of European savings," and that achieving this would require "greater liberalization of capital movements." An additional claimed benefit of capital liberalization was that "greater financial freedom leads to greater discipline in the conduct of economic policies."

In 1986 the Commission published its program for the liberalization of capital movements in the Community.[10] It was clear from this document that the Commission had taken the view that liberalization of capital movements was one of the top priorities for the EC. The legislative process required to achieve complete elimination of capital controls throughout the EC was finally completed with the adoption of two Directives — the first in 1986 and the second in 1988; both were implemented on July 1, 1990. However, four Member States — Spain, Ireland, Greece, and Portugal — are authorized to retain some type of control until somewhat later.[11]

The fact that the Commission was able to reach agreement in the Council of Ministers on the abolition of controls on capital movements, even in countries that had traditionally been strongly in favor of maintaining them, was in part due to the global integration of markets, which was taking place alongside EC developments. This had led to the realization that, in the long-run, exchange controls were likely to become ineffective.

THE MAJOR SECURITIES MARKET DIRECTIVES

The Investment Services Directive

The Investment Services Directive (ISD) is the equivalent piece of legislation to the Second Banking Coordination Directive but in respect of "investment firms" rather than "credit institutions." The need for such a Directive, in addition to 2BCD, arises because, as we have already noted, financial services firms in some Member States offer investment services through specialized securities subsidiaries rather than through credit institutions. 2BCD covers credit institutions, but ISD creates a single passport in respect of investment services provided by specialized securities firms.

As with 2BCD, the single passport is intended to achieve the removal of barriers to the establishment of branches and the provision of cross-border services throughout the EC.[12] It is predicated on the principles of harmonization of essential standards, mutual recognition, and home-country control. As firms from Member States are already free to set up subsidiaries in other member states under the Treaty of Rome, there is no need for this to be specifically legislated for in the ISD. But branches and subsidiaries are treated differently. For branches, home-country rules apply. For subsidiaries, it is the national rules of the Member State in which the subsidiary is incorporated.

The ISD is not intended, of itself, to create a "level playing field" between financial services firms incorporated in different Member States. Since institutional and regulatory frameworks and market structures will continue to differ across Member States, competitiveness, based on these factors, may also differ. Over time the effect of market forces is expected to minimize the differences, leaving factors such as financial skills and attitudes to risk-taking as the main determinants of the country's competitive advantage.

While 2BCD was implemented in time for the December 31, 1992 deadline in the White Paper, the ISD need not be implemented by the Member States until December 31, 1995. This delay arose because of the time taken to achieve the political compromises involved in obtaining final agreement on the wording of the Directive from all Member States. While the original draft of the ISD was relatively straightforward and was not highly detailed, the final version was, in some respects, highly detailed and displayed signs of political manoeuvring. Much of the delay arose from arguments between Member State government representatives seeking to ensure that the ISD was worded in a way which might give firms from their country some competitive advantage.

There were three areas which gave rise to the greatest contention and which may have the greatest influence on the ultimate shape of the EC single market in securities. The first is on the rights of access to regulated markets — principally stock exchanges. The second is on trade reporting and transparency in regulated markets. The third is on concentration of trading in a market.

Access to Regulated Markets

Under the ISD, a market may choose to be a *regulated market* which is one governed by rules approved by a competent authority in its home state and which complies with the rules in the ISD on reporting and transparency. We noted above that in some states, such as Germany, banks operate directly in stock markets, whereas in others they operate through specialized securities firms such as the French sociétés de bourse. German banks had insisted on being able to trade on stock exchanges in other Member States in the same way as they did in Germany.

In order to accommodate the universal banking model, a clause permitting direct access by banks to all EC-regulated markets was included in the ISD. To get agreement on this clause, however, it was necessary to provide derogations for a number of states. France, Italy, and Belgium do not need to allow host-country banks to trade directly on their exchanges until the end of 1996. Portugal, Spain, and Greece have until the end of the century. However, these restrictions could still be extended to a later date under Article 15 of the ISD. This permits an extension to be granted by a qualified majority vote in the Council of Ministers.[13]

Trade Reporting and Transparency

Securities market regulators are concerned to ensure that markets under their supervision are fair. One aspect of fairness is ensuring that investors are provided with the means to assess the terms of a transaction they are considering or to verify afterwards the terms at which they traded, in relation to other transactions. Facilitating this judgement requires that investors (and other market participants) be provided with pre-trade information on prices at which deals may be negotiated (quotes and limit orders) and post-trade information on price (and ideally size) of completed transactions. In the case of electronic order-matching markets operating without dealers, such as the CAC market in Paris, such information is immediately available for publication as soon as orders on the screen match and give rise to completed transactions. There is no need for the counterparties whose orders have matched to report this match to a supervisory authority, as the match has been effected by the central computer and is thus immediately available to the supervisor.

In the case of dealer markets, such as the SEAQ market in London, information on competing quotations is always available, but information on actual transaction prices is not immediately available to the supervisory authorities. This is because transactions are completed by telephone and are only then entered onto a dealing sheet (or electronic record) in a securities house. Before transactions on such a market can be published, they need to be reported to a supervisory authority. If deal capture is electronic, reporting could be immediate and publication could be achieved virtually simultaneously with completion of the transaction. However, immediate publication is generally opposed by dealers and also by some market supervisory bodies. Article 21 of the ISD has reporting and trade publication requirements (the transparency provisions) and these apply to both types of market. However, as transparency is not an issue among those who participate in order-driven markets, we discuss it in relation to competing dealer markets.

Dealers' objections to transparency, at least for large trades, arise for two principal reasons that need to be separated. First, if dealers have exclusive information on their own previous transactions in a security (no transparency), they have an information advantage over future counterparties, including other dealers. Such information asymmetry is likely to generate substantial economic rent for dealers, particularly those with a large market share and hence more private information. On the other hand, a fully transparent market with immediate trade publication would be likely to increase the efficiency of dealer markets by eliminating this source of economic rent. Such an improvement in efficiency is clearly beneficial to investors and other traders using a dealer market, but is one reason why larger dealers are clearly opposed to transparency.

The second reason why dealers oppose transparency, at least for large trades, arises from their belief that if the trades are published immediately, they are exposed to spoiling tactics from competing dealers when they take on a large position without having an immediate counterparty. They claim that when the trade is published, competitors, knowing a large block is overhanging the market, move their prices against the dealer with the position. Dealers in the London SEAQ market claim that too much transparency would reduce their willingness to take the risk of providing immediacy, therefore market liquidity would suffer. Research in this area is not conclusive but some researchers believe the market as a whole benefits from greater transparency and the widest possible dissemination of trade data. Garbade (1982) explains the importance of trade publication as follows:

> When dealers conceal their transactions, each dealer perceives the market as being thinner than is actually the case, i.e. each receives only a fraction of the total available information on public order flow. In response to this perception of thinness, each dealer individually may widen his bid-ask spread, reduce the breadth of the market, and shift his quotes more aggressively to achieve his inventory objectives. . . . Although privacy in a transaction is clearly to the advantage of the participating dealer, it is less clear that his gain outweighs the loss to his competitors and to investors generally.

Dealers on the London Stock Exchange counter arguments in favor of transparency by claiming that the provision of competing executable dealer quotations on the SEAQ screen is equivalent to the provision of pre-trade transparency. They claim this achieves, even better than post-trade publication, the information disclosure that allows investors to assess the terms of a transaction they are considering. Assuming post-trade publication is a requirement, dealers would argue that investors can also verify the terms on which they traded relative to other investors.

Evidence from Clemons and Weber undermines the claim that pre-trade quotes provide a reliable indication of the terms on which trades are undertaken, in particular the market "touch" (best bid and best offer). The Clemons and Weber Report (1989) to the the London Stock Exchange is based on research undertaken in early 1989. This showed that:

> SEAQ quotes are less meaningful than many believe. In our sample, less than half of the value of trading actually occurred at the touch price. Nearly as much trading volume is inside the touch quotes.

Clemons and Weber also found that less than one-half of trading in a sample set of stocks was executed by a market-maker quoting the best screen price at the time. Instead preferencing — directing business towards favored market-makers who are then asked to match or better the best price on the screen — is a widespread practice. This has severe implications for the price discovery process, as they note.

> The level of trading that is preferenced, and not directed to a touch market maker has implications for fragmentation, fairness and especially for price discovery. A market maker placing himself on the touch is *obligated* to deal at that price but [this] of course does not *guarantee* that he will receive the ensuing trades. A market maker on the touch has accepted a risk because he is obligated to trade at his posted price; he is vulnerable to traders with superior information. However, our numbers suggest that accepting the risk of making the touch price has far less impact on the chance of receiving trades than was intended when SEAQ was designed (Clemons and Weber 1989).

At the EC level, the French have been the most ardent champions of transparency while the British have opposed mandating more than a minimum level. The French argue on the grounds of market integrity and fairness while the British argue on the grounds of ensuring the provision of liquidity for large institutional investors. Many would agree with Steil, however, when he says:

> While one need not question the French commitment to market integrity, it is clear that the primary motivation for their position is simply fear of losing more and more large block trading to London's SEAQ International, where publication requirements are far less stringent than on the Paris Bourse (Steil 1993).

In fact, much of the argument arises because of the polarization within the EC between the pure dealer market in London on the one hand and the pure order-matching markets in the equity markets of almost all other Member States. With such limited choice of competing mechanisms, it may be necessary to mandate a minimum level of transparency. On the other hand, if Europe had a more diverse set of market mechanisms, such regulation would not be so necessary.

The philosophical difference between the two sides of the transparency debate arises from a difference between the traditional perception that views securities markets in a public goods framework (which could be said to represent the French view), and the property rights perspective of a securities exchange (a stylized representation of the UK view).[14] The public goods perspective views a country's exchange as a natural monopoly with a mandate to raise capital for that country's government and industry. Being a monopoly, it is then necessary to have regulation to enhance efficiency and ensure "fairness." In contrast, the property rights perspective views the monopoly paradigm as inappropriate in a world where technology allows competing market mechanisms to be used to trade a security. In cross-border transactions there would be no presumption in favor of using what has traditionally been considered to be the domestic exchange. In the property rights perspective, information such as trade data is something which has a value, and the sale of the rights in that information is something which should be decided on by the owners of that information. Monopoly exchanges would not be acceptable. Thus under the property rights perspective, it is essential to have competing mechanisms.

It is likely that new market mechanisms will develop in London and in Continental Europe as they have in the US, and thus offer investors a better choice between different types of transaction mechanism.[15] At present in London, for example, a dealer trade is virtually the only type available. However, the London Stock Exchange has been considering, for some years, the possibility of introducing a limit-order system, and it would seem possible that its plans for some type of order-driven facility will materialize. Tradepoint, a new trading mechanism using order matching is about to begin operating in London. This system is discussed in more detail below.

The present system in the UK, which involves the provision of dealer services for all transactions, even when the counterparty does not require immediacy, is wasteful of risk capital. Many trades could be brokered as in New York, thereby minimizing the capital employed in their execution. Greater transparency, if mandated in the future by the EC, would encourage a move to brokered trades by reducing the economic rent generated by lack of transparency. Higher capital requirements for trading books under the Capital Adequacy Directive (discussed below) would also reduce the attraction of dealer-intermediated trades. The London Stock Exchange study, *London trading in German Equities*, seems to support the case for alternative mechanisms when it notes that:

> Views varied about the value of immediacy in executing orders. Some firms always prefer immediate execution. Others prefer to see an order built up slowly over the day or even longer periods, particularly where their performance is being measured against the average price on the day or where they are trying to build a large position (Davis 1993).

The issues involved in market design and rule-making raise the question of the extent to which the Commission should be trying to determine the appropriate trade-off, and hence the exact degree of transparency, that should be required of any regulated market in the Community. The ISD in its present form requires regulated markets to publish weighted average prices, high and low prices, and aggregate trading volumes at the start of trading and on a rolling basis throughout the trading session. However, the Commission has sidestepped a decision on the real issues involved by its let-out clauses which allow the competent authority to suspend or override the agreed transparency rules in the case of "very large" trades, "illiquid" securities, or "exceptional" market conditions. The criteria for establishing what is a very large trade or an illiquid security are left to the competent authority to determine. However, the Commission intends to review the Article dealing with transparency by the end of 1995. In the period up to then, there will be considerable debate on the relative merits of the two extreme positions.

This unwillingness by the Commission and the Member States to let the issue of transparency rest may be a factor in the recent publication of a discussion paper by the SIB, the UK regulatory authority, on issues related to market design and rules (Securities and Investment Board 1994). This invites interested parties to comment on what they believe is the appropriate delay before publication of trades as well as on whether investors should be allowed to see the (finer) prices that inter-dealer-brokers (IDBs) in equities display on their screens.

Concentration

The concentration principle is based on the argument that a market in a security can be fair only if all transactions in it are undertaken on a single marketplace where every order can interact with every other order. Proponents of this view argue that a concentrated market ensures price and time priority. Thus all investors, whether large or small, are ensured a fair deal in that they can transact at the same prices if transacting at the same time. Fairness is further enhanced by the fact that the efficiency of the price discovery process is claimed to be better if all transactions are conducted in a single marketplace. The concentration provision in the ISD (Article 14) is an attempt to prevent nationals of a country which implements the provision from transacting in domestic securities away from a regulated market.

The countries which wanted a concentration provision to be included in the ISD were the so-called Club Med Group — France, Belgium, Italy, and Spain. Originally, it was thought by the Club Med Group that SEAQ International would not qualify as a regulated market, on the grounds that it would not be able to comply with the transparency provisions of the ISD. As a result, nationals in Club Med countries would have to repatriate back to the domestic market any business they undertook in London. However, it would now appear that SEAQI will qualify as regulated, thus the concentration provision may not have the effect expected by some of its proponents. As might be expected, the definition of a regulated market was a matter of heated debate, as it could have such a direct impact on the viability of a particular market design.

By definition, a competing dealer market is not a true central, or concentrated, market. Dealers can be distributed over a large geographical area and over many countries. Each can operate its own minimarket on which transaction prices need not correspond with those at which transactions are being undertaken by other dealers. On the other hand, an order-matching market, functioning on the basis of computer algorithms, such as the Paris CAC market, clearly is a true central market where all trading is concentrated and where price and time priority are achieved. This difference in market structure between the Club Med countries and the UK arises in part because of the differences in the user base of the markets. In the UK, the proportion of the total stock of securities held by investment institutions rather than by individuals is, as we noted earlier, much higher than in other Member States, leading to a much larger average size of transaction. Clemons and Weber (1989) quote a figure of 80 percent of trading volume coming from managed funds and professionals. Thus in the UK a high proportion of transactions are of a size where a dealer market may provide the requisite liquidity more easily. But in the Club Med countries institutionalization of investment is not yet so widespread, and the electronic matching mechanism may thus be more appropriate for a higher proportion of trades.

The proponents of the concentration provision argue that dispersed trading damages the price discovery mechanism, resulting in different prices in different markets for comparable transactions. However, achieving efficient price discovery does not require a monopoly exchange. It requires simply an integration of the mechanisms that compete for trading in a security (Scott-Quinn 1992). In the case of the SEAQ domestic market system in London, this integration arises through the quote display screen in dealers' and investors' offices, which lists the competing quotes of dealers in a share, and through interdealer transactions, either directly by telephone or anonymously through inter-dealer-brokers. In the case of markets in the same security in different countries and on different mechanisms, integration could be through screens (possibly provided by independent information vendors) indicating both competing quotes (from dealers) and limit orders (from traders on matching markets). Even without special screens, it is clear, as we have already noted from the London Stock Exchange study on trading in German equities, that arbitrage between the markets can be quite effective in integrating competing mechanisms. If the necessary degree of integration does not develop by itself because of technical or legal obstacles this would, however, be an appropriate area in which the Commission might act as a facilitator. Otherwise market forces might be expected to provide such services as are useful to market participants.

In addition to the London Stock Exchange SEAQI system (which is part of one of the traditional European domestic stock exchanges), there are several relatively recently established entities known in the UK as market service providers (MSPs). Although not exchanges, they offer services related to exchanges. In contrast to traditional (nonprofit) stock exchanges, which operate on a membership basis and are managed by a council of members, MSPs are organized as limited liability companies.

Instinet, a US-based electronic continuous order-driven auction market owned by Reuters, is an example of such an MSP. Another is the POSIT crossing network operated by International Technology Group. Both operate as "broker" members of the London Stock Exchange. Deals on these systems are transacted under the same rules as the London Stock Exchange, just like deals done with or through other members. As these MSPs are already members of what will be a regulated market under the ISD, there is no need for them to request the competent authority to classify them as regulated markets. Thus investors in a country which chooses to invoke the concentration provision can use such MSPs.

In addition to the services offered by Instinet and POSIT, Tradepoint intends to offer continuous electronic matching and call market services in UK and Continental European stocks (Eurolist stocks). Unlike traditional brokers who typically deal on a bilateral basis, Tradepoint intends to provide a multilateral system in which orders will be displayed in aggregate at each price and matched according to a price, time, and size algorithm. It is currently regulated by the SIB under the so-called service company regime. However, as it is not a member of the London Stock Exchange it would not, unlike Instinet and POSIT, be operating as a member firm of what will become a regulated market. It is believed that the company is currently in discussion with the UK Treasury to try to gain regulated market status as a Recognized Investment Exchange (RIE), since only by this means would it be able to compete freely against traditional exchanges for investor business in countries which choose to invoke the concentration provision.

The effect of the concentration provision is likely to be further weakened by the opt-out clause for investors, inserted as part of the compromise between the two opposing viewpoints. Under the opt-out provision, Member States, when they draft their enabling legislation, must allow a distinction between the rules applied to professional investors and those applied to individual investors. It would seem likely that some, at least, of the Club Med countries will not give professional investors much scope to opt out. On the other hand the UK will not even invoke the concentration provision. Opting out of the concentration regime would allow an investor to deal on an unregulated market. It is quite possible that Club Med countries will offer institutional investors the right to opt out, but only on a deal-by-deal basis rather than through a global opt-out provision. But if even the new proprietary markets (as well as SEAQI) are classified as regulated markets, investors may not need to choose to opt out in order to transact on their market of choice. It should be noted, however, that the International Securities Market Association has not applied for regulated market status for the international securities (Eurobond) market. Thus the transparency and concentration will not be applied to it. But in future this market may be required to comply with the transparency provisions.

The Capital Adequacy Directive

The Capital Adequacy Directive (CAD) was drafted by the EC Commission in parallel with the ISD. The preamble to the ISD notes that the two directives must be considered as a joint package and are so closely interrelated that their entry into force on different dates could lead to a distortion of competition. Thus the CAD was adopted by the economics and finance ministers in March 1993, shortly after the ISD, and must be implemented by the Member States by the same date — January 1, 1996.

The CAD aims to ensure that both investment firms and credit institutions (banks) hold sufficient capital to cover the market risks to which they are subject. At the same time, the CAD aims to ensure there is no competitive distortion between the two types of institutions as a result of differential capital requirements when they compete in the same business area (the level playing field). The approach taken by the CAD, therefore, is to regulate functions rather than institutions. For this reason, in the case of universal banks, it allows them, for the purpose of applying the capital adequacy regulations, to abstract from their balance sheet what is defined as the *trading book* (as distinct from the rest of the bank's assets and liabilities). Thus the CAD can be applied to the trading book whether this is within a company defined as an investment firm or within a credit institution (i.e., a universal bank). The Commission thus allows banks to have their securities activities regulated under the less onerous requirements of the CAD rather than under the Basle ratios (provided the domestic regulator permits this).[16] Under the CAD, a firm's trading book can be financed with a relatively high proportion of short-term subordinated debt which will, subject to various restrictions, count towards *own funds* when calculating the required capital to back the trading book. The logic behind this is that trading inventories should be marketable, hence if short-term liabilities cannot be rolled over in the market, it should be possible to liquidate the necessary proportion of the trading book without substantial loss. In order to achieve its objective, the CAD establishes four things.

- A framework to be used for the measurement and ongoing monitoring of market risks
- A "large exposures" framework
- Minimum capital requirements
- A definition of capital

The directive is primarily concerned with *position risk*, the risk of a decline in the value of an inventory of securities (including derivatives), as a result of changes in market conditions. In addition to such position risks, the directive also covers risks arising from changes in foreign exchange prices, from delayed or failed settlement and from credit risk of counterparties.

In setting capital requirements, finance theory would suggest that the amount of capital required by a regulator should reflect the risk, or volatility, of the trading book of the regulated firm. The volatility of the specific security in the portfolio is obviously one determinant of this, but finance theory would suggest two additional factors. These are the extent to which (1) short positions are offsetting long positions in similar securities and (2) the portfolio is diversified. Once position risk has been determined, it is then necessary to decide the level of capital required to cover that risk. This will be in the form of a percentage of the position risk.

There are a number of possible ways of determining position risk. The Commission has chosen to use the *building-block* approach. This bases the capital requirement partly on the net value of the trading book and partly on the gross value. It thus makes some allowance for the offsetting risks of long and short positions. In contrast, the SEC approach in the US is the so-called *comprehensive* approach. This requires capital to be set against both long and short positions and limits the extent to which offsetting positions reduce required capital. Such an approach is not as effective as alternative approaches in encouraging firms to reduce their risk by running trading books which are close to being balanced — long and short positions of the same size. The *portfolio* approach makes an extra allowance for the reduction in risk that arises from holding a diversified portfolio. While less relevant to bond portfolios, the unsystematic risk of an equity trading book can be reduced substantially by holding a diversified portfolio.

The building-block approach to measuring position risk, chosen by the Commission, is a better approach than the comprehensive method since it allows for benefits of some offsetting risks. However, it does not go as far as the portfolio approach in considering ways in which risk in a trading book can be minimized. The drawback of not taking account of such diversification is well explained by Dimson and Marsh in their study on capital requirements published as part of the City of London Research Project.

> What will be the impact of the regulators' recent preference for the building-block approach? In fairness, this methodology succeeds in incentivizing securities firms to control their net exposure to the equity market, and it can therefore be expected to have the positive effect of reducing the systematic risk which might otherwise arise. On the other hand, it fails to reward firms for running well-diversified books. The portfolio approach, in contrast, since it offers a low capital requirement for a well diversified book, can be expected to reduce, not only systematic risk, but also the risk of failure by an individual securities firm (Dimson and Marsh 1994).

Although the CAD need not be implemented by Member States until the end of 1995, there are already two other international capital adequacy regimes which apply to many of the companies affected by the CAD. The first regime stems from the Basle Accord on International Convergence of Capital Measurement and Capital Standards. Adopted by the G-10 countries in July 1988, it applies to banks in the G-10 countries and like the CAD it uses the building-block approach. The second regime stems from two EC Directives, enacted in 1989 — the Own Funds Directive and the Solvency Ratio Directive. Both sets of rules apply to banks and their requirements are stricter than the CAD. In addition, most countries have their own capital adequacy requirements which may require more or less capital than the minimum under the CAD. The UK, for example, has a regime known as the *simplified portfolio approach.* As the UK approach may require less capital for an equity trading book than the CAD, the imposition of CAD requirements could reduce the competitiveness of UK equity market-making compared with order matching. Such a conflict may arise when the UK has to implement the CAD. Dimson and Marsh observe that

> With the recent agreement (in mid-1993) that the European Community will proceed with the CAD, it is worth noting that the Directive will have to be implemented fairly quickly. For the securities subsidiaries of [UK] banks, the building-block approach is therefore likely to overtake the portfolio approach. Conceivably, these securities businesses may even find themselves subject to both sets of rules, with an obligation to observe the higher of the two requirements at any time (Dimson and Marsh 1994).

Such differences, and the ability of banks to circumvent the Basle requirements or the own funds and solvency ratio requirements in respect of their trading book through opting to apply the rules of the CAD, raise two questions. Is the level playing field appropriate from the prudential point of view? Will the CAD itself produce comparable capital requirements across the EC once implemented in each Member State?

On the question of the level playing field between banks and investment firms, it would appear that the desire on the part of those who drafted the CAD to ensure a level playing field overrode the logic behind the imposition

be more important

of capital requirements. Sir Leon Brittan noted, "Within the Community we are making good progress in the negotiations on the Capital Adequacy Directive not least in overcoming the difficult problem of providing a broadly level playing field for bank and nonbank players in the market" (IOSCO Conference Address, Washington, D.C., 1991).

Reaching agreement on the CAD was much harder than in the case of the Basle framework. This was because of the difficulty of achieving a compromise that would satisfy the competitive and market safety concerns of Member States, which encompass such a diverse range of financial market structures. The first drafts of the Directive were circulated in 1990 and drew considerable criticism from both securities firms and regulators (General Accounting Office 1992, pp. 38–40). In the UK, both firms and regulators believed that early drafts set minimum required capital too high and did not consider the effects of risk management techniques (the SFA in the UK is the only regulator which currently has rules for equity position risk based on Markowitz's portfolio theory). Initially, US securities firms in London threatened to move offshore if an acceptable solution was not found. German banks, on the other hand, were troubled by the possibility that UK firms might branch freely in German financial markets under capital rules that might require less capital than those applied to their own banks.

The level playing field concept would seem to have arisen from a dialectic between the Commission, regulators in the Member States, and the securities houses and banks themselves. The outcome has been that, to ensure competitive equality, the Directive applies to all firms. Thus, if permitted by the regulator in their Member State, banks are allowed to apply the CAD to their short-term trading book activities rather than having to apply the EC bank capital requirements. In addition, the Directive was modified to give regulators the discretion to make allowances for hedging and diversification of trading books, which reduces capital requirements and can bring them more into line with those required by the SFA in the UK.

Even if the level playing field is accepted, it is still necessary to decide what level of capital is appropriate for all regulated institutions. Regulators and banks in Germany have expressed reservations about the adequacy of the provisions (General Accounting Office 1992). In particular, they were unsatisfied with the provisions permitting a bank to apply the investment services capital requirements to their trading book rather than those of the bank capital requirements. They said that these provisions might weaken the capital base of German banks and that it would be difficult to separate a bank's securities trading book from its credit-related activities. The implication of their comments was that they were happy for the same regulatory treatment to be applied to both banks and securities houses, but that it was the bank regulations that should be applied. Once IOSCO and the Basle Committee have reviewed capital requirements for securities positions, it remains to be seen whether the EC regulations on capital for trading books will be brought into line with (possibly higher) requirements for banks.

The issue of the separate trading book could be an important one in respect of competitive equality between types of institution. Some investment firms are believed to have raised the issue of unfair competition from banks. They argue that all securities should be held on a trading book. Otherwise the same securities could appear in a universal bank balance sheet on both the trading book and the long-term investment book, and thus be subject to different rules. In practice, this issue is one which will require supervisors to police the split between the two books to ensure that competitive equality is maintained, or to eliminate the distinction. How this will be achieved in practice is difficult to know. What may be even more important, in practice, than the actual wording of implementing legislation is the extent to which national supervisors take advantage of their allowable discretion under the Directive.

The CAD requires regulators to ensure that the internal control mechanisms and administrative and accounting procedures of the "institutions" permit the verification of their compliance with such rules at all times. Price Waterhouse (1992, pp. 71–74) takes the view that an important determinant of capital requirements will, in practice, be the sophistication of the information technology (IT) that firms have installed to measure risk and permit such verification In practice, they believe the desire to mark-to-market daily and calculate their financial position at any time will move firms towards systems which report their financial position on a real-time basis. The CAD provides the possibility for firms to reduce their capital requirements if they can persuade their national supervisors of the validity, and accuracy, of their proprietary systems. Indeed, Price Waterhouse goes so far as to say, "It is understood that the European Commission's position is to emphasise the importance of traders' own systems, and to encourage firms to negotiate with national regulators with a view to having those systems accepted for supervisory purposes" (Price Waterhouse 1992). Clearly, this opens an avenue for firms seeking competitive advantage through the use of sophisticated IT systems. It also allows the competent authorities in a Member State some discretion if they choose to try to tilt the playing field to the benefit of the firms they regulate.

Other EC Securities Market Directives

The remaining securities-related Directives apply principally to securities markets, rather than to securities firms, and mostly relate specifically to stock exchanges. A majority predate the internal market White Paper and reflect the Commission's desire to provide a regulatory framework that would encourage the development of a unified stock exchange system throughout the Community. The Directives that have been agreed are designed to break down barriers between national stock exchanges both from the point of view of the investor and the issuer. The Directives establish standardization of essential requirements and, in some cases, mutual recognition of unharmonized rules, but do not integrate exchanges into a single market.

The Three Stock Exchange Directives of 1979, 1980, and 1982

Although adopted at different times, all three stock exchange Directives were implemented in mid-1983. They were not, however, based on the principle of mutual recognition, as this principle was yet to be developed.

The 1979 Directive (79/279/EEC) coordinated the conditions for the admission of securities to official stock exchange quotation in the Member States. This Directive set out conditions which have to be met by issuers. It also imposed a continuing obligation on issuers to publish, without delay, information on any important new development which might impact the share price.

The 1980 Directive (80/390/EEC) on listing prospectuses coordinated the information that was required to be disclosed at the time of admission of a security to an official stock exchange listing. The directive has schedules attached to it which lay down, in detail, the information which must be given.

The 1982 Directive (82/121/EEC) requires companies to publish half-yearly reports which include turnover and profit.

After these three stock exchange Directives were adopted, the next Directive (1985/611/EEC) was the first in the financial services field to introduce the principle of mutual recognition, thus predating the use of this principle in 2BCD. The Directive on Undertakings for Collective Investment in Transferable Securities (UCITS) was adopted in 1985 and implemented in 1989. The pressure to issue this Directive arose because of the restrictions that had been introduced in Germany, and other countries, in consequence of fraudulent activities in the 1960s of, among others, the infamous Investors Overseas Services (IOS). After its adoption, the principle of mutual recognition became established as the means by which the Commission achieved most of its single-market objectives by the end of 1992.

The 1987 Directive on Mutual Recognition of Stock Exchange Listing Prospectuses (87/345/EEC) used the 1985 (UCITS) precedent to amend the 1980 Directive on Stock Exchange Listing Prospectuses so as to allow for mutual recognition. However, the mutual recognition applies only to the prospectus document itself, not to the procedures for listing applications and acceptance. In this respect, the 1979 Directive still applies so that individual applications for listing are still needed. It is expected that an amending

Directive on listing will shortly be issued to eliminate the need for individual applications. Once this is implemented, the Eurolist project can go ahead (see below).

The 1989 Directive on Public Offer Prospectuses (89/298/EEC) also allows for mutual recognition, and provides that a new issue prospectus in the home Member State can be used for a simultaneous offer in other Member States.

The question of prospectuses is problematic for international securities market issues (Eurobond issues), where prospectuses are not issued before distribution. Requiring that the prospectus be approved beforehand by supervisors would greatly impede the swift working of the international securities market. For this reason there is a special dispensation for such issues. The Directive provides that it is only when there is a general campaign of publicity or advertising — a public issue — that a prospectus is required. Tombstone advertisements for international securities issues always note, "These securities having been sold, this announcement appears as a matter of record only." The notice is not a public solicitation.

The 1990 Directive 90/211/EEC amended 80/390/EEC in respect of the mutual recognition of public offer prospectuses used as stock exchange listing particulars. Public offer prospectuses and listing prospectuses for stock exchanges are in principle different documents. Allowing one document to serve both purposes and requiring mutual recognition of this document clearly is a useful step towards a unified market. This amendment, therefore, provided that a public offer prospectus which has been approved by the home Member State can also be used, not only for the purpose of a public offer in the host state, but also for admission to stock exchange listing on both the home and host states; a single disclosure document will suffice both for public offers and listings throughout the EC.

In addition to the above directives, there are two which relate to information disclosure by large shareholders and use of insider information. The 1988 Directive 88/627/EEC on information to be published when major holdings in listed companies are acquired or disposed of, supplements the 1979 Directive on listing conditions as regards notification of changes in major shareholdings in listed companies. Since in some EC countries shares are bearer (i.e., unregistered), the Directive puts the obligation on those persons buying or selling significant blocks of shares to inform the company. The first threshold for disclosure is 10 percent.

In 1989, a Directive on insider trading (89/592/EEC) was adopted which defined "primary" insiders and detailed what they were not permitted to do. At the same time, it recommended a system of cross-border cooperation between supervisors to enable insider trading, originating in one Member State but being carried out in another, to be pursued effectively.

The above Directives can do no more than provide a framework within which regulatory barriers to the creation of a unified stock exchange system in Europe are gradually eliminated. The task of creating a unified system remains to be undertaken by the stock exchanges themselves, should they view it as being in their commercial interest. Alternatively, proprietary mechanisms may provide such a system. During the 1980s there were attempts to unify rule books, quotation systems, and trading systems across Europe. There were also proposals for a single European stock exchange. Work on two European stock exchange projects to pool market information — Pipe and Euroquote (for an integrated European quotation system) — were abandoned as a result of the partners (all members of the Federation of European Stock Exchanges) failing to agree on how to progress. Unsurprisingly, the competing commercial interests of twelve Member State stock exchanges have precluded such developments. Instead, exchanges have been modernizing their facilities in order to remain competitive while cooperating in a way which will facilitate inter-exchange connections at a later date. Local idiosyncrasies and competition between exchanges persist.

One joint project is likely to come to fruition before the end of 1994 — Eurolist. Like Pipe and Euroquote, Eurolist, the European Stock List is an initiative of the Federation of European Stock Exchanges; it is not a Commission project though it has Commission support. Eurolist will involve the simultaneous listing of a number of major European stocks (eventually 250) on at least six EU exchanges. It was originally intended that trading could be undertaken on any of the exchanges and would take place according to the local rule book, regardless of the home country of the company which issued the shares. However, there are no plans at present to make this possible. Alongside the listing procedure will be a corporate information dissemination system which will ensure that the home exchange provides corporate news simultaneously with the other eleven exchanges. Information dissemination will be the first aspect of Eurolist to become operational. The listing and information dissemination objectives are relatively easy to achieve. Trading and settlement are much harder. Nevertheless, national clearing systems are developing links with each other so that eventually it should be possible to provide an investor with delivery in the market of choice regardless of the market of execution or the home country of the stock. At present, no such facilities will be offered. The Eurolist project may, however, act as a catalyst for the exchanges and lead quickly to one or two of them offering trading services across Europe in a wide range of Eurolist stocks.

THE SUBSIDIARITY PRINCIPLE AND SECURITIES MARKET INTEGRATION

Subsidiarity has been defined by Sir Leon Brittan as, "The principle that decisions should be taken at the lowest appropriate level: as close as possible, that is, to the people who are affected by them." In relation to the EC, the strict interpretation of subsidiarity would be that policy decisions should only be taken at the Community level if the same desired objectives cannot be achieved by action taken at national level. However, such a strict interpretation would be likely to slow down decision-making in the EC to an unacceptable degree, particularly in areas such as the single market program. An alternative interpretation would be that the EC would have powers of decision where the objectives of a particular policy can be attained better at the EC level than at the level of individual Member States. Sir Leon Brittan believes that, following the enactment of the Maastricht treaty, the limits of power of the Commission could be tested by the courts, and decisions of the EC challenged, if they were believed to infringe the principle of subsidiarity.

There are two areas relevant to the integration of securities markets which would require overall action by the EC rather than separate actions by each of the Member States.

- The creation of a single currency for the EC
- The creation of a securities commission for the EC

The US has both a single currency and a federal securities commission and thus provides a possible model for the EC. With only one currency, goods, services, and capital flow freely in a single market with all transactions denominated in this currency. In the EC, in contrast, many would argue that there cannot be a genuine single market or fair competition and a true level playing field while prices and rates of return on capital continue to be affected by exchange rate movements. While it is true that some exchange rate movements arise from changes in real underlying economic conditions, others arise from private sector speculation or active government policy such as beggar-thy-neighbor devaluations. Clearly, however, the creation of a single currency zone in the EC would involve a very substantial transfer of sovereignty. In the absence of a single currency, the single market in the EC will continue to be subject to changes in competitiveness among the member states, resulting from exchange rate changes rather than from changes in economic fundamentals. However, there would appear to be little prospect of a single currency coming into existence this century, thus the single market in the EC will continue to suffer from this imperfection.

The securities market regulatory structure in the US involves state securities commissioners and also a federal securities commission, the Securities and Exchange Commission (SEC), a statutory body responsible for regulating securities markets across all states. Some commentators have called for a similar structure for the EC.[17] At present the functions of market regulation and supervision are quite clearly in the hands of those competent authorities in each Member State that are so designated by the government of that state. The legislation that applies is drafted by the state and must be passed by its parliament. While EC Directives are binding as to (minimum) results to be achieved, the actual legislation is likely to be slightly different in each state.

In practice the powers of the SEC are less than is sometimes believed. The SEC's powers have to be viewed in the context of federal/state relations. In fact, the federal government can only legislate in matters affecting commerce between states. Whatever powers are not given to the federal government are reserved to the states. The SEC has no power to bring criminal as opposed to civil and administrative proceedings against anyone. Only the Department of Justice has that power. The US securities market regulatory system is also much more dependent on self-regulatory bodies than is often imagined. Thus US broker-dealers are not registered with the SEC but with exchange and self-regulatory organizations (SROs). All the SEC does is to adopt regulations which set the standards for the operation of exchanges and SROs.

The US structure does point up a distinction between the setting of an overall framework for securities markets (by the SEC) and the promulgation and enforcement of a detailed set of day-to-day rules (by SROs). In the case of the EC, the Directives in respect of financial markets have involved some quite detailed rule-making which makes the framework rather inflexible. It is also not yet clear how, if at all, the Commission will ensure that its rules are being implemented by Member States. Lee (1993) suggests a distinction should be drawn in the EC between "legislation" and "regulation". Legislation would establish broad political objectives whereas regulation would define the detail to achieve them. While the Commission would be responsible for legislation, another body would be responsible for regulation. This might be a body comparable to the SEC. Steil has suggested two levels of Community legislation (Steil 1993). Primary legislation would "enshrine broad political objectives which Member States could more readily agree on" while subordinate legislation, necessary to meet agreed objectives, could be subsequently negotiated. Subordinate legislation would be subject to less stringent amendment procedures than the present Directives, allowing the flexibility to make changes to enable it to be adapted to developments in the financial marketplace.

Steil suggests there is a need for a body, separate from the Commission, to supervise the implementation of legislation. This role, he believes, "would be better served by the establishment of a separate supervisory agency, comprised of industry experts, which would keep the Commission informed of progress and problems in the operation of Community legislation." At this embryonic stage, however, be believes it should be an advisory body only, without powers of enforcement or prosecution.

The Commission has in fact considered these issues in relation to securities markets, and most of the securities market directives since the 1979 Stock Market Directive have made reference to a contact committee. Article 20 of the Directive tells us that the function of the contact committee is to facilitate the harmonized implementation of Directives and the establishment of a "concerted" attitude between Member States, and to advise the Commission on any amendments to be made to the Directive. The committee is composed of persons appointed by the Member States and representatives of the Commission.

In the case of the banking (and also insurance) sector, there is a banking advisory committee which was set up under the First Banking Directive of 1977. This is a "higher level committee" which has not only advisory functions but also a limited executive role. In the jargon of the EC, this is known as a *comitology committee*. While no such committee has yet been set up, Article 29 of the ISD indicates there will be a further Directive "laying down provisions adapting this Directive (the ISD) to technical progress..." This implies at some point there will be a Directive setting up a securities market committee. This committee would have responsibility for updating the two Directives and would be a higher-level, less-technical, and more policy-oriented version of the existing contact committee (set up in 1979).

The present and proposed networks of EC committees do have the advisory authority and some of the rule-making authority vested in the SEC. The committees also provide a means for updating Directives to enable these to be adapted to reflect market changes. However, failure by a national regulator to operate in a manner consistent with the Directives is not a matter which comes before the committee, except as part of its general supervisory role; anyway, it has no teeth in this matter. Only the Commission itself — or an aggrieved individual, company, or Member State which felt harmed by the failure of a regulatory authority in another Member State to regulate properly — could take action. This approach may be in line with the principle of subsidiarity since it leaves proactive stances to be taken at the lowest level. However, when there is a dispute about, say, a transaction which can be regulated by two different national regulators, it provides no means of resolution. The committee will also be comprised of civil servants or bureaucrats appointed by the Member States, and civil servants who may not have investment industry experience comparable with some SEC commissioners.

It is not improbable that this Securities Market Committee, appointed from the Member States, will be too political and insufficiently attuned to market needs. The fact that it cannot take action against national regulators to ensure compliance with the Directives also greatly limits its value. In the US, commissioners have fixed terms of office and a specific mandate to ensure the securities markets are properly regulated.

The Commission will soon have achieved its major legislative program stemming from the Single European Act. Once it has achieved this, it will turn its attention more towards implementation and compliance. At this point, the role of the Securities Market Committee will likely be extended to functions comparable with those of the SEC. Given that each state in the EC currently has a different legal system, a different accounting system, and a different financial services industry structure, by then the Commission would be also likely to be developing its ideas for creating the legal framework for the European company. If the large companies of Europe (including banks and securities houses) were to see advantages in reincorporating in this form, then some of the arguments against more centralization would change and the subsidiarity argument would hold much less force in respect of the regulation and supervision of such firms.

AN EVALUATION OF THE NEW REGULATORY FRAMEWORK

The level playing field applies to competition between banks and securities houses in the securities trading business. However, neither the ISD nor the CAD have directly attempted to create — as from January 1, 1996 — a level playing field between Member States. The objective is only convergence over time. While the Directives are binding on Member States as to the results to be achieved, they do not have to be implemented into national law verbatim. At present it is not possible to anticipate what will happen in practice post-1996 since Member State legislation has not yet been drafted. However, it is likely that in the medium term competitive inequalities, though of lesser degree than at present, will remain. These will arise in part as a result of some countries using the available flexibility in implementation of the Directives. In addition, the framework developed by each country will leave scope for interpretation by the courts in those countries as well as by firms and their regulators.

Most Member States have started to reform their securities market regulatory framework, partly in anticipation of the requirements of the ISD and the CAD, but also because securities market regulation has, in much of the EC, either been virtually nonexistent (as in Germany) or in need of considerable updating to reflect market changes (as in France). We look briefly at these two countries to see what implications there might be from the changes. These two sections are based on the Linklater and Paines (1993) study referred to at the start of this chapter.

Germany

At present Germany has minimal securities market regulation compared to France, for example, and no securities commission. In January 1992, the Federal Government announced legislative plans for changes to the regulatory and supervisory system which, taken together with implementation of EC legislation, would result for the first time in a comprehensive securities regulation framework. In July 1993, the Federal Ministry of Finance presented a discussion draft of the proposed new legislation to be called the Second Financial Market Promotion Act. Of central importance will be the introduction of the new Securities Trading Act (*Wertpapierhandelsgesetz*) and a far-reaching amendment of the Stock Exchange Act. The principal elements of the new legislation involve the following:

- The establishment of a supervisory authority at federal level.
- The introduction of a statutory prohibition on insider dealing.
- Improving the transparency of the securities markets by introducing stricter notification and disclosure requirements in respect of major shareholdings in listed companies.
- Establishing rules of conduct for providers of investment services including the duty to act in the client's best interest. There will also be special rules of conduct such as prohibition on front-running.
- Extending stock exchange supervisory powers of the federal states to include comprehensive supervision of securities trading on stock exchanges.
- The adaptation of the law in order to provide a secure legal basis for the use of electronic trading systems such as IBIS.
- Tightening of the law on prospectus liability.

The proposed new legislation will implement the Insider Dealing Directive and the Disclosure of Major Shareholdings Directive. The government has stated that the legislative process will be carried on independently of the implementation of the ISD. In the opinion of the government, the rules of conduct pursuant to Article 11 of the ISD reflect a broadly accepted standard to be employed by persons providing investment services. These rules will therefore be included in the new legislation. All other provisions of the ISD will be implemented at a later date, including those granting investment firms free access to the domestic securities markets as long as they are authorized and supervised by the competent authority of any other Member State. Once the ISD is implemented in Germany, further fundamental changes will occur and the regulatory system will then provide for a new institutional category of market participant (investment firms) and for the regulation of investment services which are, except for securities brokerage, currently largely exempt from regulation.

France

In 1991, the Conseil des Bourses de Valeurs (CBV) commissioned a report from a working group headed by M. René La Serre which recommended a major restructuring of the securities industry and its regulators. The report concluded that the prudential supervision of all securities intermediaries should be carried out by one authority (instead of the current regulation by institution), with each intermediary having the opportunity to obtain a seat on any of the various exchanges. The group favored a separation of functions, which would be reflected in categories of membership in the exchanges. In addition, certain functions would require to be undertaken through separately incorporated subsidiaries. Principally, the report identified a need to separate the functions of dealing and clearing from safe-keeping and administration of securities and from portfolio management. To the extent possible under the EC directives, the report recommended that the creation of a subsidiary for dealing and/or clearing of transactions in securities be obligatory in France. On the regulatory side, it recommended that a new regulatory authority be created by merging the CBV with the present futures and options regulator, the CMT, to create a new authority: the Conseil des Marchés Financiers.

EC legislation contains a *general good* provision which allows a derogation from the principle of home-country regulation and the imposition of the requirements of local laws on businesses incorporated in another member state. Under the general good provision, the French banking regulators have identified twenty-seven regulations which will apply to branches of EC credit institutions operating in France under the passport. They include a regulation on risk coverage on transactions in securities and other financial products. All regulations will apply in addition to general provisions of French law (such as contract or labor law) and any provisions of French legislation which would be applicable to specific activities undertaken by the branch, including transactions in securities. This could duplicate regulations imposed by a home state, thus raising some questions as to whether the test set out by the European Court of Justice has been met. This requires that the measure must be intended to protect a legitimate interest (not as an obstacle to the freedom of establishment or to provide services), be no more restrictive than is necessary adequately to protect that interest, and must not duplicate existing home-state control.

The implementation of the ISD will make it impossible for the monopoly of French sociétés de bourse in relation to trading and transfers of quoted securities to be maintained. Not only will passported investment firms be entitled to trade in quoted securities in France, but they will have to be given direct access to membership of stock exchanges by 1997. At present, French banks cannot deal on the stock exchange. So it would seem likely that French banks, as well as passported banks, will have to be permitted to do so in order to remain competitive. However, if the La Serre recommendations are adopted, French banks will have to carry on their business through a subsidiary — a requirement that cannot be imposed on their EC counterparts. Implementing the ISD will also mean that the availability of seats on the Matif will no longer be restricted to French banks, maisons de titres, and sociétés de bourse.

The French have, as we noted earlier, been active proponents of the concentration provision, which was originally intended to prevent transactions in French stocks being conducted off-exchange. Present French rules draw no distinction between professional and less sophisticated investors. A system which will provide professional and institutional investors with the possibility to opt out of this requirement will have to be introduced to comply with the ISD. This development could increase pressure on French regulators to move away from the concept of trading on the basis of a single market price, in order to attract more business to the French regulated market. Such a development would mean that the French stock exchange could combine its present order matching system with a more developed dealer market than the contrepartie system discussed in an earlier section. Thus France might move towards the UK system at a time when the UK markets were also starting to offer a French-style order-matching facility.

General Implications for Member State Securities Industries

The Commission is clearly aware of the need to ensure that directives are uniformly implemented and enforced. At the end of December 1993, it published *Strategic Program for the Internal Market*, a sixty-five-page document which set out how it intended to achieve uniformity. It coincided with the ending of what it describes as Phase 1, during which the 282 directives on which the single market is based were developed. The so-called Phase 2 will involve "decisive action" to force members of the European Community to implement all legislation on the single market by the end of 1994. The document also makes reference to the need to create a "better legal framework for cross-border companies." Mr. Raniero Vanni d'Archirafi, the internal market commissioner of the EC, is reported as saying, "It is no longer a 'softly softly' approach: there's balance, but there will be very decisive and very severe action to enforce the application at national level of this legislation."[18] He also noted that under the Maastricht Treaty, the Commission can recommend fines for infringements.

The view of Gaddum (1992), a member of the directorate of the Deutsche Bundesbank, is that standards will become much more uniform and present differences between Member States will be ironed out.

> The regulatory level of banks in the EC will converge in future. Existing national regulations, whether more lax or more restrictive, will be called in question by competition. This has advantages and drawbacks at the same time. On the one hand, the minimum standards will ensure that offshore financial centres will come under pressure and that in future there will be little scope left

for "competition in laxity." On the other hand, stricter regulatory rules are likely in future to be increasingly called into question.

This was also the view taken by Key (1989) of the Federal Reserve System when she analyzed the reasons for the Commission's approach to achieving regulatory convergence.

The result of the EC approach [in all goods and services markets], at least in the short run, could be competitive inequalities and fragmentation of markets. However, with regard to the financial services sector, the European Community assumes that over the longer run market forces will create pressure on governments that will lead to convergence of additional national rules and practices that have not been harmonised at the EC level. In the financial sector the principle of mutual recognition is thus being used as a pragmatic tool.

In addition to the flexibility that is likely to exist in implementation, there is cause for concern that the general good provision might be used by countries in ways which are designed to give their own firms a competitive advantage. How this provision will be interpreted, and the extent to which it will be used as a nontariff barrier within the EC, remains to be seen.

CONCLUSIONS

We have noted already that, even before the Second Banking Coordination Directive was implemented, technological developments had resulted in a considerable degree of integration between EC securities markets and in particular between EC bond markets. One obvious reason for this is that the Single European Act was designed only to "complete" the single market in a specified time period, and was not the start of a process of unification. One outcome of the impending implementation of the ISD is that firms offering financial services are assessing how to determine the most appropriate structure for their organizations in the light of the additional freedoms they will have from January 1, 1996. Each firm is likely to try to make an assessment of the appropriate institutional arrangement for each country in which it offers services. This will involve issues such as the form of company (bank or investment firm), the home country for the firm, and whether to provide a service through a branch, subsidiary, or cross-border. Another important type of decision that could be affected by regulatory developments is the location of trading facilities. This involves the choice between a single location for all currencies or the location of trading in the country of the local market. It is likely that the implementation of the ISD will lead to some restructuring of the industry, but not to major structural changes.

What is more likely to create a major change in the industry is the rapid growth in securities activities resulting from global market developments and expected demographic changes in Europe over the next decade. These will interact with the ongoing integration that will result from the single market program and lead to substantial changes in the European securities industry.

The acceleration of securitization and institutionalization of investment is likely to result in the structure and practice of continental European corporate finance and investment moving more to the US/UK pattern. Privatizations in Europe are likely to be an important factor, not only in creating an increase in publicly-traded corporate securities, but also in changing the nature of the banking sector. This will be affected, firstly, because there will be a substantial number of privatizations involving banks themselves. But secondly, privatization will also lead to changes for the newly privatized banks on both the asset and liability sides of their balance sheets. This problem has been analyzed by Smith who observes

> More fundamentally for the banks being privatised, the asset side of the balance sheet could be seriously affected by privatizations of industrial concerns to which they have made facilities available. A facility that had low [CAD] risk weighting (on the strength of a state guarantee) could, on privatization of the borrower, be converted to a fully weighted claim. The situation is exacerbated where the facility concerned is a large exposure but exempted, or partially exempted, from the requirements of the Large Exposures Directive because of the presence of a State guarantee. If the guarantee is lost on privatization, yet more capital will be tied up in supporting assets that are unlikely to be particularly profitable.[19]

Privatizations are likely to increase in number in part because of the single market program itself since, under EC law, national subsidy to state industry is strictly limited, as it creates competitive inequalities between industries in different Member States. An example of this would be the airline industry, where the de Croo Report, published in February 1994 and sponsored by the European Commission, recommended that EC state airlines be privatized. If the trend toward privatization continues, this is likely to lead to the further development of securitization and other forms of structured finance that convert non-investment grade, illiquid debt into investment grade, tradable debt.

Gaddum (1993) also thinks that the new regulatory framework will lead to more securitization.

> Not only market influences, but supervisory standards, too, have contributed to the move towards securitization. In many cases securitized assets, i.e. securities positions, carry lower capital weights than traditional unsecuritized bank lending. This also applies to the future Community-wide uniform regulations on the adequacy of the banks' and investment firms' capital. They require classical bank loans to be backed by capital at the rate of 8 percent. If the bank, rather than granting a loan, acquires a debt instrument of the same borrower, the capital cost involved is much lower, depending on the maturity. There can be no doubt that this underpins the trend towards the securitization of lending. . . . Further, and perhaps more serious, consequences might result for the quality of

the banks' loan portfolios. If assets with a good rating are increasingly withdrawn from the banking sector or remain there only briefly during the issue process, the quality of the banks' balance sheets will suffer.

In addition to changes on the supply side of the securities market, there are also likely to be substantial changes on the demand side arising in part from EC Directives and in part from changes in demographics and public finances. Traditionally in most of Continental Europe, a high proportion of pension provision has been undertaken by the state rather than by private employers or by individuals directly. This provision has been organized on a "pay as you go" basis, whereby provision of pensions is funded from current taxation. This is in contrast to pension provision through schemes funded from investment portfolios. In the UK and the Netherlands, in contrast to much of the rest of Europe, the government has encouraged a move away from state pension provision and towards private provision through fully funded schemes. As a result, around 80 percent of pension fund assets in the EC are accounted for by the UK and the Netherlands. It is likely that pressure on state budgets and the demographic changes in Europe, which are resulting in a higher proportion of the population being of pensionable age, will result in similar policy moves in Continental Europe.

At a meeting of the internal market ministers of the EC held in June 1993, a proposed Directive on management and investment of retirement funds was considered. The proposal that came out of this meeting aims to apply the principle of free movement of capital to the management of retirement funds by providing for cross-border financial management and freedom of cross-border investment, though it does not cover cross-border membership of institutions for retirement provision. However, to date, it has not been possible for the Member States to reach a common position on this proposed directive.

A major area of disagreement is the question of the currency-matching requirement. At present there is a clause that could result in a UK fund manager, for example, operating in another Member State, having to invest up to 80 percent of funds in assets denominated in the local currency. Another provision, which is a hangover from the days when government finance was given special privileges, would allow Belgium, for example, to require foreign pension funds operating in Belgium to continue to include at least 15 percent Belgian government bonds in their portfolio. Another contentious issue is a suggestion that a pension fund regulatory body in one Member State should be allowed to require the freezing of pension fund assets in another Member State.

Europe's pension funds industry is generally against the adoption of the Directive in its current form because of amendments that would mitigate its original intended liberalizing effect. There has also been lobbying by non-EC corporations that wish to operate EC-wide pension schemes for all their employees. If a common position can be reached by Member States which allows a truly open single market in pension funds in Europe, this, in combination with the demographic and public finance issues discussed above, would be likely to lead to a large increase in cross-border investment, not only in debt securities but also in equities. It would also be likely to lead to a greater institutionalization of investment, and thereby to a greater influence of performance-oriented shareholders in corporate governance in Continental Europe. This influence would be strengthened by the likelihood that a higher proportion of shareholders will in future be based outside the home state of the corporation.

It is also likely that large holdings of equities by universal banks and cross-holdings between companies will be sold into the market, as the new activist shareholders pressure companies for higher returns on equity and higher dividend payouts. These changes would bring the corporate environment in Continental Europe more into line with that in the UK and the US. This, in turn, may lead to greater merger and acquisition activity as a result of the increase in shareholder power relative to established management. It is likely also, in the longer term, that the EC will achieve the objective of greater disclosure of corporate information and a more unified accounting system. Pressure on this front is likely to emerge even more strongly than at present from large institutional investors.

It is probable that market forces over the next decade — in combination with the new EC regulatory framework, state budgetary constraints, changing demographics, technology, and the globalization of securities markets — will result in the creation of a highly unified securities market in debt, equity, and derivatives in the European Economic Area. This market will also be highly integrated with the securities markets in other major centers. In parallel with this, it is likely that the structure of the securities, banking, and stock exchange industry across Member States will develop towards a more common model. In particular this will apply to the provision of dealer and order matching services by many stock exchanges. The developments we have discussed should lead to a more unified corporate governance framework over the whole geographical area. By the turn of the century meetings of regulators from the Member States may have initiated a common view on regulatory issues and structure, a view which could supplant the present "competitive advantage" approach.

ENDNOTES

1. The *European Commission* was established under Article 155 of the Treaty of Rome as the body responsible for proposing legislation and for ensuring implementation of Community law issued in the form of directives. These lay down the aim and principle of a measure but leave it up to national parliaments

to put the law into national form. Directives are required to be implemented by each Member State, i.e. turned into domestic legislation in order to achieve the Directive's objectives. An EC regulation, on the other hand, applies in detail to all Member States. The *Council of Ministers* represents the governments of the twelve countries and is an ad hoc body made up of national ministers with responsibility for the policy under discussion. The president of the Council is the prime minister of the country holding the rotating six-month presidency. The function of the Council is to examine the draft measures produced by the Commission and to amend, accept, or reject them. The *European Parliament* has traditionally been only an advisory body. Under the Maastricht Treaty it obtained some additional powers through a *negative assent* procedure. The *European Court of Justice* has thirteen judges and six advocates-general nominated by the Member States. Since EC law takes precedence over national law, one of its functions is to make preliminary rulings on cases referred to it by national courts when a point of EC law is at issue. The national court must then apply the ruling. Cases relating to infringement of EC rules, in particular, single market rules, would be brought to the court.

2. See, for example, Temperton (1993) for analyses of the EMS and the single currency.
3. Commission of the European Communities, *Completing the Internal Market: White Paper from the Commission to the European Council* (Luxembourg, Office of Official Publications of the European Communities, 1985).
4. On November 1, 1993 the *European Union* (EU) officially came into existence. This development was a result of the treaty signed by the member states of the European Community (EC) in Maastricht on February 7, 1992. The Maastricht Treaty established a European Union whose aims included the promotion of economic and social progress through the creation of an area without internal frontiers and through economic and monetary union "ultimately including a single currency." Other aims were the development of a common foreign and security policy and eventually the framing of a common defense policy. Soon after the EU came into existence, the European Economic Area (EEA) was also created (January 1, 1994). The EEA treaty extends the European Union's single market to five of the seven members of the European Free Trade Association (EFTA) — Austria, Finland, Norway, Sweden, and Iceland — thus creating a single market of seventeen nations. These countries will comply with EC legislation on the single market, including that relating to financial services. These countries (except for Iceland) are also in negotiation with the twelve about full membership of the EC by January 1995. Although Switzerland was a signatory to the EEA treaty signed in Oporto on May 2, 1992, Swiss voters rejected the Agreement in a referendum in December 1992. Nevertheless Switzerland has stated that it will broadly comply with the EC legislation in respect of the single market in financial services. Liechtenstein, which has ratified the agreement, must modify its customs union with Switzerland before it can fully participate in the EEA. These developments are the latest in a series of steps taken by European countries since the end of World War II with a view to creating greater integration of European economies.
5. This statement comes from *The Creation of a Unified Securities Market for the Community*, an unattributed speech given by a senior Commission staff member.
6. These ideas are well developed in David T. Llewellyn's paper 'Financial intermediation and systems: global integration' in Fair and Boissieu (1988).
7. See Scott-Quinn (1992) for a discussion of electronic trading.

8. From *Declaration on International Investment and Multinational Enterprises*, para. II.I, Paris, OECD, 1976.
9. The Single European Act distinguishes between the country where the head office of a company is situated and the country in which it is trading. The former is the home country of that company while the latter is the host country within which it is operating.
10. Commission of the European Communities, communication from the Commission to the Council, *Program for the Liberalization of Capital Movements in the Community* COM(86) 292, Brussels.
11. These countries were allowed to retain some restrictions on long-term capital movements until the end of 1992 (1995 in the case of the last two countries).
12. Cross-border provision of services means providing services in one Member State to purchasers in another Member State without having a branch located in the state of the purchaser. Capital controls have, in the past, limited such transactions. In addition, however, some member states have had rules which prohibit foreign companies soliciting business.
13. Each Member State in the Council has a number of votes weighted according to its population. In total there are seventy-six votes of which fifty-four are required to adopt legislation.
14. An excellent analysis of this issue can be found in Mulherin (1993).
15. See De Jong, Nijman, and Röell (1993) for a comparison of trading costs on dealer and matching markets.
16. Richard Dale elaborates on the differences between CAD and Basle in Chapter 7 of this book.
17. See the Federal Trust Study Group (1993) and also Lee (1993) as examples of perspectives in this area.
18. Quoted in *Financial Times*, December 16, 1993.
19. See article by S. Smith of Cameron Markby Hewitt, law firm.

REFERENCES AND BIBLIOGRAPHY

Clemons, E.K. and Weber, B.W. (1989) International Stock Exchange: Assessment and Recommendations, Report to the Council of the Stock Exchange, August 1989.

Commission of the European Communities. (1985) *Completing the Internal Market.* White paper from the Commission to the European Council, June.

———. (1993) *Securities Markets.* Community measures adopted or proposed together with their extension to the European economic area; situation as at June, Luxembourg.

Dale, R. (1992) 'Capital adequacy and European securities markets,' in A. Steinherr, (ed.) *The New European Financial Market Place.* London, Longman.

Davis, R. (1993) 'London trading in German equities.' (London) *Stock Exchange Quarterly*, Winter, October–December.

De Jong, F., Nijman, T. and Röell, A. (1993) 'A comparison of the cost of trading French shares on the Paris Bourse and on SEAQ International.' *London School of Economics, Financial Markets Group, Discussion Paper No. 169*, August.

Dermine, J. (1991) 'The regulation of financial services in the EC, centralization or national autonomy?' *Working Paper No. 91/35/FIN*, INSEAD, Fontainebleau, France, June.

Dimson, E. and Marsh, P. (1994) 'City research project, the debate on international capital requirements — evidence on equity position risk for UK securities firms.' *London Business School, Subject Report VIII,* February.

Fair, D.E. and de Boissieu, C. (1988) *International Monetary and Financial Integration — The European Dimension*, Financial and Monetary Policy Studies, Vol. 14. Dordrecht, Kluwer.

———. (1990)*Financial Institutions in Europe Under New Competitive Conditions*, Financial and Monetary Policy Studies, Vol. 20. Dordrecht, Kluwer.

Federal Trust Study Group. (1993) *Towards an Integrated European Capital Market.* London, Federal Trust for Education and Research.

Franks, J. and Schaefer, S (1993) 'City research project, the costs and effectiveness of the UK financial regulatory system.' *London Business School, Subject Report II,* March.

Gaddum, J.W. (1992) 'The regulation of German financial markets in an EC context.' *IFR, Journal of International Securities Markets*, **6**, Summer, 151–154.

Garbade, K. (1982) *Securities Markets*, New York, McGraw-Hill, 1982.

General Accounting Office (1992) 'Securities markets: challenges to harmonizing international capital standards remain.' *Report to Congressional Committees, GAO/GGD-92-41,* March.

George, E.A.J. (1992) 'Financial regulations: what are we trying to do?' *IFR, Journal of International Securities Markets*, **6**, Summer, 147–154.

Hawawini, G. & Schill, M. (1993) 'Current state and expectations for European equity trading within the common market.' *Working Paper No. 93/07/FIN,* INSEAD, Fontainebleau, France, April.

International Securities Markets Association. (1993) *Towards a Single European Securities Market*, Zurich.

International Stock Exchange. (1989) *Maintaining a Central Equities Market.* London, Touche Ross Management Consultants.

Kane, E.J. (1988) 'How market forces influence the structure of financial regulation,' in W.S. Haraf and R.M. Kushmeider, (eds.) *Restructuring Banking and Financial Services in America*, American Enterprise Institute for Public Policy Research.

Key, S.J. (1989) 'Financial integration in the European Community.' *International Finance Discussion Papers, No. 349,* Board of Governors of the Federal Reserve System, April.

Khan, B. and Ireland, J. (1993) 'City research project, the use of technology for competitive advantage: a study of screen *v* floor trading.' *London Business School, Subject Report IV,* September.

Lee, R. (1993) 'Supervising EC capital markets: do we need a European SEC?' *Oxford Finance Group Discussion Paper No. 1*, June.

Linklater and Paines (1993) *Securities Regulation in the Single Market*, November.

McCrone, G. (1992) 'Subsidiarity: its implications for economic policy.' *National Westminster Bank Quarterly Review,* November, 45–56.

Mulherin, J.H. (1993) 'Market transparency: pros, cons, and property rights.' *Journal of Applied Corporate Finance*, **5**, Winter.

Owen, R. and Dynes, M. (1993) *The Times Guide to the Single European Market*, 2d edn. London, Times Books.

Price Waterhouse. (1994) *The Regulation of Market Risk — the impact of the European Community's Capital Adequacy Directive and the Basle proposals.* London, Price Waterhouse.

Rose, H. 'Bank risk and the level playing field.' *London Business School, Institute of Finance and Accounting, IFA Working Paper 166–93.*

Schaefer, S. (1992) 'Financial regulation: the contribution of the theory of finance.'

London Business School, Institute of Finance and Accounting, IFA-157-92, February.

Scott-Quinn, B. (1992) 'Networks and the changing structure of the European securities industry.' *IFR, Journal of the International Securities Markets,* **6**, Spring, 11–18.

Securities and Investment Board. (1994) *Regulation of the United Kingdom Equity Markets*. Discussion paper, February.

Siebert, H., ed. (1990) *The Completion of the Internal Market, Symposium 1989, Institut für Weltwirtschaft an der Universität Kiel,* Boulder, Colorado, Westview Press.

Smith, S. (1993) 'Europe's bumpy fields.' *The Banker*, December.

Stansell, S.R., ed. (1993) *International Financial Market Integration*. Oxford, UK, Blackwell.

Steil, B. (1993) *Competition, Integration and Regulation in EC Capital Markets.* London, Royal Institute of International Affairs, International Economics Programme.

Stoll, H.R. (1993) 'Organization of the stock market: competition or fragmentation?' *Journal of Applied Corporate Finance*, **5**, Winter.

Temperton, P., ed. (1993) *The European Currency Crisis — what chance now for a single European currency?* Cambridge, UK, Probus.

7
International Banking Regulation

RICHARD DALE

Until the early 1970s banking regulation was considered to be the exclusive preserve of national policymakers. However, the growth of international lending and the emergence of multinational banks servicing this business from offices spread across the globe made regulators aware of the need to coordinate their activities. First, the interpenetration of national banking markets by foreign banking establishments called for a clear understanding as to which authority was responsible for regulating which banks. Second, the close linkages between national banking systems through the interbank market meant that financial stability in one jurisdiction could be adversely affected by problems originating in another jurisdiction. And, finally, the fact that banks from different countries were competing for business within a global market raised the possibility of competitive distortions arising from uneven national regulatory arrangements. It was against this background that regulators from the leading industrial countries felt it necessary to establish a forum to coordinate their policies.

Today, the trend towards globalization of financial markets is proceeding apace, given further impetus by the dismantling of exchange controls, a dramatic rise in cross-border investment flows, and increased access to domestic banking markets by foreign institutions. A number of other developments are also posing a challenge to regulators. First, banking is no longer a distinct financial service, but has become intermingled with other financial activities, including securities business. The process of securitization,

International Financial Market Regulation. Edited by B. Steil

by which banks repackage and sell loans to nonbank investors, has further blurred the boundaries between bank lending and securities market financing. Second, banks' heavy involvement in the explosive growth of over-the-counter derivatives markets has provoked a major controversy over the systemic risks associated with derivatives trading and the appropriate regulatory response.

Finally, and perhaps most importantly, the banking industry is facing intensified competition on a number of fronts. Within the domestic markets price cartels, administered interest rates, and other restrictive practices are being dismantled; cross-border competition is increasing due to enhanced reciprocal rights of access (notably within the single European market); and there is now a growing competitive threat from nonbank financial institutions (securities firms and insurance companies) which are eroding banks' share both of aggregate lending and of short-term savings.

The ever changing financial environment in which banks operate ensures that the regulatory problem can never be finally resolved: new issues emerge and old issues reappear in a different form. This chapter assesses the current international regulatory agenda in the light of the trends noted above. It first reviews the evolution of the Basle regulatory regime, then considers a number of issues in preventive regulation (i.e., regulation designed to prevent bank failures). Next it examines the question of supervisory standards, before dealing with some major issues in protective regulation (the role of deposit insurance and the lender of last resort). Finally it draws some general conclusions on the future direction of regulatory cooperation.

EVOLUTION OF REGULATORY COOPERATION

Until the mid-1970s there was no formal machinery for coordinating national regulation of international banks. However, the disturbances that followed in the wake of Herstatt Bank's collapse in the summer of 1974 focused attention on the interdependence of national banking systems and led, in the following year, to the creation of a standing committee of bank supervisors, under the auspices of the Bank for International Settlements (BIS), comprising the Group of Ten (G-10) countries plus Luxembourg. This Committee on Banking Regulation and Supervisory Practices (CBRSP) (called the Cooke Committee, after its first chairman) sought not to harmonize national laws and practices, but rather to interlink disparate regulatory regimes with a view to ensuring that all banks are supervised according to certain broad principles (Cooke 1981).

One of the earliest and most far-reaching initiatives of the Cooke Committee was to develop broad guidelines for the division of responsibilities among national supervisory authorities. These guidelines, which were approved by the G-10 central bank governors in December 1975, became known as the Basle Concordat (CBRSP 1975).

The Concordat embodied the key principle that the supervision of solvency is essentially a matter for the parent authority in the case of foreign branches and primarily the responsibility of the host authority in the case of foreign subsidiaries.

Although the Concordat represented a significant step towards greater international supervisory cooperation, it suffered from a number of defects which began to become apparent from 1978 onwards. In the first place, the primary supervisory responsibility accorded to host authorities for the solvency of foreign subsidiaries ran counter to another important initiative of the Cooke Committee. This was the recommendation, endorsed by the G-10 central bank governors in 1978, that supervision of banks' international business should be conducted on a consolidated basis, the object being to limit the opportunities for regulatory evasion. There was a clear danger here that host countries would look to parent authorities to supervise locally incorporated subsidiaries of foreign banks under the principle of consolidated supervision, while home authorities would rely on host countries to exercise their responsibilities under the Concordat.

The controversy surrounding the handling of Banco Ambrosiano's collapse in 1982 was one factor prompting a reappraisal of the original Concordat and the emergence of a revised version, which was approved by the central bank governors in June 1983 (CBRSP 1983). The authors of the revised Concordat clearly had the Ambrosiano case in mind when they introduced more precise guidelines for the supervision of holding companies. Apart from closing such supervisory gaps, the revised Concordat sought to address directly the question of adequacy of supervision.

The authors of the 1983 Concordat attempted to deal with the problem of supervisory standards by introducing what might be described as a *dual key* approach to the operation of foreign banking establishments. Under the revised guidelines, if a host authority considered the supervision of parent institutions of foreign banks operating on its territory to be inadequate, it should prohibit or discourage the continued operation of such offices, or alternatively impose specific conditions on the conduct of their business. In addition, where the parent authority considered the host authority's supervision to be inadequate, it should "either extend its supervision, to the degree that it is practicable, or it should be prepared to discourage the parent bank from continuing to operate the establishment in question." Each national supervisory authority therefore had to satisfy itself that its banks' foreign operations were being conducted in jurisdictions with sound supervisory practices and that foreign banks to which it was host were subject to adequate supervision within their home jurisdiction.

In April 1990 an addendum to the Basle Concordat (the Supplement) was approved (CBRSP 1990). This was designed "to supplement the principles of the Concordat by encouraging more regular and structured collaboration between supervisors." The Supplement addressed the information needs of both parent and host authorities, included recommendations on the role of external audit and urged countries whose secrecy laws inhibited the transmission of supervisory information to review these requirements.

In July 1988 the Basle Committee launched a major new regulatory initiative when it announced that the G-10 countries had approved the guidelines establishing minimum capital adequacy standards for international banks (CBRSP 1988). The purpose of this agreement is twofold: firstly, to strengthen the soundness and stability of the international banking system; secondly, to ensure competitive equality among international banks — the competitive concern being that banks operating on a low capital/assets ratio can support a higher level of banking business for any given level of capital than can more highly capitalized institutions.

The Basle Accord on capital adequacy standards should be viewed as an important landmark in international supervisory cooperation. It represents the first move towards global regulatory harmonization, as distinct from the regional harmonization initiatives introduced within the European Community. It also signifies a departure from the original purpose of the Basle Committee which was to coordinate national regulatory regimes but not to seek to impose a common regulatory framework. Common capital adequacy rules, considered in more detail below, may turn out to be only the first stage in a more comprehensive program of international regulatory harmonization.

The supervisory weaknesses revealed by the collapse of BCCI in the Summer of 1991 prompted a reassessment of the Basle approach to banking regulation. Accordingly, in July 1992 the Basle Committee, with the endorsement of the central bank governors of the G-10 countries, issued a new set of "minimum standards" for the supervision of international banks which are intended to have greater force than earlier guidelines (CBRSP 1992). These standards have been summarized by the Committee as follows:

1. All international banking groups and international banks should be supervised by a home-country authority that capably performs consolidated supervision.
2. The creation of a cross-border banking establishment should receive the prior consent of both the host-country supervisory authority and the bank's, and if different, the banking group's home-country supervisory authority.
3. Supervisory authorities should possess the right to gather information from the cross-border banking establishments of the banks or banking groups for which they are the home-country supervisor.

4. If a host-country authority determines that any one of the foregoing minimum standards is not met to its satisfaction, that authority could impose restrictive measures necessary to satisfy its prudential concerns consistent with these minimum standards, including the prohibition of the creation of banking establishments.

The key requirement is that all international banks should be supervised by a home-country authority "that capably performs consolidated supervision." This is further spelt out as meaning that the authority concerned should (1) monitor banks' global operations on the basis of verifiable consolidated data; (2) be able to prohibit the creation of corporate structures that impede consolidated supervision; and (3) be in a position to prevent banks from establishing a presence in suspect jurisdictions.

If the minimum standards are not met, the host authority is called on to exclude banks from the jurisdiction concerned or alternatively to accept responsibility for supervising these banks' local operations, subject to appropriate restrictions (which may, by implication, include mandatory incorporation of such operations).

Finally, in April 1993 the Basle Committee issued a package of proposals intended to extend the scope of the Capital Adequacy Accord by incorporating market risk and interest rate risk and clarifying permissible netting arrangements (CBRSP 1993). Under these proposals (discussed below) specific capital charges would be applied to banks' trading positions, including derivative positions, in debt and equity securities, and a measurement system would be introduced in order to identify banks that might be incurring exceptionally large interest rate risk. This latest initiative again underlines the emphasis now being given to the establishment of a common global regulatory framework for international banks, in marked contrast to the original Basle approach which specifically rejected harmonization in favor of the much looser concept of regulatory coordination based on an agreed allocation of regulatory responsibilities.

Looking back at the evolution of the Basle regulatory regime over the past twenty years it is clear that the pressures behind regulatory convergence have shifted. Initially the predominant concern was the safety and soundness of the financial system. More recently competitive equality, or "the level playing field," has become the main driving force. This helps to explain the new emphasis on harmonization initiatives designed, above all, to remove competitive disparities between rival banking systems.

However, several key issues remain unsolved. What factors should determine the boundaries between regulatory harmonization on the one hand and regulatory competition on the other? Should the Basle regime, like its EC counterpart, be based on legally binding obligations rather than, as at present, on voluntary compliance with broadly drawn guidelines? Given the new concern with ensuring minimum supervisory standards, how are such standards to be assessed, monitored and enforced? And, perhaps most important of all, has the Basle machinery itself been outdated by the globalization of financial markets, bearing in mind that the BIS has no formal supervisory authority over banks which own it or over banking supervisory authorities? Should the IMF or some other supranational agency now become involved with establishing a truly global regulatory framework for international banking? These and other more specific issues are considered in the discussion that follows.

ISSUES IN PREVENTIVE REGULATION

The distinction is made here between *preventive* regulation, intended to prevent banks from getting into difficulties, and *protective* regulation, designed to safeguard depositors and the financial system in the event of bank failures. This section is concerned with preventive regulation, a later section deals with protective regulation.

1988 Basle Accord

The central pillar of preventive regulation is capital adequacy.[1] At the international level this is embodied in the minimum risk-weighted capital ratio laid down by the 1988 Basle Accord that came fully into effect at the beginning of 1993. The Basle ratio has been widely accepted by the international financial community as an indicator of banks' financial strength. Indeed, it appears that financial markets have been rewarding banks for achieving capital ratios in excess of the regulatory minimum, thereby encouraging institutions to target ratios well above the Basle norm. For instance, one recent study suggests that US banks' capital raising since 1990, which has taken industry well beyond the Basle requirements, has been partly prompted by business strategy rather than regulatory considerations, a strategy that has been rewarded by the stock market.[2] The implication is that the Basle capital ratio may be better viewed as a form of disclosure, valued by the marketplace, rather than as a binding regulatory requirement.

Despite it ready adoption by financial markets, the Basle concept of capital adequacy is open to criticism. The risk weightings encourage banks to substitute government debt for business loans to an extent that gives public sector borrowers privileged access to credit markets at the expense of private borrowers. The fact that residential mortgage loans are given a minimum risk weighting only half that of other commercial loans may similarly give undue preference to the housing sector. More generally, the simple aggregation of risk-weighted assets under the accord gives no recognition to the potential benefits of portfolio diversification, in marked contrast to the approach of some securities regulators who make allowance for noncovariant risk exposures (although it should also be said that risk covariance is more easily measured in relation to traded securities than it is for nontraded bank loans). Furthermore the Basle distinction between Tier I (essentially equity) capital and Tier II capital, which includes eligible subordinated debt, has encouraged the growth of complex debt instruments whose contribution to the capital strength of the issuing bank may be difficult to assess.

Some critics have alleged that the phased introduction of the Basle capital adequacy regime, coinciding as it did with recession in much of the industrialized world, held back economic recovery by impeding credit growth through a capital-constrained banking sector. On the other hand, it is difficult in practice to distinguish between the role of the capital requirements and other influences (e.g., changing risk perceptions) that could have adversely affected bank credit expansion.

Perhaps the most serious concern about the Basle Accord relates to the uniform 100 percent risk weighting applicable to commercial loans to the private sector. That is to say, the capital requirement for a loan to a triple-A multinational company is precisely the same as it is for a loan of similar size to a small unquoted property developer. In this key area of loan quality there are no differential risk weightings. The result is that aggressively managed banks may be tempted to shift their loan portfolios towards high risk borrowers, while cautiously managed institutions are unrewarded for their prudence.

This problem is further exacerbated by the Basle Accord's failure to formulate specific guidelines on provisioning — deductions from profit to reflect anticipated loan losses. The approach to provisioning adopted by the Basle Committee is based on the idea of recognizable asset impairment. Provisions set aside against impaired assets are "specific" and are not eligible for inclusion in regulatory capital. On the other hand, "where ... general loan loss reserves or provisions are not allocated in any way ... to an identified deterioration in any asset or group or subset of assets, and are therefore genuinely available to meet losses which are subsequently identified wherever they may occur, ... it would be reasonable to include them in capital" (CBRSP 1991). General provisions defined in this way may therefore be included in Tier II capital.

One major drawback of this Basle approach to provisioning is that the concept of identifiable asset deterioration is essentially subjective and can therefore result in considerable latitude in banks' provisioning decisions. Indeed, disparities in national regulation, accounting practices, and fiscal incentives are reflected in significant variations in provisioning policies as between different jurisdictions (Table 7.1). From a supervisory standpoint the most worrying consequence of variable provisioning practices is that the

Table 7.1 Percent Net Provisions of Commercial Banks

		1986	1987	1988	1989	1990	1991
Australia*	bs	0.25	0.35	0.38	0.51	0.86	1.20
	gi	5.26	7.40	7.77	10.96	19.13	24.24
Austria	bs	–	–	–	0.39	0.50	0.52
	gi	–	–	–	16.35	19.49	19.62
Belgium	bs	0.31	0.28	0.40	0.43	0.20	0.31
	gi	14.18	13.93	20.46	23.61	11.54	17.13
Canada	bs	0.75	0.68	0.60	1.16	0.36	0.54
	gi	20.57	17.49	13.68	25.56	8.28	11.93
Denmark†	bs	0.39	0.70	1.09	0.87	1.21	–
	gi	18.27	20.82	24.87	26.64	40.51	37.66‡
Finland	bs	0.21	0.48	0.40‡	0.24	0.19	−0.01
	gi	6.14	13.65	10.51‡	7.43	5.86	−0.42
France	bs	0.61	0.53	0.52	0.53	0.50	0.52
	gi	21.25	19.03	19.31	21.57	21.05	22.16
Germany	bs	0.55	0.44	0.25	0.42	0.53	0.47
	gi	15.05	13.26	7.77	13.07	16.51	15.03
Greece§	bs	0.32	0.25	0.24	0.36	0.50	0.82
	gi	10.61	8.91	8.06	11.54	13.68	16.70
Italy	bs	0.58	0.49	0.56	0.51	0.54	0.50‡
	gi	12.18	11.12	12.41	11.49	11.69	10.51‡
Japan	bs	0.04	0.03	0.05‡	0.04	0.03	0.07
	gi	2.42	2.16	3.34‡	3.36	2.37	5.72
Luxembourg	bs	0.66	0.51	0.37	0.37	0.52	0.42
	gi	46.05	39.66	29.54	32.37	44.06	36.87
Netherlands*	bs	0.34	0.19	0.42‡	0.36‡	0.30‡	0.29
	gi	10.68	6.13	13.26‡	12.19‡	11.72‡	11.48
Norway	bs	0.92	0.85	1.58	1.58	1.96	4.50‡
	gi	20.69	24.12	40.16	36.04	55.14	146.01‡
Portugal	bs	0.84	1.35	1.43	1.59	–	1.79
	gi	24.90	32.35	32.07	32.36	34.43‡	29.35
Spain	bs	0.79	0.91	0.80	0.61	0.59	0.72
	gi	17.20	18.38	15.13	11.88	11.55	13.80
Sweden	bs	0.84	0.81	0.93	0.86	0.40	−3.42‡
	gi	20.94	23.45	27.20	28.64	14.10	−122.09‡
Switzerland	bs	0.51	0.51	0.47	0.54	0.55	0.96
	gi	19.00	19.06	17.82	18.90	20.70	30.26
Turkey	bs	0.67	1.62	1.69	1.20‡	1.08	1.15
	gi	12.02	22.14	20.58	16.23‡	11.76	12.55
UK	bs	0.54	1.53‡	0.31	1.60	0.95	1.32
	gi	10.95	29.98‡	6.03	31.48	19.55	26.32
US	bs	0.78	1.27	0.56	0.97	0.95	1.01
	gi	16.34	26.30	11.14	18.90	18.57	18.50

bs: as percent of average balance sheet total.
gi: as percent of gross income.
* All banks.
† Commercial banks and savings banks.
‡ Break in series.
§ Large commercial banks.
Source: OECD, *Financial Market Trends*, June 1993, 63.

concept of capital adequacy, which lies at the heart of the Basle regulatory regime, is seriously undermined. For instance, if Bank A has made cumulative general provisions of 3½ percent on its commercial loan portfolio whereas the provisioning level for Bank B, on a loan portfolio of similar quality, is only 2 percent, then Bank B's risk-weighted Tier 1 capital ratio may appear to be 1½ percentage points higher than Bank A's. If the difference in provisioning coverage relates to specific rather than general provisions then the distortion would be reflected in the total risk-weighted capital asset ratio.

In either case, the Basle capital adequacy regime will give a false reading of the relative financial strength of individual banks. This point is borne out by US research, which demonstrates that by using examiner asset classifications to identify banks that are underprovisioning it is possible to greatly enhance the ability of risk-based capital ratios to separate high- and low-risk banks (Jones and King 1992).

Market Risk Proposals

The primary objective of the 1988 Basle Accord was to establish minimum capital standards designed to reflect credit risk. In April 1993 the Basle Committee issued supplementary proposals for the supervisory treatment of market risks incurred by banks, covering open positions in debt securities, equities and foreign exchange. For this purpose a distinction is made between a bank's longer-term investment and its trading book, the idea being that the original Basle credit risk weightings should be applied to the former, and the new capital requirements for market risk to the latter.

These proposals on market risk raise a number of controversial issues. Most fundamental of these is the extent to which bank supervisors should adjust their capital adequacy standards in an attempt to achieve competitive equality between banks and nonbank securities firms. According to its authors, the Basle proposals "contain features which bank supervisors acting on their own would not necessarily favour but are prepared to adopt in the hope that further convergence with securities regulators will be achieved at some future date" (CBRSP 1993, p.2). In other words, the perceived need for a common regulatory framework for banks and securities firms has induced bank supervisors to lower the standards they would ideally wish to apply to banks. Implicitly, therefore, the prudential goal of safety and soundness is being subordinated to the broader objective of establishing a level playing field for all financial institutions undertaking securities business.

The difficulty of reconciling conflicting objectives is most clearly evident in the proposed definition of regulatory capital. The Basle Committee states that "were the Basle proposals to be designed for banks alone, [the Committee] would favour the retention of the present definition of capital"

(CBRSP, p.10). However, in the interests of establishing common capital adequacy rules for banks and securities firms the Committee proposes that banks should be permitted to employ an additional form of short-term subordinated debt for the sole purpose of meeting part of the capital requirement for market risks. In order to ensure that such short-term subordinated debt is available to absorb losses it is proposed that it should be subject to a lock-in clause, which stipulates that neither interest nor principal may be paid (even at maturity) if such payments means that the capital allocated to the trading book would fall below a specified threshold level. The difficulty here is that if the lock-in clause were triggered, and it became known that a bank had failed to repay maturing debt obligations, confidence in the bank could be severely damaged and a deposit run could develop. It is presumably for this reason that several members of the Basle Committee do not favor the use of this newly proposed Tier III capital for banks.

There are some further potential difficulties associated with the Basle proposals. The distinction between a bank's trading book and its longer-term investments is not clear-cut, raising the possibility of regulatory circumvention. Furthermore, the need for such a distinction is open to question; a persuasive case could be made for marking to market *all* banks' securities holdings and then applying an appropriate capital requirement based on market risk. This would avoid the considerable problems that are likely to arise in defining a bank's trading book.

The proposed minimum capital standard for equity positions held in the trading account is problematical. The approach used is the so-called building-block technique, based on separately calculated charges for specific and general market risk. Specific risk refers to possible adverse movements in the price of an individual security, whereas general market risk is the risk of a broad market movement unrelated to any specific securities. It is suggested that the capital charge for specific risk should be between 4 and 8 percent (see below) and for general market risk a standard 8 percent. The Basle Committee acknowledges that the choice of this building block method may conflict with the objective of securing wider convergence with securities regulators, the point here being that the US Securities and Exchange Commission applies a single risk charge or "haircut" to securities firms' equity positions. In order to meet this difficulty it is proposed that national authorities should have discretion to continue to apply a comprehensive approach, combining specific and general market risks, so long as it can be demonstrated that the alternative method, "by its very nature," requires capital charges equal to or greater than the building-block methodology. This issue of equivalence is likely to prove contentious.[3]

Finally, the Basle proposal on market risk for equities is likely to encounter serious difficulties when it comes to the treatment of specific risk. The Committee suggests that the capital charge for specific risk should be between 4 and 8 percent, depending on the diversification of the portfolio and the extent to which it contains liquid and marketable stocks. However, the Committee has been unable to formulate a clear definition of liquidity or diversification and is therefore proposing to allow national authorities to develop their own criteria. Clearly, the delegation of such a key area of risk assessment to national regulators is in direct conflict with the aim of establishing common capital adequacy standards and must inevitably lead to competitive distortions within securities markets.

Interest Rate Risk Proposals

In addition to applying capital requirements to market risk, the Basle Committee, in its April 1993 package of supervisory proposals, seeks to establish a methodology for measuring interest rate risk. It should be noted that the Basle approach adopted here is quite different to that followed in relation to other types of risk, notably market risk and credit risk. For every type of risk there is a two-stage policy problem: first how to measure the risk and second how to discourage excessive risk-taking through, for example, appropriate capital charges. In the case of market risk and credit risk the Basle Committee has formulated both a measurement system and detailed capital requirements. In the case of interest rate risk the Committee's stated purpose is quite different, namely to develop a measurement system which supervisors can use for observation purposes as a means of identifying "outliers", leaving each authority free to decide how to respond to institutions identified as high risk.

This approach immediately raises two issues. First, is it advisable on the one hand to develop a highly complex methodology for measuring interest rate risk which is to be applied internationally, and on the other hand, to leave national authorities with total discretion as to how this information should be used for supervisory purposes? In other words, may not any benefits associated with a uniform system of measurement be entirely offset by variable national treatment of the risks so measured?

A second, and related, point is that it may be dangerous to adopt different supervisory regimes for different kinds of risk. That is to say, if credit risk is subject to specific capital adequacy requirements, while interest rate risk is penalized only when a bank's exceptional exposure makes it an outlier, there could well be a tendency for banks as a whole to substitute interest risk for credit risk. And if banks are prompted to increase interest rate exposure, then the benchmark level of risk in relation to which outliers are identified will itself increase — raising questions about the effectiveness of the outlier approach.

In any event, it seems highly likely that once a measurement system for interest rate risk has been agreed, competitive pressures will eventually induce national supervisors to seek further international agreement on common arrangements for discouraging excessive risk-taking in this area.

In addressing the question of how to measure interest rate risk, the Basle Committee has focused on the extent to which the economic value (rather than the current earnings) of a bank is exposed to future changes in interest rates. The proposed measurement system involves the following stages:

1. All interest-rate-sensitive asset, liability and off-balance-sheet positions would be placed into one of thirteen time-bands based on the instrument's maturity or repricing characteristics.
2. The positions within each time-band would be netted and the resulting net position for each time-band would then be weighted by an estimate of its duration.
3. The duration weights would be adjusted to reflect the relative volatility of interest rates across the term structure.
4. The net balance of these individual weighted positions would provide the basis for measuring a bank's interest rate risk.

The Committee itself identified several key problems in this formulation which as yet remain unresolved. First, should an institution's interest rate risk be viewed on a whole-book basis, embracing both the trading book and the banking book, or should these two operations be assessed separately? In a world of universal banking, where there is no risk segregation between different businesses conducted within a single banking group, economic logic would point to a consolidated approach to risk measurement.[4] However, since a bank's trading book is to be isolated for separate treatment under the proposed capital adequacy rules relating to market risk (which in the case of debt securities incorporates interest rate risk), it might seem inconsistent to combine the trading and banking books for the purposes of calculating interest rate risk exposure.

A second problem identified by the Committee concerns the treatment of items where either the interest repricing date or the maturity is uncertain. The most obvious example is non-interest-bearing transaction deposits which, for some banks, may constitute a relatively stable core deposit base, largely insensitive to changes in market interest rates. The extent to which such liabilities should be treated as long-term for interest rate risk purposes has been left open for debate by the Committee.

Finally, there is a question as to what extent, if at all, short and long positions within and between different time bands, and in different currencies, should be treated as offsetting. Again, the Committee has yet to reach a consensus on the extent to which such offsetting is permissible. Concerning the recognition of hedging between offsetting positions in different currencies, the Committee is seeking outside views on whether there is a practical method of recognizing interest rate correlations between currencies.

Derivatives

The Basle proposals on market risk incorporate capital adequacy requirements to cover banks' debt and equity derivatives. These requirements embrace forward rate agreements, futures and options on debt instruments, interest rate and cross-currency swaps, forward foreign exchange positions, futures and options on both individual equities and on equity indices, as well as options on futures and warrants. In principle, all derivatives (except for those held outside the trading book) would be converted into positions in the relevant underlying and become subject to the proposals for applying specific and general market risk under the building-block methodology.

However, regulators' concerns over derivative products go well beyond the need to establish an appropriate capital adequacy framework.[5] In the first place there has been an explosive increase in the trading of financial derivatives (Table 7.2). In particular the outstanding volume of the over-the-counter (OTC) or customized derivatives rose nearly ninefold in the five

Table 7.2 Markets for Selected Derivative Instruments, Notional Principal Amounts Outstanding at Year-end, in Billions of US Dollars Equivalent

	1986	1987	1988	1989	1990	1991
Exchange-traded instruments*	583	725	1,300	1,762	2,284	3,518
Interest rate futures	370	488	895	1,201	1,454	2,159
Interest rate options†	146	122	279	387	600	1,072
Currency futures	10	14	12	16	16	18
Currency options†	39	60	48	50	56	59
Stock market index futures	15	18	28	42	70	77
Options on stock market indices†	3	23	38	66	88	132
Over-the-counter instruments‡	500[e]	867	1,330	2,402	3,451	4,449
Interest rate swaps*	400[e]	683	1,010	1,503	2,312	3,065
Currency and cross-currency interest rate swaps§¶	100[e]	184	320	449	578	807
Other derivative instruments§#	–	–	–	450	561	577
Memorandum item						
Cross-border plus local foreign currency claims of BIS reporting banks	4,031	5,187	5,540	6,498	7,578	7,497

[e] = estimate
* Excludes options on individual shares and derivatives involving commodity contracts.
† Calls plus puts.
‡ Only data collected by ISDA. Excludes information on contracts such as forward rate agreements, over-the-counter currency options, forward foreign exchange positions, equity swaps and warrants on equity.
§ Contracts between ISDA members reported only once.
¶ Adjusted for reporting of both currencies.
# Caps, collars, floors, and swaptions.
Source: *Recent Development in International Interbank Relations*, Bank for International Settlements, 1992, 49.

years from 1986 to 1991, representing an annual increase of well over 50 percent.

The rapid growth of any new financial market gives pause for thought, but in the case of derivatives there are a number of other concerns. It has been claimed that derivatives increase the volatility of financial markets by promoting speculation; that their intellectual complexity impedes effective risk control by senior management and regulators; that derivatives trading creates large off-balance-sheet exposures that reduce market transparency; and that the market linkages created by derivatives increase the potential for generalized financial contagion.

In June 1993, concerns of this kind prompted the following warning from former BIS General Manager, Alexandre Lamfalussy:

> . . . the phenomenal growth of derivatives and associated trading techniques has reduced the transparency of market participants' balance sheets and has obscured the transmission of disturbances across market segments and institutions. This has severely complicated the assessment of the nature and distribution of risks in financial operations, at the level of both the individual firm and of the system as a whole. The implication is that market participants may not be in a position to impose the necessary discipline on financial institutions to prevent the risk of the buildup of systemic problems (Lamfalussy 1993, p.4).

Since 1992 there have been three major supervisory reviews of derivatives — from the BIS, the US regulatory agencies and the Bank of England — each expressing concerns about potential risks in the derivatives business. The Group of Thirty (G-30), the New York-based consultancy group, has now sought to redress the balance in the derivatives debate by publishing an authoritative study of the OTC derivatives market prepared largely by market participants (Group of Thirty 1993). Among other matters on which the authors are at pains to offer reassurance are

1. *Market size.* According to the G-30 the scale of global derivatives activity is "unimposing compared to that of traditional financial activities." For instance, the value of swaps written in 1991 was less than 1 percent of the annual turnover in the foreign exchange market and swaps outstanding represented less than one-third of domestic and international bonds outstanding. Furthermore, actual risk exposures, measured by replacement cost, typically represent between only 1 and 3 percent of the notional principle value of the derivatives portfolio.
2. *Benefits of Derivatives.* Users of financial services often overlook important benefits from derivative products. In particular, the G-30 study argues

   > where financial markets are segmented nationally or internationally, whether due to market or regulatory barriers or to different perceptions of credit qualities in various markets, the use of derivatives has delivered unambiguous cost-savings for borrowers and higher yields for investors.

This assertion is supported by specific examples of the advantageous use of derivatives by corporations, government entities, institutional investors, and financial institutions.

3. *Derivative risk exposures.* While acknowledging that the management of derivative risk exposures is more complex than in the case of traditional banking products, the G-30 study states that these risks (essentially market, credit, operational, and legal) are not different in nature from those encountered in ordinary bank lending and securities business. Furthermore, a survey of industry practice conducted for the study (involving responses from eighty dealers and seventy-two end-users) suggests that most dealers have developed rigorous risk management systems for this purpose.
4. *Overall economic impact.* In examining the impact of derivatives on the overall economy, the study points out that academic research strongly indicates that derivatives trading either has no effect on, or reduces, volatility in underlying markets. On the positive side, it is argued that derivatives have expanded risk management techniques, while reducing transaction costs and increasing the liquidity of markets.

While presenting a positive case for derivatives, the G-30 study also makes twenty best practice recommendations for industry participants, focusing mainly on risk management. And although it does not examine regulatory issues in any detail (the whole question of capital adequacy is ignored) the study does make four additional recommendations aimed specifically at national authorities. In summary, policymakers should (1) recognize the benefits and promote the use of netting arrangements; (2) remove legal uncertainties relating to inter alia, the enforceability of derivative transactions and bilateral close-out netting arrangements; (3) amend tax laws that impede the use of derivatives; and (4) provide guidance on accounting and reporting of derivatives.

In the light of the G-30 study, where does the debate over derivatives now stand? It should be recognized first of all that the G-30 authors have performed a useful service in demonstrating through clear prose and intelligible examples the considerable benefits that derivatives transactions can offer to borrowers, lenders, investors, and intermediaries. Here the balance of the debate needed to be redressed. However, on the key issue of systemic risk the G-30 analysis is much less persuasive.

To begin with, official concerns about the growth, size, and concentration of the derivatives market cannot be easily dismissed. A total exchange-traded and over-the-counter (OTC) derivatives market has come from nowhere ten years ago to a position where its gross value exceeds the volume of banks' international lending (Table 7.2) and cannot reasonably be described as "unimposing compared to that of traditional financial activities" (the words of the G-30 authors).

Even when the market is netted down to reflect its replacement cost or market value, the credit exposures are hardly trivial. The G-30 study states that, measured in this way, the fifty leading US banks have an *average* OTC derivatives exposure equivalent to "only" 11 percent of their total assets or 120 percent of their total capital. However, since the study also reveals that the top eight US banks account for nearly 90 percent of this exposure, it is clear that some large banks have exposures far in excess of 11 percent of assets.

Some of the largest participants in the derivatives markets (for example, affiliates of insurance companies) are unregulated but the G-30 authors express confidence that potential counterparties can evaluate the risks of trading with unregulated entities and believe they should be free to do so. This view is in direct conflict with the Bank of England, which states in its recent derivatives review that "the unsupervised status of, for example, large swap players represents a supervisory hole at the very heart of the derivatives market" (Bank of England 1993, at 76).

The real point about the size and concentration of the derivatives market is surely this. No market can constitute a threat to financial stability merely by virtue of its size (witness the $220 trillion per annum foreign exchange market). However, when a certain category of activity represents (on whatever measurement basis) a major segment of some banks' overall business, that activity is certainly large enough to cause systemic problems if it is not conducted in a safe and proper manner.

This observation leads directly to the second major weakness of the G-30 study. The authors take comfort from the fact that their survey of market practitioners demonstrates high standards of risk control within the industry — "the risks associated with complexity, concentration, liquidity, and linkages between markets are manageable and being managed." The implication is that it is sufficient to rely on market participants themselves to regulate their activities. Yet this is surely too simplistic. For obvious reasons, responses to questionnaires are perhaps not the best way to gauge whether risks are being properly managed. This consideration apart, it only requires some large participants to behave imprudently for the stability of the entire market to be threatened. From this perspective it is insufficient that "most dealers have gone to great lengths to establish sophisticated techniques to manage their exposures" or that there is "nearly universal" (actually 85 percent) reliance on mark-to-market measures for risk management. In short, voluntary compliance with industry-led standards is no substitute for regulatory oversight, a point recently taken up by David Mullins, Vice Chairman of the US Federal Reserve Board (Mullins 1993).

The most serious weakness of the G-30 study, however, is that it does not appear to recognize, let alone address, the fundamental regulatory problem posed by banks' derivatives trading. Banks are subject to comprehensive regulation because if left to themselves *some* institutions will always incur risks that are excessive when judged by the damage which their failure can inflict on the financial system and society generally. If a major slice of the banking industry's business becomes too complex and opaque to regulate effectively, then there is a supervisory blind spot which aggressively managed institutions will undoubtedly exploit in order to escape from the regulatory constraints on risk-taking. Yet in the words of Paul Volcker's foreword to the G-30 study

> the authors believe that the amount of capital needed to support derivatives exposure is a matter of judgement for individual institutions depending on their appetite for risk and their ability to measure and manage it.

This is not a position that can be easily sustained. The stability of the financial system should not be jeopardized by those (perhaps few) institutions whose appetite for risk exceeds an appropriate level, or whose competence to manage risk falls below some appropriate standard. It may be useful to debate what those appropriate limits and standards should be and how they should be enforced; but at the end of the day risk-taking in the derivatives market, like other forms of banking risk, must surely be subject to regulatory constraints.

SUPERVISORY STANDARDS

The supervisory weaknesses revealed by the collapse of BCCI in 1991 prompted a reassessment of the Basle approach to banking regulation.[6] Two issues, in particular, had to be addressed. First, a central principle of the Basle Concordat is that the soundness of a bank cannot be properly assessed unless regulators can examine the totality of each banks' business worldwide through the technique of consolidation. Yet BCCI's complex structure enabled it not only to escape consolidated supervision but to confuse regulators deliberately by shuffling its assets between different jurisdictions.

Secondly, the BCCI collapse demonstrated the ease with which a fraudulent bank could exploit weakly regulated offshore centers in the absence of any machinery for ensuring the adequacy of supervisory standards. On this point the Bingham Report on BCCI concluded that "the need for some independent monitoring of supervisory standards is in my view clear" and that host supervisors "must be reassured by some form of independent verification that the home supervisor is really doing his job" (Bingham 1992, at 3.27).

The Basle Committee has attempted to meet these concerns by introducing the requirement that all banks should be supervised by a home-country authority "that capably performs consolidated supervision." However, the effectiveness of these new guidelines depends on the ability of national authorities to monitor each other's quality of supervision, so they can exercise an informed judgement as to whether banks from a particular jurisdiction should be excluded from their territory or subject to special restrictions imposed by the host authority.

Under the Basle guidelines one country is called upon to assess another country's quality of supervision on the basis of the latter's statutory powers, administrative practices and supervisory record. But there is no new multilateral machinery to assist in the monitoring process and it is difficult to see how bilateral relationships can provide adequate information about supervisory standards in particular jurisdictions. In order to overcome this problem, the Bank of England has proposed a system of peer group review under which each country's supervisory arrangements would be assessed by a panel of supervisory authorities from other countries. However, it is as yet unclear whether this kind of approach would have the broad support among non-G-10 countries that would be needed to make it viable. If the Basle approach proves inadequate to the task then there may eventually be pressure for the International Monetary Fund (IMF) to conduct formal supervisory reviews as part of its country surveillance procedures.[7]

Supervisory Responsibilities

The issue of supervisory standards is often discussed as if the supervisory function were the exclusive concern of regulatory authorities. Yet this is not the case. There is indeed a vigorous debate about the respective supervisory roles of regulators, market participants and bank auditors and there are also varying national practices in this area.[8]

At one extreme there are those who believe that systemic banking instability is typically the consequence of excessive regulation which raises expectations of official intervention and depositor protection in the event of bank failures. That expectation, so it is argued, undermines the disciplinary role of financial markets and removes the normal market penalties for excessive risk-taking. According to this view, bank safety and soundness would be enhanced if primary responsibility for monitoring banking risks were placed firmly with depositors. Under this regime bank regulation would be aimed mainly at enforcing stringent disclosure requirements so as to enable depositors to assess the relative riskiness of individual institutions.

The Reserve Bank of New Zealand's recent proposals on banking supervision come closest to this free-market model. In setting out its proposals the Reserve Bank explains its general approach in the following terms:

> . . . we see scope to shift the emphasis towards more market scrutiny and away from direct prudential regulation. We consider that regular scrutiny of registered banks by the marketplace can, and should, play an important role in promoting prudent banking practices. The maintenance of prudent banking practices can also be enhanced by increasing the involvement of private sector monitoring agents, such as external auditors and rating agencies. Prudential regulation and official monitoring have complementary roles to play, but are not the principal mechanism, nor substitutes for market-based private mechanisms. Our general thinking is that a rebalancing of policy which brings market-based mechanisms a little more to the fore, would enhance the overall soundness of the banking system, and at the same time afford banks greater scope to prudently respond to customer needs.[9]

In essence, the Reserve Bank's proposed regulatory regime consists of six key elements.

1. The Basle capital adequacy rules will continue to apply.
2. A US-style scheme of corrective action will be imposed, involving automatic penalties for banks with a capital deficiency.
3. Strengthened disclosure requirements for banks, including public disclosure of mandatory credit ratings.
4. A reduced role for prudential regulation by the central bank, with discontinuation of banks' existing prudential returns and residual monitoring based largely on banks' public disclosure statements.
5. An increase in the ability of the financial system to withstand individual failures by, for example, introducing a more robust payments system.
6. Limiting the role of the lender of last resort and reducing the perception that the government underwrites the prudential soundness of banks.

The underlying assumptions behind the Reserve Bank's new emphasis on market surveillance are that (1) depositors are in a position to make a realistic risk assessment of individual banks and (2) the market response to changed risk perceptions will not be seriously destabilizing. However, there must be serious doubts about both propositions.

First, it is optimistic to expect financial markets to form a realistic view of the financial standing of banks given the difficulties of assessing either the quality of banks' loan portfolios or the adequacy of provisioning policies (see above). The second area of doubt concerns the question of confidence. It is well established that when a bank runs into difficulties financial markets tend to respond by rationing credit. Put another way, the emergence of a large risk premium on a bank's borrowings may deter rather than attract potential lenders. Therefore market discipline may become destabilizing. Furthermore, if markets were heavily dependent on credit rating agencies for their risk assessments, a publicized downgrading could become the trigger for a bank run.

Notwithstanding these potential pitfalls, the New Zealand experiment in market-based supervision could provide important insights into banks' behavior in a deregulated setting. In the meantime there is continuing debate at both national and international levels about the most appropriate balance between official intervention and reliance on market discipline.

The controversy over market self-regulation versus official intervention extends to the role of auditors. There are two questions here: what obligations should bank auditors have towards the supervisory authorities; and should bank auditors owe a duty of care not only to shareholders but also to depositors, general creditors and other stakeholders? On the first point, the UK government has followed the recommendations of the Bingham Report by introducing proposals for imposing a statutory duty on bank auditors to report to the regulators information relevant to a bank's fulfilment of the authorization criteria set out in the Banking Act of 1987.

On the second point, UK case law has established that an auditor's duty of care is confined to shareholders.[10] This may leave depositors, as the predominant suppliers of funds to banks, in an unsatisfactory position since the interests of shareholders and depositors may not be the same. Furthermore, if auditors reported and owed a duty of care directly to depositors, the burden of supervision could be shifted away from the regulatory authorities. On the other hand, such a move would probably have to be accompanied by a ceiling on auditor legal liability in order to prevent the costs of professional indemnity insurance from becoming prohibitive.

To the extent that supervisory responsibility is retained by the regulatory authorities, there remains the issue of whether this responsibility should be discharged by the central bank or by a specialized regulatory agency. A recent analysis of this issue showed that the functions of banking regulation and supervision on the one hand, and monetary policy on the other, were separated in about one half of countries reviewed, but that because of the increasing scale of government support for failing banks there was a tendency for the regulatory/supervisory function to shift away from the central bank to an independent body more directly under political control (Goodhart and Schoenmaker 1993). However, there appears to be no overwhelming argument in favor of one particular approach, and, as the Bank of England has itself pointed out, where the supervisory and monetary functions are separated there still has to be very close cooperation between the two (Quinn 1993).

PROTECTIVE REGULATION

Having considered a number of international supervisory issues arising out of preventive regulation, this section addresses some key problems associated with protective regulation in the form of deposit insurance and lender of last resort arrangements.

Coordination or harmonization of national deposit insurance schemes is not currently on the Basle agenda. Nevertheless, the EC's adoption of a directive on deposit insurance, establishing a minimum level of deposit protection in all member states, raises the question of whether there is a need for a global initiative in this area. Alternatively, is it preferable to permit or even encourage a multiplicity of competing national schemes that widen depositors' choice?

The answer to this question is partly dependent on the policy underlying deposit insurance. If, as in the UK, deposit insurance is viewed mainly as a form of consumer protection then it would seem unnecessary to harmonize territorially based national deposit protection schemes. As the Bank of England recently put it

> So far there has been no international convergence of deposit insurance schemes. This is unsurprising given that they are generally a matter of social policy, which remains a national sovereign prerogative (Bank of England 1991, p.12).

If on the other hand, deposit insurance is intended to act as a safeguard against systemic risk, the case for harmonization is somewhat more persuasive. Because of the close interlinkages between financial markets, there is a common interest in the stabilization of the deposit base within the international banking system.

However, the case for harmonization also depends on whether or not national authorities seek to protect depositors in other ways. In particular, where there is a tradition sustaining banking *institutions* through officially organized support operations, deposit insurance may be largely redundant. Under such circumstances, harmonization achieves little and may indeed only serve to emphasize national differences in the handling of troubled banks.

A recent survey of bank failures demonstrates very clearly that, outside the US, deposit insurance arrangements are seldom invoked; the preference is to recapitalize failing institutions through combined official and private sector support (Goodhart and Schoenmaker 1993). That being the case, the prudential argument for harmonization of deposit insurance schemes would seem to be weak. Nevertheless, some degree of harmonization might be desirable if this were accompanied by arrangements designed to give home-country authorities an incentive to perform adequately their responsibility to undertake consolidated supervision (see below).

Prudential questions apart, it might be considered desirable to harmonize deposit insurance arrangements in order to avoid competitive distortions. But here again the issue is not straightforward. In the first place, the presence and extent of any competitive distortion will depend on precise arrangements for resourcing the insurance fund and on the level of premiums charged. For instance, it is quite possible that banks subject to a scheme offering relatively low insurance coverage for depositors could enjoy a competitive advantage over banks subject to a more protective scheme—if insurance premiums under the two schemes fail to reflect potential claims on the insurance fund. In other words, the *pricing* as well as the *coverage* of deposit insurance is crucial to the question of competitive distortion. Furthermore, even if both schemes were funded on an actuarial basis, depositors might well prefer to place their money with banks offering higher deposit interest rates, albeit with less insurance coverage.

A second complication, as explained above, is that deposit insurance may be largely redundant in those countries where other forms of protective intervention are the preferred method of dealing with bank failures. Under these circumstances, even identical insurance schemes identically priced may disguise serious competitive distortions associated with different levels of de facto protection for depositors. Put another way, competitive distortions arising from alternative protective arrangements can only be eliminated by standardizing national procedures for handling troubled banks, which is hardly a practical proposition at the present time.

In summary, the case for harmonizing deposit insurance schemes internationally, as the EC has done regionally, is not persuasive. Nevertheless it is interesting to note that while both the US and the EC have recently introduced new policy initiatives on deposit insurance, these moves are in opposite directions (Dale 1993b). The US authorities, faced with increasing financial instability, have sought to neutralize the "moral hazard" consequences of what is now seen as excessive protection for depositors. This they have done by introducing automatic penalties for banks with capital deficiencies; exposing depositors to greater risk through a limitation on the Federal Deposit Insurance Corporation's powers to protect uninsured depositors; and imposing a regime of risk-related deposit insurance premiums that seeks to penalize high-risk institutions. By contrast, the EC has adopted a directive that largely ignores the moral hazard issue by extending the scope of deposit protection within the Community without imposing any limit on the coverage offered by individual member states. While recognizing that a move towards common international standards of deposit protection may not be appropriate at this time, it is surely disquieting that different financial regions are following such divergent policies on deposit insurance.

Lender of Last Resort

Historically, central banks have preferred not to articulate their lender of last resort (LLR) policy, except in the broadest terms, on the principle that to do otherwise is tantamount to "showing the cat the way to the dairy." Yet from an international perspective cooperation in this area is important since in the absence of guidelines there is a danger that troubled institutions could be denied liquidity support in circumstances that might lead to systemic instability.

There are three key parameters governing the LLR function: the conditions that must be met before support is provided; the institutions that are eligible for such support; and the allocation of LLR responsibilities between national authorities.

The traditional role of the LLR is to provide short-term, secured credit to solvent banks experiencing temporary liquidity problems. However, there has been a growing tendency in recent years for governments, if not central banks, to provide capital infusions to insolvent institutions; the most notable recent example is the large-scale official support provided to Scandinavian banks (Table 7.3). The Bank of England, on the other hand, has stated that it will "not ordinarily" provide support to a bank facing solvency problems but it concedes that the distinction between solvency and liquidity problems is not always clear, that losses may therefore be incurred in exercising the LLR function and that its capital and reserves are therefore available for this purpose (Quinn 1993). In some other countries, notably the US, attempts are being made to curb the LLR function with a view to instilling greater discipline into financial markets, but no national banking system of any significance has been able to dispense altogether with LLR facilities.

There is also controversy as to which institutions should be eligible to receive LLR support. This issue has come to the fore with the fusion of banking and securities business within conglomerate corporate structures.[11] Where such businesses are combined within the same legal entity the LLR cannot avoid supporting the securities side of the operation as well as the bank. Where a bank's securities business is conducted in a separate subsidiary it may, in theory, be possible to segregate the risks and to confine the LLR role to the banking entity. However, in practice a bank would no doubt be obliged to support a troubled securities subsidiary or affiliate as a matter of commercial self-interest, a view upheld by the Swiss Federal Supreme Court in a recent legal ruling on the question.[12] If a bank is obliged to underwrite its securities unit's risks, then again the LLR is drawn into supporting securities activities.

Where securities and banking business is conducted by unrelated firms, the LLR function is typically confined to the banking sector. For instance, the Bank of England has argued that LLR assistance should not be extended to nonbanks, on the grounds that banks are distinct because their liabilities are uniquely volatile and only they supply the ultimate means of payment — money (Quinn 1993). Against this it could be argued that the liabilities of securities firms are also liquid, that banks are heavy lenders to the securities industry, and that the failure of a major securities firm could have destabilizing consequences for the banking system. It is no doubt partly for these reasons that the Japanese authorities have been reluctant to witness the collapse of large or even middle-ranking securities firms (witness the rescue of Yamaichi Securities in 1965 and Cosmo Securities in 1993).

The third aspect of the LLR function is the allocation of LLR responsibilities between national authorities. In the past this has been a source of contention, particularly in relation to banks' foreign subsidiaries (Dale 1984, p. 178). But now that the principle of consolidated supervision has been firmly endorsed by the Basle Committee, there would appear to be an implication that the foreign offices of multinational banks (whether branches or subsidiaries) should look to home-country authorities, not host-country authorities for LLR support. This division of responsibilities is unhelpful where, as in the case of BCCI, the home country has no LLR capacity and it may therefore be appropriate for host authorities to insist that a branch or subsidiary of a foreign bank should have access to an LLR in its country of origin as a precondition for authorization.

CONCLUSIONS

The initial focus of the Basle Committee was to reach agreement on the division of regulatory responsibilities between national jurisdictions. Subsequently attention shifted to the need to establish minimum supervisory standards. More recently concerns about competitive equality have been the driving force behind regulatory harmonization initiatives. Are we then moving towards a global framework for international bank regulation and supervision, or is there still scope for national autonomy in these matters?

In examining this question it is perhaps helpful to review alternative regimes aimed at safeguarding stability within the international banking system. Essentially, there are three possible approaches.

Firstly, countries hosting foreign banks (whether branches or subsidiaries) could rely on an incentive system designed to encourage home-country authorities to "capably perform consolidated supervision" (the key Basle requirement). The necessary incentive could be provided by making the home country responsible for insuring the worldwide deposits of both branches and subsidiaries of banks headquartered on its territory. This approach, which has been followed by the EC in respect of branches only (Commission of the European Communities 1992) would however involve international agreement on minimum standards of deposit protection in order to ensure that the incentive scheme operated effectively. Under this regime the cost of supervisory and regulatory failures would be at least partly borne by the authorities responsible for carrying out consolidated supervision.

A second approach would be to subsidiarize banks' foreign operations so

Table 7.3 Bank Support Operations in Selected Countries

Countries	Recipients			Total support[*]			Government support[†]	
	Number		Assets as Percent of Industry	As Percent of Recipients' Assets	As Percent of GDP	In billions of Local Currency Units	As Percent of Total Support	As Percent of Government deficit[‡]
	Absolute	As Percent of Industry						
Norway[§]								
1988	2	1.0	2.5	5.4	0.1	0.8	25.0	1.3[¶]
1989	7	3.8	3.9	16.5	0.6	3.9	14.6	6.5[¶]
1990	9	5.3	4.5	6.8	0.3	1.9	–	–
1991	17	10.5	59.4	4.1	2.0	14.0[#]	59.8[#]	298.9[#]
1992	11	7.4	69.8	2.8	1.7	12.0[#]	100.0	50.6[#]
Finland[**]								
1991 (individual)	28	6.3	15.7	3.7	0.9	4.6	84.5	13.2
1992 (individual)[††]	22	6.0	23.8	15.1	5.7	28.2	86.2	58.9
1992 (general)[‡‡]	135	33.0	92.4	1.1	1.6	7.9	100.0	19.2
Sweden[§§]								
1991	1	0.8	18.2	1.5	0.3	4.2	100.0	19.8
1992	3	2.7	26.9	7.1	2.0	29.3	100.0	26.0
1993[¶¶]	1	0.9	4.4	50.7	2.4	34.0	100.0	24.1
Japan								
1991–92[##]	2	0.3	0.1	3.3	0.0	28.0	–	–

[*]Total support provided to institutions in distress by private guarantee/insurance funds or by governments. It includes guarantees but excludes the acquisition of bad assets.
[†]Including the central bank.
[‡]Scaling factor only: the support granted represents in part the acquisition of assets whose eventual contribution to government revenues is difficult to quantify.
[§]Around one-eighth of the support in the form of guarantees.
[¶]Surplus.
[#]Excluding a concessionary loan programme for which all banks were eligible amounting to some NKr 15 billion.
[**]No support in the form of guarantees. Authorised support up to end-1993 not utilized by end-1992 amounts to some FM 25 billion, or around 5 percent of 1992 GDP.
[††]A single joint stock company was formed through a merger of forty-one savings banks, some of which were in distress.
[##]General capital injection.
[§§]Around one-third of the support in the form of guarantees.
[¶¶]Industry assets, total number of banks, GDP and government deficit in 1992.
[##]Only mergers assisted by the bank deposit insurance fund.
Source: Bank for International Settlements, 63rd Annual Report, June 1993, 172.

that the host authority could satisfy itself as to the financial soundness of foreign banks located within its jurisdiction, while also insulating local depositors from risks originating in the parent institution. This possibility has been examined both by the US and the UK authorities, who have concluded that mandatory incorporation of local offices of foreign banks would impose heavy costs on the international banking system without necessarily insulating local depositors from risks associated with the parent bank (Bank of England 1992).

The third approach is to harmonize both regulatory and supervisory standards in all major banking jurisdictions. This is the route currently being followed by the Basle Committee, which has sought to achieve regulatory harmonization through the Basle Accord and recent supplementary proposals. But there remain important areas of national discretion (notably on provisioning against loan losses) which create the potential for regulatory anomalies. Furthermore, harmonization of supervision remains a long way off. The BCCI collapse, which reflected supervisory rather than regulatory failures, has demonstrated very clearly that harmonization of regulation without harmonization of supervisory standards is of limited value, since capital adequacy requirements become meaningless when capital cannot be reliably measured or monitored. The logic of the present Basle approach therefore points to continuing harmonization initiatives aimed at a more complete alignment of both regulatory and supervisory arrangements.

These alternative regulatory regimes have been discussed from a prudential standpoint. However, as pointed out above, in recent years the objective of competitive equality has tended to displace prudential concerns as the main driving force behind international regulatory cooperation.

Within the international banking system the problem of competitive equality has three distinct dimensions. First, competitive equality may be applied to the relationship between rival financial centers. Here, there has been little attempt to establish a level playing field through harmonization initiatives. Instead, market pressures have brought about a gradual liberalization of monetary reserve requirements, stamp duties, withholding taxes, and other key regulatory determinants of the location of international financial activity. In this area we have seen global convergence through regulatory competition rather than regulatory coordination.

Second, the concept of competitive equality may refer to the relationship between national banking industries. The elimination of competitive distortions in this sense has been a major concern of the Basle Committee and a prime objective of the Basle Accord on capital adequacy. Yet it is worth noting that the potential for competitive distortions between banks of different nationality arises partly because of the official safety net (deposit insurance and LLR support) that underlies all banking systems. If the risks incurred by highly leveraged banks were reflected in higher default rates, correspondingly poor credit ratings, and higher risk premiums on deposit rates, then poorly capitalized institutions would enjoy no obvious competitive advantage over their more heavily capitalized counterparts. Viewed in this way, it is the official protection afforded to banks and their creditors, rather than differential capital requirements per se, that is responsible for competitive distortions.

Recent history suggests that most, though not all, national authorities are inclined to strengthen rather than weaken the official safety net (see above). Against this background it seems likely that the Basle Committee will come under pressure to extend the boundaries of regulatory harmonization in an attempt to remove any remaining sources of competitive inequality between banks of different nationality.

Competitive equality concerns the relationship between banks and nonbanks undertaking similar business. Here, the main focus is on securities operations, regulators having made it an explicit objective to establish a level playing field between institutions undertaking securities business in the belief that to allow securities firms to compete on more favorable regulatory terms than banks, or vice versa, would be both inequitable and damaging to the efficient operation of financial markets. The reasoning here is open to criticism, since the objectives of bank regulators and securities regulators are quite different. A troubled securities firm is expected to wind down its business, which can generally be accomplished quite rapidly because of the marketability of the firm's assets. By way of contrast, a bank is most emphatically not expected to respond to financial problems by going out of business since if it were to do so its nonmarketable assets could be sold quickly only at a heavy discount, which would leave depositors and other creditors exposed to losses. Therefore the main objective of bank regulators is to sustain banks as going concerns and in the event of capital impairment to allow them time to raise new capital, strengthen management, and conserve financial resources by, for instance, cutting dividend payments.

Partly for the above reasons, threats to bank solvency are more damaging socially than threats to the solvency of securities firms. Therefore there is a case for saying that securities business should be more highly regulated when undertaken by banks. By insisting on a level playing field regulators must *either* relax their preferred regulatory requirements for banks (as the Basle Committee has acknowledged in relation to its market risk proposals) or else impose needlessly stringent controls on nonbank securities firms. Either way, the emphasis on competitive equality gives rise to operational inefficiencies and social costs. If, at the same time, banks and their creditors are given official LLR protection that is denied to nonbank securities firms, there is a further inducement for securities business to be routed through the banking sector.

In summary, because banking is a protected industry national differences in regulatory arrangements and supervisory standards are not reflected in banks' funding costs. Uneven prudential regulation may therefore give rise not only to systemic concerns but to concerns about competitive equality between rival national banking industries. It is against this background that the Basle Committee has shifted its focus from regulatory cooperation to regulatory harmonization. To date these harmonization initiatives have not prevented the emergence of potentially important regulatory anomalies. In the case of the 1988 Basle Accord the unitary risk-weighting for commercial loans and the scope for divergent provisioning practices are hardly consistent with the notion of common capital adequacy standards. The Basle Committee's proposals on market risk fail to address the concepts of diversification and liquidity which have a key bearing on capital adequacy; and the Committee's proposals on interest rate risk develop a methodology for measurement without considering an appropriate regulatory response. The policy of partial harmonization has therefore resulted in important gaps which, over time, may have to be addressed. On the supervisory side the Basle Committee is still feeling its way, the major question here being whether a more formal mechanism for assessing national supervisory standards may have to be introduced in due course. These issues, together with intractable problems associated with the attempt to create a level playing field for banks and nonbanks, are more than enough to fill the regulatory agenda until the end of the millennium.

ENDNOTES

1. Schaefer (1992) examines the case for capital regulation from a finance theory standpoint.
2. See Cantor and Johnson (1992). However the fact that banks issue capital in excess of the Basle requirements is not necessarily inconsistent with the view that they are capital constrained. For one thing, the Basle ratios are minimum standards and individual banks may be subject to national requirements above the minimum. Secondly, banks may themselves wish to maintain a cushion of capital above the regulatory minimum so as to avoid future supervisory constraints.
3. For a critique of the building-block approach see Breeden (1992).
4. On the issue of risk segregation see Dale (1991).
5. The discussion of derivatives in this section draws on Dale (1993c). See also IMF (1993), Deutsche Bundesbank (1993).
6. For an assessment of the national and international supervisory response to BCCI see Dale (1993a).
7. On this point see Office of the Comptroller of the Currency (1991).
8. For a general discussion of these issues see US Treasury (1991).
9. Cited in *Financial Times Financial Regulation Report*, 1993, 3.
10. In *Al Saudi Banque v. Clark Pixley* (1989) it was held that the company's auditors owed no duty of care to lending banks. In *Caparo Industries v. Dickman* (1990)

the House of Lords determined that the auditor's duty of care is confined to the general body of shareholders.

11. For a general discussion of the LLR implications of the mixing of banking and securities business see Dale (1991).
12. For a summary of the court's decision see IBCA (1991).

REFERENCES

Bank of England. (1991) *Response to Treasury and Civil Service Committee, Issues Relating to BCCI*, September.

———. (1992) *Further Response to the Treasury and Civil Service Committee's Fourth Report on Banking Supervision and BCCI*, October.

———. (1993) *Derivatives: Report of an Internal Working Group*, April.

Bingham. (1992) *Inquiry into the Supervision of the Bank of Credit and Commerce International*. London, HMSO, October.

Breeden, R. (1992) 'SEC letter to IOSCO on capital adequacy.' *International Securities Regulation Report*, November 3, 11–12.

Cantor, R. and Johnson, R. (1992) 'Bank capital ratios, asset growth and the stock market.' *Quarterly Review of the Federal Reserve Bank of New York*, **17** (3) 10–24.

CBRSP. (1975) *Report to the Governors on the Supervision of Banks' Foreign Establishments*, September.

———. (1983) *Principles for the Supervision of Banks's Foreign Establishments*, May.

———. (1988) *International Convergence of Capital Measurement and Capital Standards*, July.

———. (1990) *Supplement to the Concordat: the ensuring of adequate information flows between banking supervisory authorities*, April.

———. (1991) *Proposals for the inclusion of general provisions — general loan loss reserves in capital*, February.

———. (1992) *Minimum standards for the supervision of international banking groups and their cross-border establishments*, June.

———. (1993) *The Prudential Supervision of Netting, Market Risks and Interest Rate Risk*, April.

Commission of the European Communities. (1992) 'Proposal for a council directive on deposit guarantee schemes.' *Official Journal of the European Communities*, **(C163)**, June.

Cooke, P. (1981) 'Developments in co-operation among bank supervisory authorities.' *Bank of England Quarterly Bulletin*, **21**(2), June.

Dale, R. (1984) *The Regulation of International Banking*, Cambridge, UK, Woodhead-Faulkner.

———. (1991) 'Regulating banks' securities activities: a global assessment.' *Journal of International Securities Markets*, Winter, 277–290.

———. (1993a) 'Bank regulation after BCCI.' *Journal of International Banking Law*, January, 8–17.

———. (1993b) 'Deposit insurance: US-EC policy clash.' *Journal of International Securities Markets*, Spring/Summer, 5–15.

———. (1993c) 'How risky are derivatives?' *Journal of International Banking Law*, September, 345–348.

Deutsche Bundesbank. (1993) 'Off-balance-sheet activities of German banks.' *Monthly Report*, October, 45–67.

Goodhart, C. and Schoenmaker, D. (1993) 'Institutional separation between supervisory and monetary agencies.' *Special Paper No. 52*, LSE Financial Markets Group, April.

Group of Thirty. (1993) *Derivatives: Practices and Principles*, New York, July.

IBCA. (1991) *Credit Suisse Loses its Supreme Court Appeal*, London, January.

IMF. (1993) *The Growing Involvement of Banks in Derivative Finance — A Challenge for Financial Policy, Systematic Issues and International Finance*, Washington, D.C., August.

Jones, D. and King, K. (1992) 'An analysis of the implementation of prompt corrective action.' *Finance and Economic Discussion Series, No. 204*, Federal Reserve Board, Washington, D.C., July.

Lamfalussy, A. (1993) *Capital Allocation and Risk Management.* Remarks at the International Monetary Conference, Stockholm, June.

Mullins, D. (1993) *Remarks on the Global Derivatives Study Sponsored by the Group of Thirty.* Before the International Swaps and Derivatives Association, New York, July 28.

Office of the Comptroller of the Currency. (1991) Evidence submitted to the House of Commons Treasury and Civil Service Committee.

Quinn, B. (1993) *The Bank of England's Role in Prudential Supervision.* Speech before the conference organized by Westminster and City Programmes, 'Re-examining City Regulation,' London, March 24.

Schaefer, S. (1992) 'Financial regulation: the contribution of the theory of finance,' in J. Fingleton and D. Schoenmaker, (eds.) *The Internationalisation of Capital Markets and the Regulatory Response*. London, Graham and Trotman.

US Treasury. (1991) *Modernizing the Financial System*, Washington, D.C., February.

8
International Securities Markets Regulation

BENN STEIL*

An American broker in London buys German "Bunds" for a Mexican client from a Japanese trading house in Paris and clears the trade in Brussels. This sort of story line is not simply plausible, but is on the verge of becoming commonplace.

The securities industry features standardized products, trivial distance costs, and exceptionally mobile production factors. With the removal of technological and political barriers to international trade, the industry has been able to adapt at impressive speed to the enormous international investment opportunities that have been created. Regulation naturally tends to lag behind the markets, but the gap is growing at an accelerating pace. This is in many ways a very welcome development for market participants, who have long felt shackled by regulations perceived as outdated and misguided. On the other hand, market integrity and stability are essential to the industry's continued prosperity, and few would argue with the principle that regulation must also adapt to cross-border market integration.

In this chapter, we examine the complex and often controversial area of international securities markets regulation. In the first section, we discuss the formal institutional umbrella under which national regulators cooperate and coordinate their activities. In the second section, we provide a detailed

*Funding for the research from The Leverhulme Trust and the Institute of Fiscal and Monetary Policy of the Japanese Ministry of Finance is gratefully acknowledged.

International Financial Market Regulation. Edited by B. Steil

analysis of four major international issues confronting securities regulators. These are:

- Capital adequacy
- Derivatives
- Clearance and settlement
- Multinational disclosure and accounting

This list should certainly not be considered exhaustive, but merely illustrative of the types of problems posed by cross-border market integration. In the concluding section, we look broadly at the question of regulatory harmonization in light of political as well as economic realities.

THE INTERNATIONAL ORGANIZATION OF SECURITIES COMMISSIONS

A large number of private sector, international, and intergovernmental organizations are actively involved in the area of what may loosely be called "international securities markets regulation." Only the European Community (EC) has achieved a supranational legislative umbrella for international market operations, and such an arrangement is highly unlikely to be duplicated by other regional groupings or extended into a multilateral setting for the forseeable future. Formal cooperation among national regulators is slowly being advanced, however, through the International Organization of Securities Commissions (IOSCO).

IOSCO was established as an inter-American organization in 1974. Originally called the Inter-American Association of Securities Commissions and Similar Organizations, the institution was initiated by the World Bank and the Organization of American States in order to assist in the development of Latin American securities markets. Its activities during its first decade of existence were limited to annual conferences. The decision to become a global organization was taken in 1983, and the first annual conference held outside North America was in Paris in 1986. It was at this conference that the decision was taken to create a secretariat, and Canadian Paul Guy was named to the new post of secretary general. It took several years more until the organization could claim at least to comprise all the world's major markets; Japan and Germany were only admitted as members in 1988.

IOSCO Functions and Structure

The member agencies of IOSCO have proclaimed four broad aims for the organization:

- To cooperate together to ensure a better regulation of the markets, on the domestic as well as on the international level in order to maintain just and efficient securities markets.
- To exchange information on their respective experiences in order to promote the development of domestic markets.
- To unite their efforts to establish standards and an effective surveillance of international securities transactions.
- To provide mutual assistance to ensure the integrity of the markets by a rigorous application of the standards and by effective enforcement against offences.[1]

IOSCO should not be seen as a sort of Basle Committee for securities regulators.[2] Both the organizational structure and operating procedures of the eleven-member Basle Committee are extremely opaque, reflecting the Committee's desire to operate secretly, outside the glare of public scrutiny. This has undoubtedly contributed to its ability to produce relatively detailed international agreements and to promote a reasonable semblance of compliance among members. IOSCO, in contrast, is a rapidly growing, loose-knit, global organization comprising 110 regulatory, self-regulatory, and market "development" organizations, sixty-eight of which are full voting members.[3] Its general secretariat is extremely small, having very little formal influence over the activities of the Organization. Formal IOSCO agreements, which appear in the form of resolutions of the Presidents Committee, can only be concluded once a year at the annual conference. Resolutions are approved by majority voting in the Presidents Committee,[4] but must first achieve consensus in the Technical Committee or Development Committee.

Eight formal resolutions have been adopted as of the end of the 1993 annual conference: these cover principles of international business conduct (1990), money laundering (1992), international auditing standards (1992), supervision of financial conglomerates (1992), clearance and settlement (1992), international accounting standards (1993),[5] coordination between cash and derivatives markets (1993), and transnational securities and futures fraud (1993). Tremendous media attention was focused on the organization's unsuccessful attempt to agree on a resolution endorsing minimum international capital standards for securities firms at the 1992 conference. As we discuss further on, the economic significance of this particular failure has been greatly exaggerated, although the implications for how IOSCO is seen *vis-à-vis* the Basle Committee—within the organization as well as outside it — were substantial.

It is unfortunate that the success of international organizations is frequently measured by their ability to secure what are nominally considered "binding" agreements or resolutions. It is much more difficult to measure success in terms of informal promotion of cross-border information sharing, cooperation, and coordination of activities, although this may in fact be of considerably greater importance than achieving formal consensus. The emphasis on harmonizing market rules and standards, characteristic of the EC approach, may serve to entrench *existing* practice rather than promote *best* practice, and all too often brings to the fore national political concerns rather than economic imperatives.[6] The work of the IOSCO Technical Committee and the IOSCO Development Committee often goes unnoticed when it does not result in an official resolution, but much of it has been invaluable in facilitating the cataloging and dissemination of regulatory information. This information may then be used as an aid in cross-border surveillance and enforcement operations, and in adjusting national regulations and practices in light of the accumulated experience of other markets.

The Technical Committee is, putatively, comprised of the securities agencies of the world's most developed markets. The controversial addition of Mexico in 1993, bringing the total membership to fifteen, is raising concerns about the Committee's size and accession criteria. The Technical Committee is where most of the organization's knottiest conflicts arise, since it is the locus of debate on the establishment of common rules and standards for securities markets operations. The Committee's specific mandate is to study regulatory problems related to international securities transactions and to propose appropriate solutions. The Committee currently has five Working Parties, composed of representatives of the member organizations: these cover multinational disclosure and accounting, regulation of secondary markets, regulation of market intermediaries, enforcement and exchange of information, and investment management. The Development Committee is comprised of IOSCO members regulating so-called "emerging" securities markets. Its primary objective is to promote the development of such markets, in particular through the collection and exchange of information and the implementation of common standards. It has had considerably more success with the former task. The Committee presently has forty-six members, including the director of the Central Capital Market Department of the International Finance Corporation (an arm of the World Bank). Six Working Groups are presently operating under its auspices, covering clearing and settlement, internationalization, disclosure, institutional investors, privatization, and derivatives. Reports and studies of Technical and Development Committee Working Parties and Groups are published and distributed at each annual conference.

MAJOR ISSUES IN INTERNATIONAL REGULATION

In this section, we examine four major issues of concern to regulators in light of the rapid growth in cross-border activities — capital adequacy, derivatives, clearance and settlement, and multinational disclosure and accounting.

Capital Adequacy

Banks

Concern began rising in the early 1980s over the relatively weak capital positions of major international banks, providing the impetus for the Basle Committee on Banking Supervision to work toward the establishment of minimum international capital standards for banks. The result was the Basle Accord, reached in July 1988, which devised a framework for measuring regulatory capital and set minimum capital standards for banks in the Group of Ten (G-10) countries and Luxembourg.[7] The accord mandated a minimum 8 percent ratio of "recognized" capital to "risk-weighted" credit exposures by the end of 1992.

While risks to bank solvency derive from a number of sources, the Basle Accord focused on linking capital requirements specifically to the *credit risks* borne by banks in the building of their loan portfolios. The exclusive focus on credit risk and the methodology developed to measure it have been the subject of considerable criticism,[8] although the Accord was undoubtedly valuable in focusing widespread attention on the increasingly *international* nature of systemic risk in financial markets. The Basle Committee has attempted to address concerns over the limitations of the 1988 Accord by issuing a proposed set of revisions in May 1993. These covered the market risk of equity and debt securities, foreign exchange risk, interest rate risk, and bilateral netting arrangements for over-the-counter (OTC) derivatives positions.

Securities Firms

Pressure began building shortly after the signing of the Accord for a similar international agreement on minimum capital requirements for securities firms. From the perspective of the Basle Committee, there was concern that extending capital requirements to cover market risks stemming from banks' securities activities would, in the absence of a coordinated move with securities regulators, induce a shift in securities activities from banks to less-regulated securities firms. Simultaneously, there was growing concern within IOSCO that international capital standards were needed for securities firms, regardless of further developments in international banking regulation. The IOSCO Technical Committee released a paper in September 1989 drawing attention to the possibility of "serious disruption to the markets" from the failure of a securities firm in an "unregulated environment," and calling for "a common conceptual framework regarding the capital requirements for securities firms."[9] The push to move from the "conceptual framework" outlined in the paper to a formal IOSCO endorsement of minimum international capital standards was perhaps fuelled as much by organizational politics as by perceived economic imperatives. The professional standing of various IOSCO personalities stood to benefit from the production of an international agreement comparable to the Basle Accord.

The IOSCO Technical Committee and the Basle Committee began formal coordination of their efforts in 1991. All members of the Technical Committee were prepared to back the Basle Committee's so-called "building-block" approach to determining capital requirements for debt securities, but the Technical Committee was split on the appropriateness of this approach for equities. The building-block methodology attempts, in principle, to distinguish between the risk of a specific equity and the risk of a broad market movement. It achieves this in practice through a rough-and-ready formula which applies separate risk weights to the *gross* equity portfolio position (long and short positions added together) and the *net* position in a well-diversified portfolio of highly liquid equities (where long and short positions are treated as fully offsetting). A capital charge is then calculated for the *gross position* (intended to cover the specific risk of each individual security position) and the *net position* (intended to cover the market risk of the portfolio as a whole); these two charges are then added together to produce the total required amount of "regulatory capital" for the firm. Recognized regulatory capital for securities firms generally includes shareholder equity and a limited amount of subordinated debt.

Many readers familiar with portfolio theory will undoubtedly find the building-block methodology crude and simplistic for measuring the risk of an equity portfolio. The UK Securities and Futures Authority (SFA) and Securities and Investment Board (SIB) do in fact apply a simplified Markowitz portfolio approach, but other national regulators use some variation on the building-block approach or the so-called comprehensive approach used in the US and Japan. There are many reasons why portfolio theory is not more widely used, but the main ones are that the inputs are considered difficult to estimate and that direct applications of the theory are believed not adequately to account for "systematic risk," or risk which cannot be diversified away.[10]

While differences remain between the Technical Committee and the Basle Committee over a number of specific areas,[11] the split within the Technical Committee itself is far more serious. The US Securities and Exchange Commission (SEC) in particular has been steadfastly opposed to the building-block approach, insisting that even the more conservative versions would not yield capital requirements capable of ensuring sufficient liquidity in the face of a major market disruption. The proposal supported by the UK and France, known as "2+8," would mandate a 2 percent capital charge on the gross equity position plus an 8 percent charge on the net position. This means that a completely balanced portfolio of longs and shorts would yield the minimum capital charge of 2 percent, while a portfolio of all long positions, with no offsets, would yield the maximum capital charge of 10 percent. The IOSCO compromise proposal, known as "4+8," would raise the gross capital charge to 4 percent. Capital charges under this proposal would therefore range from 4 percent to 12 percent. The SEC believes that the netting provisions in both these proposals are far too liberal, and that the assumption that offsetting positions will move in lockstep and remain equally liquid in distressed markets is inappropriate. The SEC further believes that the netting provisions would encourage firms in financial difficulty to start adding short positions merely as a means of reducing capital requirements. They have therefore stated that any compromise would have to include a minimum "floor" flat rate percentage for all equity portfolios, which would have the effect of greatly reducing the deductions to capital requirements which firms would be able to claim by having offsetting positions. The SEC has made two counter proposals. Under its preferred arrangement, there would be a basic minimum 15 percent charge on initial positions plus 15 percent on any offset position exceeding 25 percent of the initial position. As can be seen from Figure 8.1, the SEC proposals treat netting with a far more sceptical eye than the 2+8 and 4+8 proposals. Beyond a certain point, increasing the offset position will *increase* capital requirements under the SEC proposals, while it will always *reduce* them under the building-block proposals.

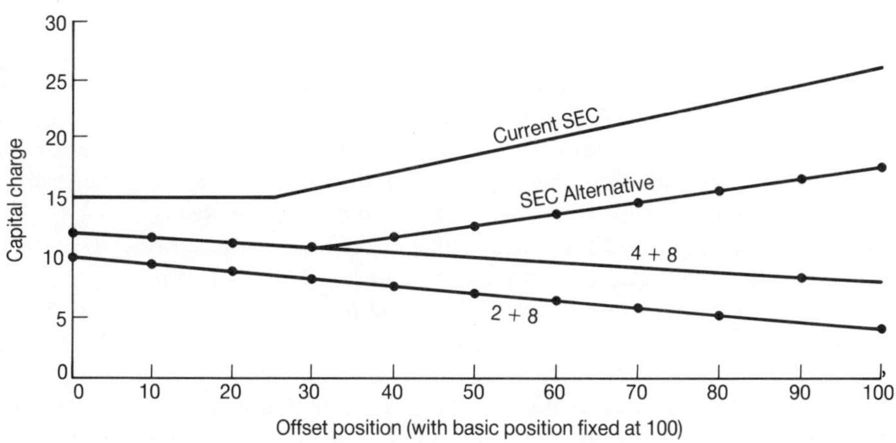

Figure 8.1 IOSCO Minimum Capital Standards. Assumes a well-diversified highly liquid portfolio. Source: Albrecht (1993).

The controversy came to a head at the IOSCO annual meeting in October 1992 in the form of an open row between the then SEC and Technical Committee chairman, Richard Breeden, and a number of his Technical Committee colleagues. Breeden insisted that the SEC would not endorse a minimum standard which could "have led to a systemic catastrophe in 1987,"[12] while SIB chairman Andrew Large refuted this claim and stressed that the SEC was not being asked to alter the US domestic standard. No agreement was reached in 1992, and the issue was virtually wiped off the IOSCO agenda in 1993. The immediate effect of the very public failure to reach an accord was a purely political one. The ambitions of those in the Technical Committee and the General Secretariat who wished to see IOSCO assume the role of an international rule-making body, comparable to the Basle Committee, were dealt a severe blow. The SEC's forthright rebuttal of the need for harmonized capital standards well illustrated the difficulties in establishing effective multilateral regimes when the dominant actor sees no benefit from abandoning unilateralism.

The Economics of Capital Standards

Systemic risk. The perceived need for minimum capital standards in banks and securities firms is based on the primary assumption that there are serious *systemic risks* in the operation of financial markets. If this is so, a strong case can be made for regulators taking measures to reduce the risk of liquidity or solvency problems in financial intermediaries, since these are liable to be spread contagiously through settlement and payment systems and panic withdrawals of investor funds.

If the famous Modigliani–Miller theorem were actually to hold, then a firm's weighted average cost of capital would be independent of its capital/asset ratio, and the firm would suffer no cost from the regulator setting capital standards so high that solvency risk would be virtually zero. There are many reasons why the Modigliani–Miller theorem may not hold in the real world, and, whatever the most salient ones may be in a given jurisdiction, firms do not generally accept the proposition that increasing their capital/asset ratios is costless. Assuming that the firms are correct, regulators are faced with the difficult task of defining capital standards which balance the need to mitigate systemic risk with the need to avoid unduly raising operating costs in the financial services industry. With financial services becoming an increasingly international business, concerns over systemic risks are naturally spilling over into the international regulatory fora, and the difficulties inherent in balancing the costs and benefits of capital requirements are being highlighted in the EC, Basle, and IOSCO debates.

Level playing fields. The problems involved in devising appropriate capital standards are compounded by the fact that securities markets activities are now undertaken by a number of different types of financial institution. The regulatory barriers between banking and securities business are breaking down, and are indeed irrelevant in countries such as Germany with universal banking systems. Many regulators and commentators are therefore claiming that international capital standards must be set so as to create a "level playing field" between banks and nonbank investment firms dealing in securities. This objective is consistent with a widely held view that regulators should be regulating "activities" rather than "institutions," so that two institutions engaged in an identical activity should, in respect of that activity, be subject to identical regulation.

This view underpins the EC's Capital Adequacy Directive, although it cannot be upheld on other than political grounds.[13] Capital standards, as we discussed above, are imposed as a means of limiting systemic risk. The problem with the level playing field concept is that an institution's trading book, viewed in isolation from its other activities, is not the relevant measure of its contribution to systemic risk. The performance of an institution's trading book influences its ability to carry out its other activities; activities which differ between bank and nonbank investment firms, and which have very different implications for the stability of the financial system.

The composition of bank asset and liability bases can differ markedly from that of securities firms. Banks' primary assets are generally illiquid loans, rather than liquid securities, while a major component of their noncapital funding derives from retail deposits which can be withdrawn on demand. The nonmarketability of a large segment of assets means that banks in financial distress cannot be wound down quickly without jeopardizing the claims of depositors and other creditors. At the same time, this ever present risk to depositors means that any hint of financial difficulty has the potential to provoke a contagious withdrawal of funds from the entire system. While the risk of contagion may be reduced dramatically through government deposit insurance, this comes only at the cost of encouraging excessive risk-taking particularly by financially tenuous institutions.[14] Combine these bank-specific risks with their exclusive direct access to national payment systems and it becomes clear that banks do not merit the same type of regulation as securities firms. The level playing field principle cannot be justified so long as banks are playing with wider boundaries.

Securities firms perform only a subset of the financial activities performed by universal banks, and forbearance from engaging in the full range mitigates their contribution to systemic risk. Securities firms are less liable to large and rapid withdrawals of core nonequity funding, are much less reliant on a lender-of-last-resort function, require no government insurance guarantees, and are a step removed from the payment system. Regulatory capital therefore plays a very different role in banks and securities firms. For banks, sufficient *permanent* capital is required to meet the regulatory imperative of keeping them solvent in difficult circumstances, since the systemic implications of bank failures are generally more serious than those of securities firm failures. For securities firms, on the other hand, more reliance on *temporary* capital, such as subordinated debt, is appropriate given their greatly fluctuating needs for capital and the relative ease with which regulators can wind them down without a significant systemic impact.[15]

These difficulties with the level playing field concept have important implications for the setting of international capital standards. From an economic perspective, nonbank investment firms require less stringent capital regulation than universal banks. More generous provisions for the use of subordinated debt as regulatory capital, for example, are appropriate for nonbanks. To the extent that universal banks find more stringent capital standards costly, this would merely reflect the fact that when systemic costs are properly accounted for, banks are inherently higher-cost producers of securities services. Setting aside any political damage which IOSCO or its members may have incurred by the failure to reach an agreement on minimum international capital standards, the economic imperative for achieving such an agreement should be considered low.

Derivatives

There is no other single issue that seems to worry and baffle regulators, in equal measure, quite as much as the explosion in derivatives trading. Since 1992, studies of the derivatives markets have been undertaken by, among others, the New York Federal Reserve, the US Securities and Exchange Commission (SEC), the US Commodity Futures Trading Commission (CFTC), the US General Accounting Office (GAO), the Bank of England, the Bank for International Settlements (BIS), the International Organization of Securities Commissions (IOSCO), and the Group of Thirty (G-30).

Derivative contracts comprise primarily futures, options, and swaps, whose values are "derived" from the prices of underlying assets, such as equities, bonds, currencies, and commodities. Most of the trading in derivatives is accounted for by interest rate contracts, volume in which has risen spectacularly since 1988 (Figure 8.2). The US Federal Reserve estimated that the total notional value of derivatives contracts in the US banking system was approximately $7 trillion in the first quarter of 1993, while the total credit exposure (based on replacement value) was about $140 billion. Although this level of credit exposure should not be of great concern if it were spread over the entire industry, it must be recognized that approximately 90 percent of it is concentrated in just *six* US banks.

There are a number of critical reasons for the marked rise in derivatives

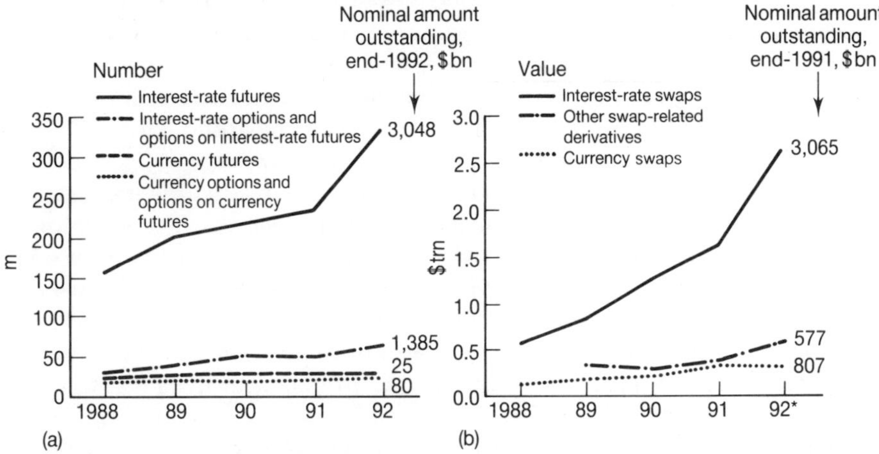

Figure 8.2 Derivatives Contracts Traded (a) On Exchanges and (b) Over the Counter. *First Half at Annual Rate.
Source: *The Economist*, June 26, 1993; BIS.

activity over the past fifteen years. A significant early impetus was surges in interest rate and exchange rate volatility in the 1970s, which gave rise to a demand for new risk-reduction products. The famous Black–Scholes option pricing formula, published in 1973, and the numerous refinements in valuation models which followed provided the essential technical tools to support the burgeoning industry. Tremendous advances in the areas of information processing and telecommunications provided the necessary technological infrastructure. Rapid technological improvements relentlessly drove down trading costs, and in turn made new techniques in risk reduction, financing cost reduction, yield enhancement, and arbitrage cost-effective. Finally, deregulatory initiatives throughout the developed markets fuelled the integration of different product markets and national markets, and thrust questions of regulatory implications into the international arena. In what follows, we examine the major issues of concern to regulators, and how these are and are not presently being addressed.

Market Risk

Market risk refers to the risk of an unanticipated change in the value of an open position deriving from a change in the price of the underlying asset. The oft-cited Group of Thirty (G-30) derivatives study (1993) rightly emphasizes that this risk is generally managed on a portfolio basis, meaning that the market exposure risk of major derivatives users is far less than is often implied by commentators referring simply to the notional value of outstanding contracts. Of course, hedging asset portfolios as a means of reducing market risk implies taking on more credit risk, and this fact cannot be ignored by market participants or regulators.

Putting aside the credit risk problem for the moment, there remains a huge question mark as to how the market risk of a hedge portfolio is actually to be measured. Consider an options portfolio. In a world which operated according to pure Black–Scholes principles, the only risk with which a trader would need to concern himself is *delta risk*, or the risk that the value of the options portfolio changes with the value of the underlying asset. In practice, however, maintaining a delta-neutral options book requires constantly rehedging the position, since the delta *itself* changes with movements in the value of the underlying (*gamma risk*). Option values also change with shifts in expected volatility (*kappa* or *vega risk*) as well as with the simple passage of time (*theta risk*).

Since traders cannot rehedge their positions from moment to moment, they try to neutralize certain risks while limiting others to "acceptable" levels, which are generally defined according to statistical confidence levels. So long as the markets operate according to the principles assumed by a trader's risk management models, the market risks the trader takes on are, statistically speaking, clearly and unambiguously quantifiable. If his market assumptions are wrong, however, the risk measures he relies upon may considerably understate the actual risk he is bearing.

How significant is the risk that traders' risk management models are wrong? Some instruments involve risks which are not traded in the market, and for these instruments "risk model risk" is considerable.[16] For those instruments which do involve directly hedgable risks, moderately underestimating volatility may result in considerable losses, but is unlikely to generate serious liquidity or solvency problems. In abnormal market conditions, however, such as those experienced during the 1992 European Exchange Rate Mechanism (ERM) crisis, the risks are far more serious. In September of that year, currency and interest rate volatility surged to exceptionally high levels, while a number of governments raised overnight borrowing rates to over 100 percent. Many institutions engaged in dynamic hedging were caught with portfolios hedged on the basis of grossly inappropriate risk models, and were forced to scramble in the markets to cover themselves.[17] Unfortunately, when almost all major market participants are trying to do the same thing at the same time, market risk becomes overwhelmed by *liquidity risk*. The combination of the two produced serious losses at a number of major institutions.

Liquidity Risk

The use of dynamic hedging models relies fundamentally on the existence of liquid derivatives markets, yet widespread use of such strategies can actually have the effect of undermining the liquidity of the markets. Often these strategies entail selling securities specifically when prices are falling, meaning that waves of sell orders hit the markets simultaneously, thereby collapsing prices and breaking down the market. This is precisely what happened during the ERM crisis, when market liquidity dried up and institutions were left holding massively exposed derivatives books. In the aftermath of the crisis, the then BIS general manager, Alexandre Lamfalussy, stated that he believed bank senior management were generally unaware of the limitations of their traders' risk management systems, and severely criticized derivatives specialists for not making explicit the risks they run in their activities. Market risk and liquidity risk are inextricably linked; traders across the industry tend to use very similar risk management systems — many rely on the same off-the-peg technology — and widespread miscalculation of market risk invariably implies liquidity risk in a market where too many large traders are looking to make the same corrections simultaneously.

Credit Risk

Credit risk derives from the fact that counterparties may fail to meet their contractual obligations. In the exchange-traded derivatives markets, positions are marked to market daily, while centralized clearinghouses protect members against the risk of any one participant failing to meet commitments. In the OTC markets, there is presently no central clearinghouse, and credit exposures are difficult to measure owing to the fact that contracts are customized rather than standardized. The most significant market innovation which has developed specifically to address the credit risk problem is the establishment of separately capitalized triple-A rated derivatives subsidiaries. Three US securities houses— Merrill Lynch, Salomon Brothers, and Goldman Sachs — have established such subsidiaries to support their growing swaps business, and a number of other institutions are likely to follow suit. Swap market quotes are now generally applicable only to triple-A counterparties, and lower-rated players will often face wider spreads. The G-30 derivatives study found that dealers have certainly not abandoned more traditional means of managing credit exposures: two-thirds of dealers surveyed were prepared to accept cash or securities as collateral, and over three-quarters were willing to accept third-party guarantees.

There remain many difficulties in establishing the credit-worthiness of a counterparty, since it is generally impossible for participants to know the parameters of the huge and complex derivatives positions often being carried by others. Referring specifically to this problem, Lamfalussy has called for standardized disclosure of off-balance-sheet positions. The US Financial Accounting Standards Board (FASB) has recently adopted a number of new rules designed to increase disclosure of derivatives positions, and the International Accounting Standards Committee (IASC) is looking to adopt a new International Accounting Standard for financial instruments. In addition to better disclosure, credit risk can also be significantly reduced through netting arrangements: the International Swap Dealers Association (ISDA) estimates that bilateral netting reduces swap dealers' credit exposures by 40–60 percent.[18] The problem with relying on netting arrangements, however, is that they often involve a significant degree of *legal risk*.

Legal Risk

Netting is a legally recognized practice in the US, but in other jurisdictions it is generally not clear how such agreements would stand up in a bankruptcy court. This problem was a subject of the 1990 BIS study commonly known as the "Lamfalussy Report" (Bank for International Settlements 1990). Other examples of significant legal risk are also to be found in major markets. In the US, the Commodity Exchange Act prohibits off-exchange futures trading. The CFTC officially exempted swaps and related derivatives from most of the Act's provisions in February 1993, but many restrictions apply. If a major OTC derivative instrument were suddenly declared to be in violation of the Act, all such contracts would immediately become legally unenforceable. There also remain dangerous ambiguities over what sorts of customers should and should not be allowed to deal in derivatives. In the UK, the country's highest court, the law lords, ruled in January 1991 that local government councils had no legal authority to enter into interest rate swap agreements. Over one thousand swap agreements involving 130 authorities were immediately annulled, causing losses at seventy-eight UK and foreign banks amounting to hundreds of millions of pounds. The 1992 ISDA default survey found that UK local authorities were the source of almost half of the cumulative default losses suffered by dealers since they began swaps trading. To date, legal uncertainties have been responsible for the most significant losses in derivatives markets, and growth in international trading will only magnify the risks they pose for the markets.

Systemic Risk

There are a number of factors fuelling concern about threats to the safety and stability of the financial system deriving from the massive growth in derivatives activity. We discuss the major concerns below, illustrating their relevance with specific reference to hedge funds and stock index trading.

- Derivatives trading, as we have discussed, involves considerable market risk, liquidity risk, credit risk and legal risk. The existence of such risks does not in and of itself imply a systemic threat, but concern is justified when large risks are concentrated in a relatively small number of institutions dominating the OTC markets, and when the scope of derivatives activities in these institutions is so exceptionally opaque. One concern is that major derivatives players may have to be accorded "too big to fail" status by government authorities. Another is that the financial safety net may have to be extended beyond the banking system to nonbank financial intermediaries. A third concern is focused on the activities of large so-called "hedge funds," which are briefly discussed below.

Hedge funds. Hedge funds are aggressively managed private investment pools, which create highly leveraged positions through the use of substantial borrowed funds, short selling, and derivatives transactions. The leverage they apply makes the funds far more risky than standard mutual funds, and the investment capital they attract is naturally committed with the expectation of achieving considerably higher than average returns. The activities of US-based funds came under intense central bank scrutiny in late February and early March 1994, when European government bond prices fell sharply under a reported wave of hedge fund selling.

Regulators are growing increasingly concerned about hedge fund trading for a number of reasons. First of all, there is a fear that the funds will substantially and permanently increase market volatility, particularly in government bonds and currencies. Estimates from March 1994 suggest that US hedge and futures funds control about $100 billion in assets, although their highly leveraged trading means that their average exposure would be roughly ten times nominal assets. Secondly, the funds are extremely difficult for regulators and creditors to monitor. Many are setting up offshore or as limited partnerships (with under one hundred participants) specifically to avoid SEC regulation, while at the same time they are not credit rated and often impossible to evaluate in terms of net asset positions. Thirdly, hedge funds prompt liquidity fears by dumping huge positions on the market simultaneously. It is difficult to estimate how far the financial shock waves could extend if a number of large funds were to become unable to settle their contracts. Finally, and most critically, banks are highly exposed to hedge funds as both creditors and counterparties. Bankers Trust and JP Morgan shares fell sharply in early March amid fears of massive trading losses and credit exposures. The two banks at the time had credit exposures of about $70 billion between them.

Most of the systemic risk fears deriving from hedge fund activities appear to be significantly exaggerated, but they are bound to boil over periodically. This is because there are so many sources of risk in the rapidly growing derivatives business, and therefore so many potential sources of error in market pricing. As one banker explained it

> When you have indeterminate credit, uncertainties over netting, and ambiguous accounting standards, as well as trading risk and the cost of regulatory capital, how do you price these products?[19]

The critical task for regulators is, in the first instance, to agree on mechanisms to encourage and facilitate better disclosure of derivatives exposures. This would at least make the distribution of risks in the markets more transparent.

- Derivatives enable traders to unbundle and repackage financial risks, and to mimic the risk-return structures of regulated cash instruments while reducing trading costs and frictions. By eliminating costs, isolating and reallocating risks, and creating arbitrage possibilities, derivatives serve to break down the barriers between product markets and national markets, and to transmit financial asset flows more widely, cheaply, and quickly than ever before. This fact raises concerns among regulators as to whether derivatives have the potential also to transmit disruptions across markets which might previously have remained localized. Much of this concern focuses on stock index derivative trading.

Stock index derivatives. "No empirical study over the past 20 years has yet shown that derivatives increase volatility" according to a March 1994 *Financial Times* article.[20] This statement has been repeated many times over in the popular business press, but it is simply not accurate.

There is fairly strong evidence that the first-time listing of options on individual exchange-traded stocks leads to a *reduction* in price volatility on these stocks.[21] This result does not, however, extend to derivatives on stock indexes. There is considerable empirical evidence that underlying stock price volatility *increases* after index derivative listing, and that index stocks are excessively volatile *vis-à-vis* nonindex stocks.[22] Regulatory concern with the effects of index derivative trading on cash markets is certainly justified, but responses to date have generally been counterproductive.

Let us briefly consider how index arbitrage operates. Index arbitrage serves to link markets which differ significantly in terms of participants, trading costs, and the speed of price movements, and this is likely the root of the volatility problem. Firstly, index futures and options are used mainly by institutional investors and professional traders hedging market risk or trying to profit from broad market moves. The stock market, on the other hand, is used mainly by institutional and individual investors looking to trade in individual company risk. Secondly, the costs of trading large portfolios using index options and futures are considerably lower than the costs of similar trades in equities. Since index derivatives are inherently cheaper to trade, information relating to the general economic climate or the broader market will tend to move index derivative prices first. The impact of this same news will, of course, also affect the cash market, but it will typically be transmitted through index arbitrage. Futures price changes, therefore, will generally "lead" changes in the value of broad-based cash indexes. Finally, while derivatives markets are generally organized so as to allow prices to adjust rapidly, stock exchange rules often deliberately attempt to slow down price changes. The derivatives markets therefore generally reflect the view that rapid price adjustment to new information is essential to efficient markets, while stock exchanges take the opposing view that investors require some measure of imposed price stability. Observers are therefore divided between those who insist that futures price movements are excessive, and that index arbitrage transmits excess volatility to the stock market, and those who insist that stock exchange stabilization efforts cause prices to adjust much too slowly, and therefore give rise to index arbitrage opportunities.

The evidence is now very strong that these tremendous differences between the derivatives and cash markets were the primary cause of the market delinkage that fuelled the 1987 US stock market crash. Studies show that prior to the crash the cash, futures, and options markets were highly integrated. Interestingly enough, even *during* the 1987 crash, the US futures and options markets retained much of their usual linkage. The problem appears to lie in the cash market. The primary cause of the delinkage was a physical order-processing problem on the NYSE during the crash.[23] The NYSE order-routing systems then in place meant long delays between the submission and execution of limit orders. This meant that limit buy orders were reaching the market too late—after the current-information price had already dropped below the limit order price—and thereby creating a market full of "stale" prices. The extraordinary volume on October 19, 20, and 21 and the consequent delays in processing orders severely exacerbated this stale price problem. By noon on October 19, order queues at the NYSE specialist posts had reached seventy-five minutes. Differential degrees of staleness across individual stocks then resulted in nonsynchronous prices across stocks. Arbitrage between the derivatives and cash markets thus became impossible because of a combination of inadequate technology and anachronistic regulation. Once the possibility of effective arbitrage is removed, market prices no longer function to provide accurate measures of supply and demand for securities, and the risk of holding securities rises massively. This encourages the sort of mass flight to liquidity which we witnessed in the '87 stock market crash. Laying the problem at the door of index arbitrage is misguided. Likewise, circuit breakers, margin adjustments, and changes in regulatory jurisdiction will do nothing to prevent another crash. Even if one accepts that equity derivatives trading increases cash market volatility, the odds of precipitating a major destabilizing event will only increase with measures which prevent the normal operation of index arbitrage, and thereby delink the cash and derivatives markets.

The Japanese authorities, unfortunately, have been implementing precisely these sorts of measures. Unlike in the US, however, inefficient trading mechanisms have been imposed on the futures markets rather than the cash markets. Nikkei 225 index futures trading has been subject to highly restrictive tick size rules, time interval rules on quote renewals, and daily price limits, all of which operate to hinder efficient price formation in the futures market. More importantly, they seriously damage the ability of futures contracts to perform their most important economic function: that is, as a hedge against financial risk. A Normura Research Institute report has documented several episodes between 1990 and 1992 when futures price movements could not keep pace with stock price movements because of trading restrictions.[24] This delinkage of the two markets served to trigger massive selling in a largely illiquid stock market, which further intensified stock market volatility. In a misguided effort to reduce volatility and support share prices, the Ministry of Finance doubled fixed brokerage commissions on Nikkei 225 futures in March 1992. While this did indeed reduce short-term futures trading in Osaka, it did so simply by pushing such trading to foreign markets, particularly SIMEX in Singapore. And the effect of futures trading on the stock market is obviously the same whether they are traded in Osaka or Oklahoma. There is certainly no evidence that futures trading restrictions dampened stock market volatility, halted share price declines, or boosted trading volume.

The essential message for regulators is that derivatives markets and their underlying cash markets are *one market* from an economic perspective, and that interventions should be geared to ensuring that trading links across markets are strengthened rather than weakened. Differential restrictions serve to disconnect markets, rendering complex hedging strategies inoperative and market prices meaningless, and may ultimately fuel panics leading to major price collapses. Regulatory authorities also have a legitimate role to play in scrutinizing equity index design, in order to ensure that index trading does not exacerbate volatility in the underlying stocks. To this end, the IOSCO Presidents Committee endorsed a resolution at the 1993 conference urging authorities to consider the number, liquidity, dispersion, replacement, and selection of component stocks; the method of calculation; and clearance and settlement mechanisms.

Clearance and Settlement

Clearance and settlement represent the "guts" of the capital markets. If the massive daily volume of trades cannot be properly digested, the markets may simply grind to a halt. In the worst case scenario, failures at one point in the system undermine confidence throughout the system, and liquidity problems are transformed into solvency crises. As international trading continues to expand rapidly, the problems associated with different currencies, time zones, legal and regulatory systems, and clearance and settlement arrangements will likely be thrust to the top of the international regulatory agenda. A number of examples serve to illustrate the types of problems market participants and regulators face:

- On November 20, 1985, the Bank of New York (BONY), a US government securities clearinghouse, suffered a major computer system failure after a record clearing volume exceeded the limitations of its operating system software. BONY's inability to make deliveries without the computer system necessitated a daylight overdraft authorized by the Federal Reserve Bank of New York which reached $30 billion — more than thirty times BONY's primary capital — before the problem was finally repaired that evening. After borrowing reserves from other banks, BONY still required an overnight loan from the Fed equivalent to twenty-four times BONY's primary capital. While BONY pledged all of its domestic assets and customer securities which could be pledged, the Fed could not have calculated the value of the collateral at the time. The Fed thus assumed a potentially massive credit risk in order to prevent a systemic risk to the government bond market.[25] The crisis illustrates the vulnerability of a major clearance and settlement system to a single technological fault within a single market participant, and raises critical questions about the way in which implicit or explicit government safety nets alter the incentive structures within private clearing networks. If market participants believe that the government will be forced to play the role of ultimate guarantor against systemic risk, the structure of the private networks which develop will likely reflect private underinvestment in mitigating systemic risk. This in turn effectively transfers massive credit risks over to the taxpayers implicitly underwriting government guarantees.

- On October 20, 1987, the morning after the US stock market crash, the stability of the US financial system was resting on the proper functioning of a settlements system involving hundreds of billions of dollars of transactions. Market participants could not have known whether many of the largest brokerage houses, commodities traders, and commercial banks were still solvent after the huge losses that had been inflicted the previous day, and were therefore reluctant to make deliveries or payments without knowing whether their counterparties could complete their side of the deals. Billions of dollars worth of perfectly functioning settlements technology could not have prevented a solvency crisis had the participants been unwilling to assume the massive credit risk involved in making deliveries and payments. What apparently persuaded the banks and securities firms not to take defensive action were personal phone calls from the president of the New York Federal Reserve, Gerald Corrigan. Corrigan has never publicly revealed what promises of central bank support he did or did not offer, but it is humbling to contemplate what might have been had Corrigan been less persuasive. Technological advances should continue to improve the efficiency and reliability of clearance and settlement networks, but the '87 crash should serve as a grim reminder that even the most perfect technology cannot eliminate systemic risk.

- When the German Bankhaus Herstatt failed in 1974, its receiver claimed the right to all payments received on foreign exchange transactions settled before its closure, but refused to honor its obligations to counterparties which were scheduled to be settled after the closure. This classic example of cross-currency settlement risk is now known as "Herstatt risk." A more recent case involves the failure of the Bank of Credit and Commerce International (BCCI) in July 1991. Just before BCCI's official closure, a large Japanese bank had made a yen payment to BCCI's Tokyo branch as one leg of a foreign exchange transaction. The Japanese bank was to receive BCCI's dollar payment through Chase Manhattan Bank in New York during the New York business day, but BCCI was shut down before the payment was made. Since a yen–dollar trade presently requires that the yen payer make his irrevocable payment six to fourteen hours before he can receive dollars from his counterparty, this credit risk could only be reduced if the Bank of Japan and the US Federal Reserve were to agree to extend the operating hours of their payment systems.

Components of the System

Clearance refers to the process of determining accountability with regard to the exchange of funds and securities, while *settlement* refers to the actual crediting and debiting of cash and securities accounts. The way clearance and settlement operates differs considerably across markets for different securities and across national boundaries. The process, including all its associated components, can in principle be carried out within a single institution, while in practice it is often completely disaggregated.

After two parties agree to a trade, the terms of the trade may first have to be confirmed by a trade comparison system, which may be run by a specialized institution. Clearance — establishing accountability — may then be carried out by a separate clearinghouse according to a number of different mechanisms, such as trade-for-trade and various forms of bilateral and multilateral netting. Settlement will then take place on the basis of "account day" settlement cycles or some form of "rolling" settlement. Since in many countries clearinghouses are not permitted direct access to the central bank's national payment system, clearinghouses are often forced to rely on the participation of separate settlement banks, which transfer funds between one another through the national payment system. In some settlement systems, delivery of securities and payment of funds can occur simultaneously, known as "delivery versus payment" (DVP), while in others there is a time gap between them. Finally, the participation of a separate securities custodian may be required to take responsibility for the safekeeping and administration of "immobilized" or "dematerialized" securities[26] owned by market participants.

Risks in Clearance and Settlement

The disaggregated nature of many clearance and settlement processes gives rise to a large array of risks, some of which may be more effectively mitigated than others.

Counterparty risk exists anytime one party has a cash or securities exposure with another, since obligations may not be settled on time or at full value. **Replacement cost risk** and **liquidity risk** are counterparty risks deriving from the time gap between trade *execution* and *settlement*. Since one party may fail to meet its obligations, this time gap produces an exposure risk equivalent, at any given time, to the difference between a security's market price and the price at which the trade was executed. A counterparty may either default on its obligations (replacement cost risk) or simply fail to make delivery or payment on time (liquidity risk). **Principal risk** derives from the time gap which often exists between *payment* and *delivery*. When one party makes payment or delivers securities before the counterparty performs, a credit risk arises equivalent to the entire principal amount of the asset transferred. The "Herstatt risk" described above is an example. **Interclearinghouse risk** refers specifically to the credit risk involved in a clearance and settlements transaction requiring the participation of multiple clearinghouses. Particularly when a bilateral link involves non-home-market securities for either clearinghouse, risk is associated with the timing of cash and securities transfers between them.

There are other sources of risk in clearance and settlement which apply to the operation of the system as a whole, rather than to any specific bilateral link in the chain. **Operational risk** is the risk associated with the breakdown of some technological component of the clearance and settlement system, such as a computer or communications failure. Such failures have the potential to transmit liquidity risks throughout the system in the absence of lender-of-last-resort intervention. The BONY computer failure described above is a perfect illustration. **Legal risk** in clearance and settlement derives from ambiguities in legal ownership rights that can exist in complex transfer and custodial arrangements. Such risk is particularly serious where the obligational restructuring resulting from private netting arrangements conflicts with the provisions of bankruptcy law. If netting arrangements are not legally enforceable, the possibility of strategic behavior on the part of market participants can undermine the effective operation of the entire system.

Reducing Risks in Clearance and Settlement

Counterparty risks can be significantly mitigated if clearance and settlement systems are properly structured. First of all, the time gap between *trade execution* and *settlement* should be made as short as possible. The US government securities market, for example, utilizes a completely integrated system which allows for same-day settlement, but few securities markets achieve this level of centralization and automation. Thus the realistic objective must be to collapse the comparison, clearance, and settlement functions into the shortest period feasible. Secondly, even without a fully integrated system the settlement mechanism can and should be structured so as to achieve *delivery versus payment* (DVP). Where delivery and payment occur simultaneously, principal risk is eliminated. Finally, for most high-volume markets the only way significantly to reduce counterparty risk without undermining transaction efficiency is to utilize transaction *netting* arrangements. Trade-for-trade clearance and settlement requires brokers to maintain large cash balances to cover the total value of trades — even offsetting trades — due for settlement on a given day. At the same time, trade-for-trade systems result in the maximum possible number of trades to settle, and any faulty link in a chain of trades can transmit liquidity problems throughout the system. Where a *centralized securities depository* (CSD) can be established — integrating the functions of custodianship, clearance, settlement, and postsettlement activities — the use of *continuous net settlement* (CNS) maximizes the consolidation of transactions, and thus minimizes interdependency risk in the system.

Consolidated Clearance and Settlement

There is a strong case to be made that the establishment of a fully integrated CSD actually maximizes transaction processing efficiency as well as minimizing interdependency risk. The existence of positive network externalities in consolidating clearance and settlement functions across markets for different securities and across national markets would appear to support the case for the eventual creation of a single "Worldclear" organization, which would effect all necessary transactions among the world's wholesale market participants. Setting aside the all too obvious political and financial difficulties implied by such a massive venture,[27] it is worth asking why we do not in fact witness considerable consolidation in the industry at the impetus of market forces. One compelling explanation would suggest that market competition among exchanges and trade support institutions leads to the erection of barriers preventing such externalities from being exploited.[28] The case for government intervention to effect industry consolidation is obviously muted by the reduction in incentives for efficiency and innovation implied by the removal of competition.

It must be recognized that however large the net benefits of consolidated clearance and settlement may be, it will never be cost-effective to try to eliminate all shades of credit and liquidity risk. Even in a fully integrated real-time settlements system featuring continuous DVP, risk must be absorbed by some participant(s) if interest costs and borrowing fees are to be minimized for the vast majority of participants. The US Federal Reserve's Fedwire system for government securities and dollar payments is the epitome of a completely integrated settlements system, where transaction efficiency is maximized by transferring all credit risk to the Federal Reserve (i.e. the US taxpayer). The Fedwire operates a gross settlements system with continuous DVP on securities and cash. Settlement banks hold reserve accounts at the Fed which are credited (irrevocably) and debited as transfer instructions are received. If a sending bank has insufficient funds in its reserve account, debits will result in negative balances, subjecting the Fed to daylight overdraft exposure. The Fed allows debits resulting in overdrafts in order to maintain an efficient payments system, and guarantees its credits as a means of achieving settlement finality — the key to removing systemic risk. The aggregate daily credit exposure risk which this mechanism entails for the Fed is roughly $115 billion: $55 billion in funds overdrafts and $60 billion in book-entry securities overdrafts.[29] Whether this credit risk is sufficiently outweighed by efficiency gains and systemic risk reduction is actually a subject of considerable debate.[30]

International Clearance and Settlement

Cross-border transactions are growing at a rapid pace. The aggregate annual volume of cross-border transactions settled through Euroclear and Cedel, the two principal international CSDs, increased more than threefold between 1987 and 1992: from $4.6 trillion to $14.4 trillion.[31] This pace looks set to accelerate over the coming years.

Accompanying the growth in cross-border transactions is rising concern among market participants and regulators over the costs and risks involved in settling cross-border transactions, which are considerably greater than those normally encountered within a single domestic market. A 1993 study by Morgan Guaranty, the Euroclear operator, examined the tremendous difficulties involved in reducing what it calls "pipeline liquidity risk" in an international setting. This risk derives from delays in the settlements "pipeline" which are caused by time gaps between the processing cycles of the different CSDs involved, and between the processing cycles of CSDs and those of national payment systems. Narrowing these gaps requires addressing a number of major difficulties; among them, multiple currencies and multiple time zones, localization of CSDs and national payment systems, and different settlement practices that have developed in different national contexts. International fragmentation also makes it impossible to establish efficient risk-transfer mechanisms for cross-border settlement.

Even without major structural changes in international settlement, there are a number of ways in which risks may be significantly reduced:

- Legal risk could be eliminated in several areas if national governments would take appropriate steps. As indicated above, private netting arrangements should be set on sound legal foundations in all major markets. Equally important, national laws must be modernized to address the multiple tiering of intermediaries required in securities transactions. If ownership rights cannot be clearly and uniformly established across national boundaries, cross-border trading will be subject to a considerable element of legal risk.
- Settlement time frames should be reduced and standardized internationally. This recommendation was a major feature of the famous 1989 Group of Thirty report, and has been echoed in a decision by the International Securities Market Association (ISMA) to shorten the Euromarket settlement period to trade date plus three working days (T+3) by June 1, 1995. Collapsing settlement cycles should reduce the number of failed trades by encouraging early submission of instructions to clearing systems, as well as reducing counterparty risk. The Bachmann Task Force on US Clearance and Settlement (1992) estimated that shortening the settlement period from T+5 to T+3 would, in the event of the failure of a large clearing member under normal market conditions, reduce market risk to the clearinghouse by 58 percent. The benefits should be even greater in a cross-border context.
- CSDs should work to synchronize processing cycles, and should add an additional cycle for each settlement date to reduce the costs and risks deriving from CSDs operating in different time zones. An eventual move to real-time processing, assuming the costs could be justified, would be the most effective solution.[32]
- Central banks should extend the operating hours of their payment systems to reduce the time gap between payments in different currencies. There are a number of ways in which central banks could operate their funds transfer systems safely and efficiently twenty-four hours a day.[33]
- Eliminating principal risk in international settlement requires achieving DVP in cross-border and multicurrency transactions. However, there are no simple or inexpensive means of operating international DVP arrangements, and without structural changes in domestic markets

establishing cross-border DVP may require lengthening the settlements process. The result may simply be to increase credit and liquidity risks between CSDs and their participants and between different CSDs, while imposing higher costs on market participants required to preposition securities or funds in advance of settlement. The difficulties involved and possible solutions are examined in three recent BIS reports.[34]

While problems of cross-border clearance and settlement will undoubtedly command a higher place on the international regulatory agenda in the coming years, sight should not be lost of the fact that most of the work which needs urgently to be done remains on the national level.[35] While clearance and settlement may have been considered a mundane back-office issue a decade ago, the efficient and reliable functioning of these systems is becoming increasingly important to the competitiveness of securities markets within and across national boundaries. Much of the difficulty in modernizing settlements systems derives from the fact that the interests of existing institutions do not always correspond to the capabilities of new technologies. Technology does not simply speed up existing tasks, but actually serves to *redefine* them. Failure to come to grips with this fact lay behind the costly collapse of Taurus, the London Stock Exchange's proposed paperless settlements system, in March 1993. Anachronistic functions like independent share registrars were kept alive through effective lobbying, and forced into an unnecessarily complex systems architecture.[36] In struggling to move from T+5 to T+3 settlement by 1995, the US securities markets are facing similar problems. Commenting on the fact that T+3 settlement would still leave the US behind emerging markets like Hungary and Thailand, a US settlements expert explained that

> What it demonstrates is that it is easier to build a system from scratch than to change the existing system and long-standing practices and procedures in our own market.[37]

Multinational Disclosure and Accounting

The internationalization of securities markets is illustrated by the steady rise in international equity issues, the value of which reached an all-time high of $36.5 billion in 1993. Multimarket offers are being driven by a number of factors, foremost among them the desire of firms trading globally to expand their shareholder base, the growing diversification needs of rapidly expanding institutional investment funds, and the rise in large-scale government privatizations beyond the absorption capacity of domestic stock markets.

Firms wishing to list their shares in foreign markets often face considerable barriers, however, in the form of disparate national disclosure and accounting standards. The investment required to reconcile accounting figures to different national standards on an ongoing basis can be considerable, and therefore represents a significant deterrent for firms considering a foreign public offering or exchange listing. While many national jurisdictions already accept financial statements prepared according to International Accounting Standards or US Generally Accepted Accounting Principles (GAAP), the US SEC will not, as a general rule, accept statements which do not accord with US GAAP. This is said to be necessary to ensure adequate disclosure and protection for US investors. SEC Rule 144A, adopted in 1990, allows foreign issuers to make private placements with large institutional investors without the necessity of reconciling financial statements to US accounting standards, but exemptions for full public offerings and exchange listings must be negotiated with the SEC on a case by case, item by item basis.

The establishment of a single set of universal accounting standards would, in greatly facilitating international offerings, represent a considerable step toward the creation of a more global marketplace for capital. The reality is, however, that there is nothing akin to an international consensus on what such a set of standards should comprise. American and German accounting standards, for example, reflect very different notions of what investors have the right to know, what public companies have the responsibility to disclose and in what form such disclosure should be made, and how different disclosure standards ultimately affect the efficiency of the equity market. Such divergent views will not be reconciled either through a deductive search for rational accounting principles or through the discovery of definitive empirical relationships between disclosure rules and efficient markets. Instead, we can expect disparate national accounting standards to continue to coexist, but with measures taken by regulators and public companies to facilitate cross-border public offerings and exchange listings. Three distinct processes are developing simultaneously.

International Accounting Standards

The International Accounting Standards Committee (IASC) was established in 1973, with the stated purpose of working for the improvement and harmonization of financial reporting worldwide. As of the end of 1992, IASC was comprised of 107 professional accountancy bodies in eighty-one countries. The Board of IASC has approved thirty-one International Accounting Standards covering the vast majority of reporting areas required of business enterprises in the preparation of financial statements. Many national authorities use IASC Standards as the basis for some or all of their national requirements, or as an acceptable basis for foreign companies to make a public offering or secure an exchange listing in their jurisdiction.

Table 8.1 Core International Accounting Standards

IOSCO List	IASC Current Status
GENERAL	
Disclosure of accounting policies	IAS 1/Presentation of Financial Statements
Changes in accounting policies	IAS 8 (revised 11/93)
Information to be disclosed in financial statements	IAS 5/Presentation of Financial Statements
INCOME STATEMENT	
Revenue recognition	IAS 18 (revised 11/93)
Construction contracts	IAS 11 (revised 11/93)
Production and purchase costs	IAS 2 (revised 11/93)
Depreciation	IAS 4/IAS 16 (revised 11/93)
Impairment	IAS 4/IAS 16 (revised) — PP&E — plus all specific IASs
Taxes	IAS 12 (under review)
Extraordinary items	IAS 8 (revised 11/93)
Government grants	IAS 20
Retirement benefits	IAS 19 (revised 11/93) — Board identified need for further review
Employee benefits	IAS 19 (revised 11/93) — Board identified need for separate project
Research and development	IAS 9 (revised 11/93)
Interest	IAS 23 (revised 11/93)
Hedging	E48, Financial Instruments
BALANCE SHEET	
Balance sheet impact of income statement items listed above	Various IASs and current projects
Property, plants and equipment	IAS 16 (revised 11/93)
Leases	IAS 17
Inventories	IAS 2 (revised 11/93)
Deferred taxes	IAS 12 (under review)
Foreign currency	IAS 21 (revised 11/93)
Investments	IAS 25/E48, Financial Instruments
Financial instruments/off-balance-sheet transactions	E48, Financial Instruments
Joint ventures	IAS 31
Contingencies	IAS 10
Events occurring after the balance sheet date	IAS 10
Current assets and current liabilities	IAS 13/Presentation of Financial Statements
Business combinations (including goodwill)	IAS 22 (revised 11/93)
Other intangibles	DSOP (1/94)
CASH FLOW STATEMENTS	
Cash flow	IAS 7 (revised 12/92) — Endorsed by IOSCO 10/93
OTHER STANDARDS	
Consolidated financial statements	IAS 27
Subsidiaries operating in hyperinflationary economies	IAS 21 (revised 11/93)/IAS 29
Associates/equity accounting	IAS 28
Segments	IAS 14 (under review)
Interim reporting	
Earnings per share	DSOP 9/93
Related party disclosures	IAS 24
Discontinued operations	IAS 8 (revised 11/93) — Disclosure only; Board identified need to deal with recognition and measurement issues
Fundamental errors	IAS 8 (revised 11/93)
Changes in estimates	IAS 8 (revised 11/93)

Source: "Agreement on Cash Flow Statements and Core Standards," *IASC Insight*, December 1993, 4–5.

The IOSCO Technical Committee Working Party on Multinational Disclosure and Accounting has been studying IASC Standards with a view to producing IOSCO endorsement of existing or modified versions for cross-border offerings and multiple listings. The Working Party has drawn up a list of accounting issues which it says "have to be included in a core of international accounting standards for these standards to be recognized by the members of the Technical Committee for use by issuers in connection with cross-border offerings and multiple listings." This list and the corresponding IASC Standards are shown in Table 8.1. The Committee, despite the wording of the statement, is not clearly following an "all or nothing" policy on endorsing IASC Standards. In one of IOSCO's most significant formal agreements to date, the Presidents Committee passed a resolution at the 1993 conference endorsing a single IASC Standard, IAS 7. The resolution calls on IOSCO members to accept cash flow statements prepared in accordance with IAS 7 as an alternative to statements prepared in accordance with domestic standards for public offerings and continuous reporting by foreign issuers. IOSCO has been working in close association with IASC to produce revised standards, which may then receive IOSCO endorsement. Ten such revised standards are now at the top of the Technical Committee's agenda, and five or six more are understood to have secured the approval of the Working Party. Depending upon whether the Technical Committee has in fact decided to abandon the stated "all or nothing" policy, up to sixteen IASC Standards could be endorsed at the 1994 conference.

In and of itself, the acceptance of IAS 7 for foreign firm cash flow statements will not greatly ease the burden on foreign issuers. The more standards which IOSCO members can agree upon, however, the easier it will be for firms to overcome the accounting barriers to tapping foreign equity markets. Such IOSCO endorsements may be particularly welcome by firms seeking a US listing, who have heretofore been deterred by the high cost of having to meet the full panoply of SEC accounting requirements. IASC is obviously aiming at securing IOSCO acceptance of its complete list of Standards, detailed in over four hundred pages of text, although no one is under the illusion that this will be an easy task. Many IASC Standards are the subject of considerable controversy, and it is likely that substantial revisions will have to be negotiated. As usual, SEC concerns represent the most difficult obstacle to overcome.

While the establishment of universally accepted international accounting standards may be a worthy goal, it should be recognized that major compromises will be necessitated by the difficult international negotiation process, and that a likely result will be standards which are so broad as to be, effectively, a menu of standards. If this is the case, the objective of making financial statements comparable internationally will not be achieved.

Mutual Recognition Agreements

The rise of major international equity offerings in the early to mid-1980s focused the attention of national regulators on how such transactions could be facilitated. The SEC issued a concept release in 1985 reviewing the major issues involved, and produced two alternative recommendations. The first was to create a "common" prospectus for major jurisdiction offerings, and the second was to establish a mutual recognition system in which participating jurisdictions would agree to recognize prospectuses from each other's jurisdiction. Commentators were generally more favorable toward the latter approach, leading the US, Canada, and the UK to try to establish such a mutual recognition system. In the end, a bilateral pact was agreed by the US and Canada to establish the Multijurisdictional Disclosure System (MJDS), which has been in operation since July 1991.[38]

The purpose of the MJDS is to facilitate cross-border transactions through the elimination of redundant regulation. The agreement covers public equity and debt offerings, rights offerings, takeover bids, issuer bids, and business combinations, and simplifies continuous disclosure obligations for foreign issuers. Under the MJDS, qualified US and Canadian issuers will be able to issue securities in each other's markets using only their home-market prospectuses, which will not be subject to review by the host-market regulator. The SEC and the Canadian Securities Administrators (CSA) released draft proposals to amend the system in the spring of 1993; proposals which generally broaden its applicability, reflecting satisfaction with the system's operation in its first two years. The SEC would like to draw other countries into the system, while the CSA is looking to go beyond it by extending unilateral foreign prospectus recognition for substantial international equity offerings by major jurisdiction issuers.

The mutual recognition approach is also applied in a number of EC securities markets directives,[39] and would appear to be a promising mechanism for facilitating cross-border transactions without the need for prior regulatory harmonization. There are limitations to its effectiveness, however, which need to be highlighted. The MJDS, for example, does not change the liability provisions of US or Canadian securities legislation, meaning that while a foreign issuer can use home-country documents as an entry visa into the host-country market, civil claims by host-country investors against that issuer will be decided by host-country courts in accordance with host-country civil liability law. The prospect of facing a damage claim to be deliberated by an unpredictable host-country jury will remain a significant concern for many international issuers. More importantly, bilateral and multilateral mutual recognition arrangements generally involve long and complex negotiations, are subject to very different interpretation and implementation, and tend necessarily to be somewhat limited in scope. The

SEC noted that the MJDS was relatively simple to establish because of the great similarity between the US and Canadian regulatory systems, but such similarity is uncommon. Reciprocity negotiations between the EC Commission and the SEC, for example, have made little progress. Thus, a web of bilateral or multilateral agreements will take a very long time to emerge, and can only represent a second-best approach from the perspective of international issuers.

The American Way

Worldwide recognition of international accounting standards for foreign issuers is akin to establishing an "Esperanto" accounting language, serving to facilitate international communication of essential corporate financial information. However, if international issuers find that host-country investors cannot actually make sense of such Esperanto, it will be of little use to them that the host-country regulators accept it as a legal language. Germany, for example, has liberal reciprocity provisions for financial disclosure, thereby encouraging foreign share listings. However, while foreign companies accounted for 43 percent of Frankfurt Stock Exchange listings in 1992, they only generated two percent of total turnover. In the US, by contrast, where only US GAAP is spoken, foreign companies accounted for only 5.7 percent of listings, yet generated almost 7 percent of turnover.

Particularly given the fact that small investors represent a much larger percentage of shareholders in the US than in most other markets, raising capital efficiently in the vast US markets is probably not as simple as just securing a New York Stock Exchange listing; it requires communicating to American investors in the language they understand: US GAAP. Thus, even if the SEC were to embrace the full panoply of IASC Standards or extend recognition to all the world's accounting languages, foreign issuers might still find it necessary to address American investors in US GAAP. Likewise, regulators, issuers, and investors around the world have become familiar with the US standard, and increasingly comfortable with its use in cross-border transactions. In the words of a Daimler-Benz executive,

> Just as English has become the international language used for communication throughout the world without being elevated to this position by a formal decree, US GAAP are slowly developing into the world's accounting language. They are accepted by more and more countries around the world. Apparently stock exchange authorities and regulatory agencies feel comfortable with the level of investor protection offered by these standards.[40]

The essential point is that market forces may ultimately yield a universal disclosure standard that effectively ignores the efforts of national regulators to produce an Esperanto accounting language or to patch together a network of reciprocity arrangements.

CONCLUSIONS

The rapid growth in cross-border trading and investment is presenting major new challenges to national securities regulators, since their concerns must necessarily extend well outside their limited geographical areas of jurisdiction. We have focused on four major areas of international concern — capital adequacy, derivatives, clearance and settlement, and multinational disclosure and accounting — although there are many other areas where the effectiveness of national regulators is strictly limited when operating in isolation. This is particularly true with regard to issues relating to fraudulent business practices, which are aided and abetted by the difficulties involved in regulators pursuing investigations outside their national jurisdiction.

In examining the proper regulatory response to the tremendous growth in cross-border activities, it is imperative that commentators maintain a sober debate about market "globalization." Integrated markets should not necessarily imply legally integrated regulation.[41] While securitization, information technology advances, and high factor mobility are rapidly increasing the global supply-side potential of the securities industry, we must consider the configuration of the demand side before declaring the "End of Geography"[42] and its regulatory implications. The poor trading volume thus far achieved by the Globex after-hours electronic futures trading system, launched in June 1992, may simply indicate insufficient demand conditions to support a global twenty-four hour securities supermarket.[43] There is a limited number of commodities for which demand is genuinely global.[44] For most equity and debt instruments, demand sufficient to maintain liquid cash and derivatives markets is still concentrated in specific regions and time zones. When we further consider that national economies remain embedded in distinct sociolegal frameworks, we cannot conclude that nationally based regulation is simply a historical artifact: it continues to have a compelling economic rationale.

The question then becomes where we actually require harmonized international regulations and standards, and where we can safely leave matters to the regulatory "marketplace."

We have discussed the issue of *systemic risk* in a number of its guises, and to the extent that systemic risk can be transmitted cross-border — much like acid rain — harmonized standards may well be necessary. The problem with determining the appropriate international response to systemic risk is that we are far from clear as to its precise sources. The capital standards debate is premised on the belief that systemic risk derives primarily from excessive credit and market risks taken on by financial institutions, yet this concern is far less relevant for securities firms than for banks, for reasons we have discussed. Attention should rather be focused on risks in cross-border clearance and settlement, where extended interdependencies have the potential to translate localized liquidity problems into widespread solvency crises. IOSCO should give cross-border clearance and settlement issues highest priority.

Harmonized standards can also, in principle, improve the *efficiency* of the markets by breaking down barriers to the free movement of capital. The efforts to promote widespread recognition of international accounting standards for cross-border issues provide an excellent example of how international organizations can facilitate market integration without undermining market stability or muting the benefits of international competition. Such efforts should be contrasted with EC Member State initiatives to promote trading "concentration" on a single "regulated" market, or to impose identical trade reporting and publication requirements across national markets and market structures.[45] These provisions were intended largely to restrict intermarket competition; an *economic* justification for such uniform standards would have necessarily to be based on a highly restrictive and incomplete definition of "market efficiency."[46] Many of the arguments for regulatory harmonization actually have little to do with efficiency concerns, and are instead based on highly idiosyncratic conceptions of a "fair market." Consider "insider trading," a practice whose efficiency effects have been hotly debated among economists for decades. Insider trading is first and foremost a fairness issue, and it is not surprising that the SEC has had difficulty securing the cooperation of other IOSCO members — who have very different views on the practice — in devising cross-border enforcement and information exchange procedures. Actually trying to *harmonize* insider trading rules would not only prove intractable, but would be of little or no economic value. Efforts to harmonize fairness-related regulations should be avoided: the costs of inadequate or misguided fairness-related regulation will only be borne by those falling under the jurisdiction of the responsible authority.

It must be stressed that international rules and standards do not necessarily enshrine "best practice;" rather, they often entrench existing practice. International agreements emerge from an inherently political process in which national actors are seeking to protect perceived national competitive interests, often regardless of whether these may be reconciled with the stated goals of increasing efficiency and promoting stability in the larger market. For this reason, *mutual recognition agreements* and *memoranda of understanding* (MOUs) between national regulatory authorities should be seen not as inferior alternatives to harmonization, but rather as valuable regulatory aids in their own right. They promote cross-border market access and information sharing without constraining innovation in product design and trading practices. The US initiated the MOU process in the mid-1980s, although the growth of international MOUs has taken on a life of its own under the IOSCO umbrella since 1989. Since

1989, there has been a considerable rise in bilateral MOUs not involving the SEC as a counterparty, indicating that the process is becoming more internationalized.[47] As international market integration continues to grow, such formal cooperative links among national authorities will become increasingly essential to effective market regulation.

ENDNOTES

1. International Organization of Securities Commissions (1992).
2. See Chapter 7, this volume, on the Basle Committee.
3. IOSCO presently consists of sixty-eight *regular members*, eight *associate members*, and thirty-four *affiliate members*. Regular members are generally the primary securities commission of each member country; associate members are generally subordinate authorities; and affiliate members are generally self-regulatory and international bodies.
4. The Presidents Committee is comprised of all the presidents of regular and associate member agencies. Resolutions are agreed by majority voting among the regular members only.
5. The IOSCO endorsement of International Accounting Standard 7 (IAS 7) is discussed further on p. 224.
6. See Steil (1993a).
7. See Chapter 7.
8. See, for example, 'A Who's Who on the BIS,' *The International Economy*, November/December 1992, 11–27; Schaefer (1992); and Steil (1992).
9. International Organization of Securities Commissions (1989, 10, 7).
10. See, for example, McKenzie, Thomas, and Clare (1991).
11. The main disagreement is over capital standards for banks' bond holdings. The Basle Committee supports an exclusion on bond holdings for "investment purposes," as opposed to "trading purposes," while the IOSCO Technical Committee rejects the relevance of this distinction.
12. From an October 21, 1993 letter from the SEC to the IOSCO Technical Committee, reprinted in the *International Securities Regulation Report*, November 3, 1992, 11–12.
13. See Steil (1993a).
14. This is the classic moral hazard problem which featured prominently in the US Savings and Loan disaster.
15. See Dale (1992).
16. One such instrument is the "diff swap," which involves exchanging cashflows on an asset or liability in one currency for those on another. Diff swaps involve "correlation risk," or the risk that the assumed correlation between interest rate and currency movements will not hold. Such risk cannot be directly hedged.
17. Option positions must be rehedged continuously as market conditions change; thus the term "dynamic hedging." "Synthetic option" positions, constructed using cash and underlying securities, are used in such strategies. If the hedging models are based on wildy inaccurate volatility assumptions, as they were during the ERM crisis, portfolios are subject to far more market risk than the models would indicate.
18. For more details on credit risks in derivatives markets, see International Monetary Fund (1993).

19. Bob Brookes of NatWest, quoted in 'You'd better ask Murphy.' *The Banker*, February 1993, 48–51.
20. 'On Trial for Dangerous Dealing,' *Financial Times*, March 21, 1994, 13.
21. See Damodaran and Subrahmanyam (1992) for a useful summary of the literature.
22. See in particular three studies based on the Standard and Poor's 500 (S&P 500) index: Harris (1989), Damodaran (1990), and Blume, MacKinlay, and Terker (1989).
23. See the excellent study by Kleidon and Whaley (1992).
24. See Arai, Akamatsu, and Yoshioka (1993).
25. See Herring (1993) for further details on the BONY crisis and other examples of systemic risk in financial markets.
26. An "immobilized" security exists in physical certificate form, but its legal transfer is effected merely by accounting entries. A "dematerialized" security is transferred in the same way, but does not even exist as a physical certificate.
27. The Morgan Guaranty report (1993) provides a summary of the development obstacles and costs involved in the "Worldclear" model.
28. See Kyle and Marsh (1993) and Steil (1993b, 11–12).
29. Angell (1991).
30. See, for example, Kane (1992).
31. Morgan Guaranty (1993). Figures include domestic, foreign and international securities.
32. See Morgan Guaranty (1993).
33. See, for example, Angell (1991, 1992).
34. Bank for International Settlements (1992, 1993) and Borio and Van den Bergh (1993).
35. A rapidly growing library of reports and studies is available to readers wishing to follow developments more closely. For international issues, see 'Improving International Settlement,' *Fédération Internationale des Bourses de Valeurs*, June 1989, in addition to sources previously referenced. For the US markets, see Parkinson et al. (1992) and Rutz (1989), in addition to sources previously referenced. For the Japanese markets, see Bank of Japan (1992). For the EC, see Banca d'Italia (1991). For Latin America and the Caribbean, see International Organization of Securities Commissions (1993), or the summary in 'IOSCO 18th Annual Meeting,' *FT Financial Regulation Report*, November 1993, 2–6.
36. Steil (1993b).
37. Executive Director, Margaret L. Koontz, of the US Working Committee of the Group of Thirty Clearance and Settlement Project, in an interview with *Global Investment Technology*, October 18, 1993, 4–6, 'Fixed Income Trades May be Achilles Heel as US Market Prepares for T + 3 Settlement.'
38. For details on the MJDS, see Drinkwater (1993).
39. In particular, two directives covering "Mutual Recognition of Public Offer Prospectuses for Public Offerings" and "Mutual Recognition of Listing Particulars."
40. Kühne (1993).
41. See Steil (1992) and White (1994) for perspectives on the regulatory harmonization debate.
42. *The End of Geography* is the clever subtitle of Richard O'Brien's (1992) concise account of global financial market integration.
43. For an account of Globex's difficulties, see 'Globex Faces Major Restructuring,' *FT Financial Regulation Report*, January, 1994, 26–28.

44. The New York Mercantile Exchange's (NYMEX) Access energy futures trading system is a much smaller operation than Globex, but it would appear to have excellent potential. Unlike with Globex's predominantly nationally based products, demand for Access's petroleum-based contracts is genuinely global.
45. See Steil (1993a) and Chapter 6, this volume, on the Investment Services Directive.
46. See Steil (1992, 1993b) on multiple and conflicting definitions of market efficiency.
47. A large proportion of the agreements signed in 1990 and 1991 which did not involve the US had the UK as one party (Porter 1993).

REFERENCES

Albrecht, W.P. (1993) *IOSCO Capital Standards Update*. Presentation made before the American Bar Association Section on Business Law Committee on Futures Regulation, January.

Angell, W.D. (1991) 'A proposal to rely on market interest rates on intraday funds to reduce payment system risk' in C. England, (ed.) *Governing Banking's Future: Markets Versus Regulation*. Boston, Kluwer.

———. (1992) 'Cooperative approaches to reducing risks in global financial markets,' in F.R. Edwards and H.T. Patrick, (eds) *Regulating International Financial Markets: Issues and Policies.* Boston, Kluwer.

Arai, T., Akamatsu, T., and Yoshioka, A. (1993) 'Stock index futures in Japan: problems and prospects.' *NRI Quarterly*, **2**, Spring, 28–57.

Bachmann Task Force. (1992) *Clearance and Settlement Reform in US Securities Markets*. Submitted to the US Securities and Exchange Commission, May.

Banca d'Italia. (1991) *Payment System Issues in the Perspective of European Monetary Unification*, November.

Bank for International Settlements. (1990) *Report of the Committee on Interbank Netting Schemes of the Central Banks of the Group of Ten Countries*, November.

———. (1992) *Delivery Versus Payment in Securities Settlement Systems*, September.

———. (1993) *Central Bank Payment and Settlement Services With Respect to Cross-Border and Multi-Currency Transactions*, September.

Bank of Japan. (1992) *Functions of and Risks in Payment and Settlement Systems in Japan*, June.

Blume, M.E., MacKinlay, A.C., and Terker, B. (1989) 'Order imbalances and stock price movements on October 19 and 20, 1987,' *Journal of Finance*. **44**, 827–848.

Borio, C.E.V. and Van den Bergh, P. (1993) 'The nature and management of payment system risks: an international perspective.' *BIS Economic Papers*, **36**, February.

Dale, R. S. (1992) 'Capital adequacy and European securities markets,' in A. Steinherr, (ed.) *The New European Financial Market Place.* London, Longman.

Damodaran, A. (1990) 'Index futures and stock market volatility.' *The Review of Futures Markets*, **9**(2), 443–457.

Damodaran, A. and Subrahmanyam, M.G. (1992) 'The effects of derivative securities on the markets for the underlying assets in the United States: a survey.' *Financial Markets, Institutions and Instruments*, **1**(5) December, 1–21.

Drinkwater, D.W. (1993) *The Canada–United States Multijurisdictional Disclosure System*. Paper presented at the 2nd International Capital Markets Seminar, Mexico City, October.

Group of Thirty. (1989) *Clearance and Settlement Systems in the World's Securities Markets*, March.
———. (1993) *Derivatives: Practices and Principles*, July.
Harris, L. (1989) 'S&P 500 cash stock price volatilities.' *Journal of Finance*, **44**(5), December, 1155–1175.
Herring, R.J. (1993) 'Innovations to enhance liquidity: implications for systemic risk.' *Discussion Paper 93–10*, Weiss Centre for International Financial Research, The Wharton School, University of Pennsylvania, October.
International Monetary Fund. (1993) *International Capital Markets: Part II. Systemic Issues in International Finance*.
International Organization of Securities Commissions. (1989) *Capital Adequacy Standards for Securities Firms*. Report of the Technical Committee.
———. (1992) Annual Report.
———. (1993) *Clearing and Settlement Systems in Emerging Markets: The Case of Latin America and the Caribbean*. Report of the Development Committee Working Group on Clearing and Settlement, October.
Kane, E.J. (1992) 'Government officials as a source of systemic risk in international financial markets,' in F.R. Edwards and H.T. Patrick, (eds.) *Regulating International Financial Markets: Issues and Policies*. Boston, Kluwer.
Kleidon, A.W. and Whaley, R.E. (1992) 'One market? Stocks, futures, and options during October 1987.' *Journal of Finance*, **47**(3), July, 851–877.
Kühne, W. (1993) *International Equity Offerings: Advantages, Obstacles and the Interest of the Market*. Paper presented at the 18th Annual Conference of the International Organization of Securities Commissions, Mexico City, October.
Kyle, A.S. and Marsh, T.A. (1993) *On the Economics of Securities Clearing and Settlement*. Working Paper, Duke University and the University of California at Berkeley, December.
McKenzie, G.W., Thomas, S.H., and Clare, A. (1991) 'The regulation of securities firms: some key issues.' *Revista Internazionale di Scienze Sociali*, January/March, 119–133.
Morgan Guaranty Trust Company of New York. (1993) *Cross-Border Clearance, Settlement, and Custody: Beyond the G30 Recommendations*, June.
O'Brien, R. (1992) *Global Financial Integration: The End of Geography*. London, The Royal Institute of International Affairs and Pinter Publishers.
Parkinson, P. et al. (1992) *Clearance and Settlement in US Securities Markets*, Board of Governors of the Federal Reserve System, March.
Porter, T. (1993) *States, Markets and Regimes in Global Finance*. London, St. Martin's Press.
Rutz, R.D. (1989) *Clearance, Payment, and Settlement Systems in the Futures, Options, and Stock Markets*, Board of Trade Clearing Corporation, February.
Schaefer, S.M. (1992) 'Financial regulation: the contribution of the theory of finance,' in J. Fingleton and D. Schoenmaker, (eds.) *The Internationalisation of Capital Markets and the Regulatory Response*. London, Graham and Trotman.
Steil, B. (1992) 'Regulatory foundations for global capital markets,' in R. O'Brien, (ed.) *Finance and the International Economy: 6*. Oxford, Oxford University Press.
———. (1993a) *Competition, Integration and Regulation in EC Capital Markets*. London, The Royal Institute of International Affairs (Special Paper Series).
———. (1993b) *Taking Efficient Markets Seriously*. Working Paper, The Royal Institute of International Affairs.
White, L. (1994) 'International regulation of securities markets: harmonization or competition?' Paper presented at the National Bureau of Economic Research conference, *The Industrial Organization and Regulation of the Securities Industry*, January.

Index

Index compiled by Geoffrey C. Jones